Saving Places That Matter

To Lee and Russ Pye of Adams Run, South Carolina,
who don't need it, this book is respectfully dedicated.

Saving Places That Matter

A Citizen's Guide to Using the National Historic Preservation Act

Thomas F. King

Left Coast Press Inc.

Walnut Creek, California

Left Coast Press inc.

LEFT COAST PRESS, INC.
1630 North Main Street, #400
Walnut Creek, CA 94596
http://www.LCoastPress.com

Copyright © 2007 by Left Coast Press, Inc.

All rights reserved. No part of this publication may be reproduced, stored in a retrieval system, or transmitted in any form or by any means, electronic, mechanical, photocopying, recording, or otherwise, without the prior permission of the publisher.

ISBN 978-1-59874-084-4 hardcover
ISBN 978-1-59874-085-1 paperback

Library of Congress Cataloguing-in-Publication Data:
Saving places that matter : a citizen's guide to the National Historic Preservation Act / Thomas F. King.
　　p. cm. — Includes bibliographical references and index.
　　　ISBN 978-1-59874-084-4 (hardback : alk. paper)
　　　ISBN 978-1-59874-085-1 (pbk. : alk. paper)
　　　1. United States. National Historic Preservation Act of 1966.
2. Historic preservation—Law and legislation—United States. I. Title.

KF4310.A316K56 2008　　　344.73'094—dc22
　　　　　　　　　　　　　　2007032741

Printed in the United States of America
The paper used in this publication meets the minimum requirements of American ∞ National Standard for Information Sciences-Permanence of Paper for Printed Library Materials, ANSI/NISO Z39.48-1992.

07 08 09 10　　5 4 3 2 1

Contents

Preface 9

Chapter One **Saving Places—Introduction** 11

    Saving Your Place 11
    Consider Section 106 11
    Other Laws 13
    Some Success Stories 14
    The Purpose of Section 106 18
    Achieving Preservation 18
    Knowing Your Place 19
    The National Register of Historic Places 22
    The Letter of the Law 24

Chapter Two **Words, Regulations, and Laws—Understanding the Context of Section 106** 26

    Definitions 26

Chapter Three **The Cast of Characters** 39

    The Project Proponent 39
    Federal Agency Overseers 43
    Government Review Agencies 45
    Indian Tribes and Native Hawaiian Groups 49
    Architect/Engineering/Planning Firms 50
    Environmental Impact Assessment Firms 51
    Cultural Resource Management Firms 52
    Project Supporters 53
    Local/Neighborhood Opposition Organizations 53
    National Advocacy Groups 54

**Chapter Four How Section 106 Is Supposed to Work—
And Why It Often Doesn't** 56

   Section 106: A Thumbnail Sketch 56
   A Quick Digression into NEPA 59
   How Agencies Abuse Their Responsibilities A Summary 61

Chapter Five Place-Saving Strategies—Getting Into the Action 73

   Strategics 73
   How Section 106 Review Gets Started 79
   Becoming a Consulting Party 88
   Asserting your interest 89

Chapter Six Place-Saving Strategies—Getting Your Place Noticed 95

   Strategics 95
   "Historic Properties" and the "Identification Effort" 96
   Scoping 98
   Real Scoping 102
   The Results of Scoping 110
   What's Really Supposed to Come Out of Identification 117
   Historic Property Identification and NEPA 120

**Chapter Seven Evaluation—Is Your Place Eligible for the
National Register?** 123

   For Those Who Just Tuned In ... .123
   Register Eligibility is *Really* Important 124
   What the Register Is 125
   What Agencies Are Supposed To Do 126
   Regarding as Eligible, Determining Eligibility, Listing 127
   The Criteria 129
   What the Criteria Mean 129
   Strategics 135
   What To Do 136
   Common Proponent Dodges 140
   Playing the Criteria Considerations 147
   Back to the Process 154
   Don't Forget NEPA 157

Chapter Eight **Will There Be an Adverse Effect on Your Place?** 160
    So Your Place Is Eligible 160
    What Being Eligible Means 161
    "No Historic Properties Affected" 161
    Determining Adverse/No Adverse Effect 162
    The Upshot 175
    Don't Forget NEPA 176

Chapter Nine **"Resolving" Adverse Effects on Your Place** 179
    Strategies 179
    What the Agency Has To Do 180
    Consultation: Avoiding and Climbing Out of Pitfalls 182
    Don't Shoot Yourself in the Foot 185
    The Memorandum of Agreement 190
    If There Is an MOA 190
    NEPA Coordination 192

Chapter Ten **Endgame – and Further Complications–
How You Got To This Point** 196
    Stop the MOA 196
    And Then? 199
    Convincing the Council 200
    But.... 201
    Playing By Other Rules 201
    An Example: The Trail of Dreams 205

Afterword **Now That We Understand the System—Let's Fix It** 210

Appendix **–Section 106 Memorandum of Agreement
for the Broad Run Bridge** 212

Resources 218

Glossary 222

Index 235

About the Author 240

Preface

Since leaving government in 1989, I've worked as a consultant in "cultural resource management" (CRM). Mostly that's meant helping clients work their way through a complex of government procedures designed to make sure that places thought to have cultural significance aren't ignored when things like highways and power lines are planned. Like most who work in the "CRM" game, I've mainly had change agents for clients—highway builders, mine diggers, military services personnel, hydroelectric project managers. That is, after all, where the money is.

In the last few years, though, I've found myself working more and more often for and with people who are trying to stop projects, or redirect them. Whatever other interests these clients have had, they came to me because they wanted to save places that play some role in their lives. They've engaged me to advise them about using Section 106 of the National Historic Preservation Act—the primary "CRM" law in the United States—to help protect such special places.

Two things dawned on me as I tried to explain Section 106 to clients and would-be clients. First, the process is pretty complicated, and second, there's nothing in print that helps regular people understand it. Virtually all the books and journal articles—my own books included—are written for professional practitioners, most of whom get paid to learn about it. About the only exception is the Advisory Council on Historic Preservation's Citizens Guide to Section 106, which is pretty good, but necessarily hews to the government's party line. The Advisory Council can't very well squeal about how its fellow federal agencies subvert the Section 106 process to permit the thoughtless destruction of special places, so it can't tell you what to do in response.

This book—which during its composition has passed under such working titles as Section 106 for NIMBYs and How to Monkey-Wrench a Project Using Section 106—is my attempt to remedy this deficiency.

Acknowledgments

I'm especially grateful to my recent non-governmental clients for helping me see the need for such a book, and for helping me—sometimes forcing me, and thankfully often hiring me—to think through the strategies they can use to make Section 106 work for them. Luis Rosas and Jean Sawyer-Rosas of Dripping Springs Ranch, David Blake and Linda Wright of the Buckland Preservation Society, Geoffrey Sea of SHIP-SONG and Sargent's Pigeon, David Nickell of Between the Rivers, and Kathleen Hayden, Jennifer Foster, and their colleagues of (among other things) the Backcountry Horsemen of California have inspired me immeasurably. For the most part, their stories are not told here—not because they are not worthy but for two other reasons. First, the stories have not yet completely played out—Luis and Jean, David and Linda,[1] Geoffrey and David and Kat—have not yet vanquished their foes in the railroad industry, the suburban sprawl/highway construction axis, the nuclear waste business, the recreation management bureaucracy, and state park management, respectively. Second, each of their tales is worthy of a book in itself, which I hope someday they'll write.

I'm also grateful, as always, to my Indian tribal, Native Hawaiian, and Micronesian clients, colleagues, and friends, who continue to teach me new ways of looking at preservation/development conflicts and to inspire me with their dedication and wisdom. The Historic Preservation Officers of the governments of Micronesia, the groups and individuals who fight for the cultural rights of Native Hawaiians, and such Indian tribes as the Mississippi Choctaw, the Tuolumne Mewuk, the Big Pine Paiute, the Pitt River Nation, the Yurok, Karuk, and Hoopa, the Mole Lake, Bad River and Red Cliff Bands of Great Lakes Ojibwe, the Yuki, the Quechan, the Caddo, and the Fort Mojave Tribe have for many years kept me largely out of the increasingly polluted mainstream of CRM-for-profit, and taught me a great deal about special places and their care. I am only beginning to understand how much I owe them.

My friend and sometime co-author Greg White, archaeologist at California State University, Chico, has graced the pages of the book with his sprightly line drawings, and made it immeasurably more human in the process; for this I'm very much in his debt. I'm also grateful to photographer Tom Semple, to Anita Canovas of the National Trust for Historic Preservation, and to Massachusetts State Historic Preservation Officer Brona Simon for the images they contributed.

Finally, I'm thankful to Mitch Allen of Left Coast Press, Inc. for investing in another of my books, to both Mitch and Joan Gatterer for critical reviews and comments, and to Carol Leyba for her skillful copy editing and production work.

– NOTE –

1. The story of one of David and Linda's cases, the Broad Run Bridge, is told here, but it's only one skirmish in their long-term, multi-front war with the forces of urban sprawl in northern Virginia.

Chapter One

Saving Places

Introduction

SAVING YOUR PLACE

You've probably opened this book because a place that's important to you is threatened. Maybe your home, your neighborhood, your farm, your village. Maybe a treasured landscape or stretch of shore. Maybe a hill or mountain, a forest, a piece of desert. Maybe a spring, or a trail, or the place where your ancestors are buried, or the place you collect mushrooms or maple sap or arrowheads. You're trying to save it from some threatened change—urban sprawl, a highway, a power plant, a national park—or from some change in the policies of a government agency.

CONSIDER SECTION 106

If you're in the United States, there are federal—that is, national-level—laws that may help you, by subjecting potentially damaging projects to environmental impact review. One of the most useful in saving a treasured place is Section 106 of the National Historic Preservation Act (NHPA). Section 106 says that a federal agency considering something that may change the environment must "take into account" the effects of that something on "historic properties."

"That's nice," you may say, "but the place I'm trying to save isn't a historic landmark, so that law can't help me."

Don't jump to that conclusion. NHPA isn't just about historic landmarks, whatever those may be. NHPA deals with historic places of all kinds, significant to all kinds of people, very explicitly including local communities. A place that's significant in the history of Almira, Washington—population 302—gets about the same consideration under NHPA as does a place important to the whole nation. It simply has to be eligible for inclusion in the National Register of Historic Places—a list of significant places that's maintained (though the places are not) by the National Park Service.

Saving Places that Matter

Your treasured place may very well be eligible for the National Register, and if it is—*whether it's actually been included in any historical register or not*—it has to be considered by any federal agency involved in a project that may do something to it.

Your place doesn't have to be fancy or associated with great events to be protected (to the extent anything is protected) by Section 106.

That doesn't mean that your place has to be saved, preserved, left undisturbed. When all is said and done, a federal agency can decide to let it be destroyed. But a lot may have to be said and done before the agency can decide, and that's what gives someone like you some power. If you can use it.

"Well," you say, "the place I want to save isn't threatened by the federal government; it's the county/city/local developer who wants to destroy it for a road/sewer plant/housing development. So a federal law isn't going to help me."

Don't jump to that conclusion, either. Section 106 of NHPA applies not only to things that the feds do themselves, but also to things they assist or permit, and you might be surprised at the length of the federal government's arm.

For the last 40 years or so, I've been advising people on how to work with "the Section 106 process"—the process by which projects are reviewed under Section 106 to control their impacts on historic places. Sometimes I've advised government agencies, sometimes non-governmental project proponents, sometimes Indian tribes, sometimes local governments, sometimes organizations and individuals trying to stop projects. I've come to realize that while there's a lot of guidance—regulations, government guidelines, textbooks, learned and not-so-learned journal articles—about Section 106 for professionals who work with the law all the time, there's almost nothing to help the ordinary citizen who wants to use it for saving a place.

Saving Places – Introduction

I'll try, in this book, to fill that gap. We'll look at:

- What does it mean for a place to be a "historic property" in the U.S.?
- How can you get your special place considered such a property?
- What does Section 106 require federal agencies to do?
- What does it require of other people?
- How can you use Section 106 to advance your interest in saving a place?
- What tricks do agencies and project proponents use to short-circuit or thwart the Section 106 process?
- What are some strategies for thwarting *them*?

I'll try to explain Section 106 in a human a way, rather than in lawyer-talk or bureaucrat-speak. I'll describe how agencies and project proponents deliberately or inadvertently circumvent the law, or interpret it in ways that—while they may not be entirely unreasonable—are probably contrary to your interests. I'll suggest things you can do about such circumventions and problematical interpretations.

Of course, maybe you're *not* trying to save something. Maybe, to put it crudely, you're trying to destroy something, or simply trying to do something that requires somebody—maybe you, maybe some agency from whom you need money or a permit—to comply with Section 106. That's fine; whatever destruction you're contemplating may be perfectly justifiable—the world or the nation or the region doubtless *needs* that new road or apartment building—and you're to be commended for trying to avoid conflict over it. I hope this book will help you work with people who treasure special places, rather than fighting it out in the courtroom or in the streets. Or maybe you have an academic interest in how Section 106 works, and that's fine too. The system can be esoteric, and in this book I'll try to demystify it.

OTHER LAWS

Section 106 isn't the only law that can be used to save special places. In the United States there's also—very importantly—the National Environmental Policy Act (NEPA). NEPA requires attention to impacts on the whole human environment. There are also laws, executive orders, and regulations dealing with specific aspects of the environment—endangered species and their habitats, air and water quality, Indian tribal and Native Hawaiian sacred places, wetlands, floodplains, toxic waste sites—all of which can be used in their own ways to help protect the places that matter to you. When I started writing this book, I thought I'd deal with all these legal authorities but quickly found that task to be far, far too complicated. So I scaled back to dealing just with Section 106 and NEPA and wrote quite a bit before I realized that it was *still* too complicated. There were too many different possibilities, permutations, relationships between this regulatory requirement and that. So this book focuses on Section 106, with only occasional excursions into other federal requirements. But let's be clear about this—*those other authorities can be very important*. They're worth knowing about; I just can't discuss them all in a sensible way between these two covers.

Besides the federal laws, there are also state laws, tribal laws, county and city ordinances, and the regulations that spring from them. They're worth knowing too; they can, in fact, be more powerfully protective than Section 106. But they vary tremendously one from another; even if I knew them all I wouldn't be able to explain them all in a single book. So I'll touch on them as we go along and suggest ways to use them, but only in a general way.

Some Success Stories

What kinds of places can be saved using Section 106? Here are some examples:

- **The Forest Glen Seminary** is a collection of strange and wonderful old buildings that make Forest Glen, Maryland, unlike anyplace else in the world. The U.S. Army acquired the seminary before World War II but then neglected it. The buildings were falling apart when local residents, organized as "Save Our Seminary" (SOS), stepped in. Using Section 106 and other legal tools, and with help from the National Trust for Historic Preservation, they prevailed on the Army to do some interim preservation, but more importantly to move out altogether and let the seminary pass to the National Park Service. In partnership with the community and private developers, the Park Service is now overseeing its preservation, rehabilitation, and mixed-use redevelopment.

    See: **http://www.saveourseminary.org/News%20folder/what_is_the _national_park_semina.htm** for information.

Saving Places — Introduction

One of the many buildings at the Forest Glen Seminary saved by SOS and the National Trust using Sections 106 and 110 of NHPA, now being rehabilitated by a private developer in partnership with the National Park Service. Photo by the author.

- **The Medicine Lake Highlands** are the remains of a gigantic collapsed volcano in northern California, mostly controlled by the U.S. Forest Service. Indian tribes of the area, notably the Pit River tribe, regard the highlands as an intensely spiritual landscape and have strongly opposed plans for geothermal energy production there. Using Section 106, the tribe and its allies were able to stop one drilling operation, but another was allowed to go forward. The tribe then took the involved federal agencies (Forest Service and Bureau of Land Management) to court and showed that their compliance with Section 106 and other laws was flawed; this halted the remaining project.

  See: http://www.mountshastaecology.org.

- **The Stillwater Bridge** is an important part of Stillwater, Minnesota, an old mill town whose people value and have preserved its historic commercial core. When a new highway was built around Stillwater, the bridge technically became surplus, and because it crossed a designated scenic river, U.S. government policy demanded its demolition. Using Section 106, the people of Stillwater were able to negotiate successfully with the National Park Service, Federal Highway Administration, and Minnesota Department of Transportation, prevailing on them to retain and rehabilitate the bridge.

See: http://en.wikipedia.org/wiki/Stillwater_Bridge.

Medicine Lake Highlands. Photo courtesy Tom Semple.

- **Kahoolawe Island** figures heavily in Native Hawaiian tradition and is loaded with ancestral Native Hawaiian residential, burial, and spiritual sites—but for many years it was used by the U.S. Navy for target practice. Using Section 106 and other laws, Native Hawaiians persuaded the Navy to move its bombardment exercises elsewhere and to clean up the unexploded ordnance on the island. The island is now controlled by the State of Hawaii and is visited regularly by Native Hawaiians to carry out ceremonial and cultural activities.
See: http://www.kahoolawe.org/.

- **Hingham, Massachusetts** is a well-preserved old town in Plymouth County, Massachusetts. The railroad used to run through Hingham, but the rail line was abandoned in the 1950s. The residents of the town were quite happy not to have trains rumbling through the middle of town—a historic area called the Lincoln Historic District—and were startled when the Massachusetts Bay Transportation

SAVING PLACES — INTRODUCTION

Authority (MBTA) proposed to "restore" train service in the form of a high-speed commuter line. Using Section 106, they fought it out with the MBTA and the federal agencies whose funds or permits MBTA needed to build the line. They eventually succeeded in getting it put in a tunnel under the historic district, greatly reducing disruption to the community.

See: **http://experts.about.com/e/h/hi/hingham,_massachusetts.htm**.

The Lincoln Historic District in Hingham, Massachusetts, was saved from a bisecting commuter rail line through the skillful citizen use of Section 106. Photo courtesy Massachusetts Historical Commission.

- **The Coalition of 9/11 Families** used Section 106 to force an unwilling Port Authority of New York and New Jersey to pay attention to the coalition's concerns about how their loved ones should be memorialized on the site of the World Trade Center. Despite widely felt sympathy for the coalition's members, the bureaucracy wouldn't give the coalition an actual seat at the table to bargain over memorial design, until the coalition was able to assert itself through the Section 106 process.

See: **http://www.coalitionof911families.org/default.asp?Page%20Name= News%20Story&Mode=Build&NewsID=60**.

In each case of these cases and hundreds, if not thousands, of others, concerned people knew or learned enough about Section 106 and its related legal requirements to make them work in their favor. Usually this involved getting—sometimes forcing—everyone to sit down and negotiate, reach agreement about what to do, and stick to it. Usually the result was some kind of compromise—often not pure and absolute protection, but not complete destruction either. And often enough, the result was something with which both the project proponent and those trying to protect things could be satisfied.

THE PURPOSE OF SECTION 106

That sort of compromise—let's be very clear about this—is what Section 106 review is supposed to accomplish. It's supposed to achieve *accommodation* between preserving significant places and other important public interests—national defense, transportation, economic development, property rights. The National Historic Preservation Act does not place historic preservation over all other interests. It simply requires that the value of preserving historic places be weighed and balanced along with all other values when a federal agency makes decisions about whether and how to do something. If you're looking for a law that gives your special place absolute, 100 percent inviolable protection, Section 106 is not the law you're looking for. But you'll look long and hard without finding such a law, at least at the federal level.

ACHIEVING PRESERVATION

Although Section 106 doesn't provide absolute protection to historic places, it is possible to use it to achieve that objective. How? By being smarter than the other guy in your use of the law. Some hard-core preservationists sneer at Section 106 as being "toothless," and they're right; the jaws of Section 106 can't clamp shut and rip out a project's guts. But those toothless jaws can gum a project to death—tie it up in knots and keep it tied up while it bleeds itself dry. The power of Section 106 is largely the power to delay a project and make it more costly than its proponents can tolerate, giving time for you to put other strategies, other tools into play. Strategies and tools like purchasing the place, purchasing easements or getting them donated, convincing local planning and zoning bodies that the project is a bad idea, electing new local or state government officials, convincing stockholders that the plan their company officials are pushing isn't such a good one after all.

But Section 106 review isn't *designed* to delay projects; it's supposed to be a smooth, efficient process. It creates delay largely when somebody screws up. Luckily for those whose interests are served by delay, project proponents and federal agencies screw up a lot. I'll try to identify the ways this usually happens, and how you can exploit the vulnerabilities such screw-ups create.

So far I've made the process seem like an awfully antagonistic, adversarial one. It often is, and I don't think there's any realistic alternative to planning for it to be that way. But there is another way that Section 106 review achieves the preservation of important places—and that's the way it's designed to work. Section 106 review is all about *good-faith consultation* among project proponents, people who want to preserve places, and other interested parties. It's amazing how effective such consultation can be at achieving solutions that let projects go forward while preserving places people care about. Often, I find, people on opposite sides of an argument simply aren't listening to each other, and when something like Section 106 forces them to pay attention, they find there are compromises that can be worked out. But—I'll harp on this a lot—the failure to consult in good faith, exercising a dislike for such consultation, an arrogant insistence on bullying through and having one's own way regardless of what others think, is one of the most common ways that project proponents and federal agencies screw up. It's especially satisfying when *that* gets them in trouble.

So, how can you use Section 106 to save your special place? Let's start by thinking about the place itself, what it is, and how it might relate to the kind of place Section 106 is designed to deal with—the *historic property*.

KNOWING YOUR PLACE

Why do you want to save the place you're concerned about? In my experience working with all kinds of people and groups around the country, I've found that reasons for wanting to save a place fall into the following categories:

- *It's sacred.* There's a spiritual quality to the place. Maybe it's believed that it's where God, or the gods, or some other expression of the eternal speaks to people. Maybe it's where religious rituals are carried out. Maybe it's where supernatural creatures are thought to live. Maybe it's just a place that feels like it has some kind of power.

- *It's historic,* in the sense of being associated with some more or less specific event (the battle of Buckland Mills; the landing place of the explorer Francis Drake) or some more general pattern of historical development (your town's main street; the wide open ranges of the East Fork Ranch).

- *It's architectural.* It's a fine example of a Dog-Trot cabin or a Romanesque railroad station, or the work of Frank Lloyd Wright or Louis Sullivan or an unknown artisan whose buildings are typical of a time, a style, or an area.

- *It's natural.* It's the last stand of old-growth timber in the area, or a pristine spring, the river on whose shores you've always lived, the canyon where you ride your horses and see the wild burros.

- *It's beautiful.* It's a lovely unspoiled vista, a stately streetscape, an imposing mountain, a peaceful lake.

- *It's scientific.* It's an archaeological or paleontological site, or an unusual geological formation, or the place where animals or plants important to science live.

- *It belongs to the ancestors.* It's the place where they're buried, or a place that tradition passed down from the ancestors tells us has to be respected.

- *It's simply familiar.* It's always been here; you're comfortable with it; you'll really miss it if it goes away. It's the dock where everyone goes fishing, the park where everyone plays softball and checkers on Sunday afternoon. Or it's your town, your village, your neighborhood, the holler in the Appalachians where your people have always lived, mined coal, played the fiddle.

Any one of these reasons for wanting to save something is a perfectly fine justification for doing so, and Section 106 may very well help you. Of course, some kinds of places are easier than others to get considered under Section 106. Explicitly historic places are pretty easy, but if the value of the place lies in its natural qualities, its scientific characteristics, or its familiarity, you're going to have to find some way to connect the place to history or culture. If it's a place that you think is sacred, you're going to have to be careful not to run afoul of the Constitution's separation of church and state—the "establishment clause" in the First Amendment. Whatever it is that makes the place important to you, you're going to have to make that importance understandable to the people who manage the National Register of Historic Places and who

Mushgigagamongsebe—"Little River of Medicines" in Ojibwe—in Wisconsin. The whole landscape through which this stream flows is a historic place because of its importance in Ojibwe traditional ways of life. Photo by the author.

Japantown in San Jose, California, is historically significant for its association with the city's Japanese-American community. Photo by the author.

carry out Section 106 review. That can be a challenge; it can even be terribly frustrating, but it can be done.

THE NATIONAL REGISTER OF HISTORIC PLACES

So what is this *National Register,* and why is it so important? The Register is two things: a list, and a bunch of people.

The list—the formal list of places known as the National Register—is maintained by the National Park Service, but it has nothing to do with national parks. Some national parks, and lots of places *in* national parks, are listed in the Register, but so are lots of places in national forests (administered by the Forest Service, a totally different agency than the Park Service), on other federal lands, on state lands, tribal lands, local government lands, and private land. The Park Service maintains the list simply because over the years since its creation in 1916, Congress has given the Park Service responsibility for promoting and administering programs of *historic preservation,* both inside and outside the national parks. One of those responsibilities is to manage the National Register.

The Register is maintained in a huge bunch of file cabinets in Washington, DC, though it has a rather cumbersome and limited cyber-presence that can be accessed via the Internet (at *www.cr.nps.gov/nr/research/nris.htm*). At this writing, it includes something over 80,000 *properties*—that is, places (and things like ships and airplanes)—each of which is documented in the files in text, maps, and images.

Properties are added to the register through *nomination.* To nominate something, you fill out a detailed form, many pages long, following precise standards that the Park Service puts out. You compile images and maps, establish boundaries, describe the property in detail, and explain its significance. Once the form is done, if you're a private citizen you send it to the *State Historic Preservation Officer (SHPO)*—a state official who also has a role in Section 106 review, so we'll talk about him or her a lot—who has it reviewed by a panel of experts in academic fields such as history, architecture, and archaeology. If it passes muster, it goes on to the Park Service for further review and, unless some problem is found with the documentation, inclusion in the Register.

This brings us to the other thing the Register is—a bunch of people. The people are Park Service employees who make up a division or office that, like the list, is referred to as the National Register of Historic Places. This bunch of people is headed by an official called the *keeper.* Yes, keeper, because he or she "keeps" the Register, and the people who created the Register back in the 1960s thought it was an impressive, old-worldy sort of title. The keeper and his or her staff process nominations, maintain the files, answer public inquiries, promote use of the Register for educational purposes, and—very importantly for Section 106 review—make binding determinations where a property's *eligibility* for the Register is in dispute.

It's important to keep this human aspect of the Register in mind. People can be biased, they can be influenced, and they can be unpredictable. People can get up on the wrong side of the bed and make grumpy, thoughtless decisions. People can make snap judgments and say dumb things. And when they're government officials, they tend to find it very hard to back down and change their minds, even when quite thoroughly proved wrong. There are times when it's useful, even necessary, to ask the keeper for an opinion, but you want to do it carefully, watching your language, and knowing that the potential for weird responses is high.

> CONTACT: For the text of the National Historic Preservation Act (16 U.S.C. 470), see **http://www.cr.nps.gov/local-law/nhpa1966.htm**

Should I nominate my place to the National Register?

If you ask the Register's staff, or most other Park Service historic preservation people, or most State Historic Preservation Officers, they'll probably tell you that nomination is absolutely, always, and invariably a good idea. But it's not. Sometimes it's a very bad idea from the standpoint of protecting the place. And—a very important point that many people don't know, don't understand, or forget—*it's not necessary for purposes of Section 106 review*. Federal agencies are required by Section 106 to consider the impacts of their actions on places both *included in* and *eligible for* the Register. It's *their* responsibility to figure out what's eligible—*not* the responsibility of those who want to protect a place.

Why can nomination be a bad idea? In practical terms, because it's a pain to do. The forms you have to use are so complicated, so counterintuitive, that they might have been created by the Internal Revenue Service, and you have to fill them out just so. You end up spending a lot of time, and probably a lot of money, because you usually need to hire some pricey consultant like me[1] to finish them up. And then you put yourself and your place at the mercy of the State Historic Preservation Officer, his review board, and the keeper. That's a chancy business. Plus, it may be that your place is one you don't want to tell people about. Maybe it's a sacred place to you, a spiritual place, a more or less secret place, or a place that thoughtless or ill-intentioned people can mess up. The last thing you want to do is try to capture it on paper and share it with others.

That said, there are reasons for nominating a place. Sometimes it qualifies the property owner for federal or state income tax benefits, and that can help motivate him or her to preserve it. Sometimes it's a precondition for acquiring a protective easement, or a grant. Sometimes it has a useful psychological effect. Sometimes it's the only way to get the significance of the place recognized.

But—let me say it again—*for purposes of Section 106 review, nomination is not necessary.* Remembering that can simplify a lot of things.

What makes a property eligible for the Register?

A property is eligible for the Register if it meets certain criteria published in regulation by the National Park Service. There can be a lot of argument about whether a given place does or does not meet any of the criteria; such arguments play themselves out in a part of the Section 106 review process referred to, naturally, as *determining eligibility*. Determining eligibility, which is supposed to follow some pretty definite rules, is one of the major sources of complexity and delay in Section 106 review. It's a part of the process that agencies and project proponents screw up a lot, and hence it's an area where they display vulnerabilities that you can exploit. In Chapter Seven, we'll go into detail about the Register criteria and how to use them.

THE LETTER OF THE LAW

Lawyers often refer to Section 106 as 16 USC 470f. That means Title 16, Section 470f of the U.S. Code—the massive compilation of all U.S. laws. What does Section 106/Section 470f say, and how can it help you save your special place? Let's look at the letter of the law. Section 106 of the National Historic Preservation Act says:

> *The head of any Federal agency having direct or indirect jurisdiction over a proposed Federal or federally assisted undertaking in any State and the head of any Federal department or independent agency having authority to license any undertaking shall, prior to the approval of the expenditure of any Federal funds on the undertaking or prior to the*

Saving Places — Introduction

issuance of any license, as the case may be, take into account the effect of the undertaking on any district, site, building, structure, or object that is included in or eligible for inclusion in the National Register. The head of any such Federal agency shall afford the Advisory Council on Historic Preservation established under Title II of this Act a reasonable opportunity to comment with regard to such undertaking.

A mouthful, I know. This is what it means: In any "state"—of which there are fifty-nine[2]—a federal agency must "take into account" the effects of its actions on places included in or eligible for the National Register, elsewhere in the law referred to as "historic properties" or "historic resources." The action (or "undertaking") can be something a federal agency itself considers doing, or something someone else wants to do that requires federal funding or a federal permit. "Taking into account" means to consider, think about, reflect upon, the action's effects. The agency also has to give the Advisory Council—a tiny independent agency created by the law—a "reasonable opportunity to comment" on the undertaking.

So—it's pretty simple, really. If a federal agency is thinking about doing something, or helping somebody do something, or licensing somebody to do something, it has to think about its effects on historic properties. And it has to give the Advisory Council an opportunity to advise.

How does an agency do these things? It follows *regulations* issued by the Advisory Council, which are published at *36 CFR 800*—that is, Title 36, Part 800 of the Code of Federal Regulations. Those regulations have the force of law; agencies must follow them. And they're the regulations you can use to help save your special place.

Before we go into what the regulations require, and how to make those requirements work for you, there are some more basic things we need to be sure we understand—about government, about places, about people and roles and jargon. These are what the next chapter is about.

— Notes —

1. Though I try to avoid getting involved in nominations, I hate them so.
2. The fifty states plus the District of Columbia, Puerto Rico, the U.S. Virgin Islands, American Samoa, Guam, the Commonwealth of the Northern Mariana Islands, and the three freely associated nations of Micronesia—the Federated States of Micronesia and the Republics of the Palau and the Marshall Islands.

CHAPTER TWO

Words, Regulations, and Laws

Understanding the Context of Section 106

DEFINITIONS

I've been using some words, perhaps expressing some ideas, that mean different things to different people. Before we go on, let's make sure we share an understanding of some basic terms and concepts.

Federal agencies

The U.S. government, as we all know, is divided into three parts—executive, legislative, and judicial. The *executive branch*—which runs the government day to day and whose people report up a long chain of command to the president—is made up of *departments*, each headed by a presidential appointee who is part of the president's *cabinet*. Most of these people are called *secretaries*—the Secretary of the Interior, the Secretary of Housing and Urban Development, and so on. Each department is made up of units called *agencies*, though they're often called other things as well. In the Department of the Interior, for example, one agency is the *Bureau* of Land Management; another is the National Park *Service*.

To complicate things a bit, there are *regulatory* and *advisory* agencies that are independent of the executive departments. The Federal Communications Commission (FCC) is an independent regulatory agency, for example, while the Advisory Council on Historic Preservation (ACHP) is an advisory one. Like the mainstream executive branch agencies, they report to the president, though they often have equal reporting responsibilities to Congress. There are also more or less hybrid agencies; the Federal Energy Regulatory Commission

(FERC), for instance, operates like an independent regulatory agency but is lodged within the Department of Energy.

This can be pretty confusing, but the thing to remember at this point is that all these creatures are *federal agencies*. Both the National Historic Preservation Act (NHPA) and other federal laws refer to them that way. When a law requires a "federal agency" or a "federal agency head" to do something, that requirement is imposed on the Bureau of Land Management, the Fish and Wildlife Service, the Department of Defense and its subdepartments (Departments of the Army, Navy, Air Force), FERC, FCC, and so on.

The National Historic Preservation Act is all about preserving the character of our communities, both urban and rural. Chattanooga, Tennessee. Photo by the author.

Intergovernmental relations

The fact that something is done or planned by a *government* agency doesn't necessarily mean that a *federal* agency is involved. *State* governments, *tribal* governments, and *local* governments are typically divided up into departments and agencies, too, and there are *intergovernmental* agencies as well—regional planning bodies, for example, and coastal commissions. On the other hand, the fact that a state or local or intergovernmental agency is responsible for something doesn't mean that the federal government is *not* involved. For example, highways are built primarily by state departments of transportation, but they almost always use federal funds, and this brings the Federal Highway Administration (FHWA)—a federal agency, part of the U.S. Department of Transportation—into the picture.

Federal involvement

Section 106 of NHPA applies *only to activities in which a federal agency is somehow involved.* That may mean that the agency is actually *taking* the action—the Army, let's say, is planning a training exercise somewhere, or the National Park Service is planning a new visitor center in Greatgreen National Park. Or it may mean that the agency is *assisting* someone else in taking the action—FHWA may be assisting the state transportation department in constructing a highway from here to there, or the Farm Service Agency (FSA) in the Department of Agriculture may be providing a grant to farmer Smith to improve her stock pond. Or the agency may be considering *licensing* or *permitting* someone to do something. If farmer Smith wants to dump dirt in a marsh, for example, she's likely to need a permit from the U.S. Army Corps of Engineers under Section 404 of the Clean Water Act, so the Corps will be involved in her project. All these kinds of involvement bring Section 106 into play.

Projects

Another term we should be clear about is the word *project*. The technical term used in Section 106 is "undertakings," but for purposes of simplicity I'm going to use *project* as the general term for things that agencies and others propose to do, assist, or license. For our purposes, building or widening a highway is a project. Building, demolishing, or rehabilitating a building is a project. Filling a wetland—like farmer Smith's marsh—to put in a new housing tract is a project. A military exercise is a project. Managing a national forest is a project. But agencies and others often distinguish between projects and other things such as *programs*, or even *non-projects*. And sometimes they prefer to call everything *actions*, or to focus on *decisions*. It's important to understand what they mean by the words they use, and to use words that they understand, but unless there's some reason to do otherwise, in this book *project* is the word I'll default to. All such projects—even those an agency refers to as *non-projects*—require the federal agencies responsible for them to comply with Section 106, unless Congress explicitly *exempts* a particular project or program from its requirements.

Places

We need a word for the places you or somebody else wants to save from destructive projects. In general, I'm just going to call them *places*, and talk about how you can get them regarded as *historic places*, requiring consideration under Section 106. Historic places are referred to in the National Historic Preservation Act (NHPA) interchangeably as "historic properties" and "historic resources." Both terms mean "districts, sites, buildings, structures, and objects included in or eligible for the National Register of Historic Places."

The National Register, as we discussed in the last chapter, is simply a list—albeit a pretty complicated list—that's maintained by the National Park Service. At some bright, shining, and entirely fictitious time in the future, the Register is supposed to contain all the significant historic places in the nation. Right now—in 2007—it includes over 80,000 properties, many of them "districts" made up of multiple buildings, structures, sites, and/or objects.

Since it's the National Register of *Historic* Places, many, if not most, of the places on it reflect specific historical events or people, or broad patterns of international, national, state, regional, tribal, or local history. But properties can also be eligible for the Register if they have other values, such as:

The desire to protect architectural character was one of ideas that motivated the drafters of the National Historic Preservation Act. Fort Leavenworth, KS. Photo by the author.

- *Architectural* value—as fine, or interesting, typical or atypical pieces of grand or humble architecture, the work of great and well-known architects or "vernacular" artisans whose identities may have been forgotten.
- *Engineering* value—importance in the history and development of civil, mechanical, electrical, aerospace, and other kinds of engineering.
- *Archaeological* value—value as subjects for study by archaeologists to learn about the human past, including both the distant, "prehistoric" past of Native American cultures before Columbus and the more recent "historic" past.
- *Cultural* value—importance for association with the cultural traditions, beliefs, practices, or identity of a community, a group, a tribe, or the whole nation or world. It's not uncommon for a cultural place to be a *spiritual place*—a place, that is, that someone values for spiritual, more or less religious reasons.

Archaeological sites are among the places considered under Section 106. Cabrillo College excavations near Santa Cruz, California. Courtesy Rob Edwards, Cabrillo College.

There are other kinds of places that federal law protects. Wet places, for example, called *wetlands*, are protected, in some cases and to some extent, under the *Clean Water Act*. The *habitats* of endangered plants and animals are protected—to some extent—under the *Endangered Species Act*. But this book is about protecting places (which sometimes *are* wetlands and habitats) that people value for some kind of historic or cultural reason.

A historic place can be a particular building or other structure; a group of structures, such as a neighborhood or a downtown, a village or town; or a huge (or not so huge) piece of land with or without structures on it—a mountain, a forest, a farm landscape, a river. Or it can be a specific location or site—your grandfather's farmstead, your ancestors' village site, your tribe's sacred grove, the wreck of your pirate ancestor's ship. It may even be a somewhat movable place—maybe a boat, a ship, an airplane—but if it's *very* movable, if you can just pick it up and walk away with it without changing it or diminishing its importance to people, then it's probably not eligible for the National Register because there's no need to use laws like Section 106 to protect it in place.

Historic rural landscapes are often threatened by federal government actions. Buckland, Virginia. Photo by the author.

Impacts on large natural areas can be the subjects of Section 106 Review. The Klamath River in Northern California is a cultural place of great importance to the Karuk, Yurok, Hoopa, and Shasta tribes. Photo by the author.

Laws, executive orders, regulations

I keep talking about "laws," but I'm simplifying—maybe oversimplifying—when I do so. Federal agencies—and those like you or me who want to influence agency decisions—have to deal with a complicated body of legal direction that generally breaks down as follows:

Federal laws are enacted by Congress and signed by the president. NHPA is such a law, of course, and Section 106 is one section of it. The National Environmental Policy Act (NEPA) is another federal law we'll touch on a good deal. NHPA was enacted in 1966, NEPA in 1969, and both—like other laws—have been amended now and then by subsequent acts of Congress. State laws—which we're not going to discuss much in this book—are created in the same way by state legislatures and governors. Local laws are enacted by local governments—cities, counties, parishes. Indian tribes also enact laws, binding within the boundaries of their reservations.

Regulations direct agencies and others (for example, those seeking federal funds or permits) in how to comply with laws. They're issued by rulemaking agencies specified in the laws to which they relate. The rulemaking agencies for different parts of NHPA are the National Park Service and the Advisory Council on Historic Preservation, but the Council is the rulemaker for Section 106. The Advisory Council's regulations for Section 106 are called 36 CFR 800—which means Title 36, Part 800, of the Code of Federal Regulations. The rulemaking agency for NEPA is the Council on Environmental Quality (CEQ), in the executive office of the president. CEQ's regulations are 40 CFR 1500–1508—that is, Title 40, Parts 1500 through 1508 of the Code of Federal Regulations. Various National Park Service regulations (especially 36 CFR 60) govern the National Register. Regulations have the force of law—they must be complied with by whomever they apply to.

Executive orders in the U.S. government are issued by the president and give special direction to agencies about how to interpret and carry out various aspects of various laws. Often they aren't derived very directly from any specific law's particular requirements, but they have to be somehow grounded in law. For example, Executive Order 12898—the 12,898th executive order issued by a president of the United States (Bill Clinton)—deals with "environmental justice." It's grounded in Title 6 of the Civil Rights Act, but it also relates to NEPA, NHPA, and other laws that deal with the environment. It directs agencies to be alert to environmental issues affecting low-income groups and minority communities, and to try to avoid undue environmental impacts on them. Executive orders don't exactly have the force of law—you can't take one to court all by itself—but they do represent the chief executive's direction to the executive branch, and that makes them important. And by the way, they don't disappear when a new president is elected, unless the new president explicitly rescinds them. Governors and Indian tribal leaders issue executive orders, too, which are binding on agencies of the state or tribe in which they're issued.

Case law is the body of court cases interpreting laws and regulations. When a case is adjudicated—decided by a court—the decision becomes part of case law and provides precedent for later decisions. There are several levels to our courts. In the federal system, there are district courts, appeals courts, and the Supreme Court. State courts are organized in roughly the same way, and generally so are tribal courts. A decision made by a district court provides precedent only in that district, though other district courts may refer to it for advice. In other words, if the district court for the Northern District of California interprets some provision of NHPA, subsequent decisions in that district are pretty much bound to interpret it the same way, but a court in the Southern District of California or the District of New Mexico doesn't have to. If (in the case of California) the case is appealed to the Ninth Circuit Court of Appeals, then the decision of that appeals court will be binding on all district courts in the Ninth Circuit but not in the Tenth Circuit where New Mexico is located. If the appeals court's decision is appealed to the Supreme Court, the decision of that court is binding on everybody. A decision of a state court isn't binding on any federal court, and neither is the decision of a tribal court, but they are binding within their own jurisdictions. Some agencies also have internal court—like bodies, whose administrative law judges (ALJs) interpret agency regulations and procedures. Their determinations are relevant within their agencies' jurisdictions only, subject to review by actual courts of law. The military services administer their own legal systems, under the direction of Judge Advocates General (JAGs).

The Constitution. Underlying all this is the U.S. Constitution; everything the federal government and state or local governments do must be constitutional. Much of the federal authority to regulate activities in places not owned by the federal government—for example, in navigable waterways and in wetlands like marshes somehow connected to such waterways—springs from the Constitution's Commerce Clause, which reserves to the federal government the regulation of interstate commerce. Waterways are necessary to commerce; wetlands keep the waterways healthy, so the federal government has the authority and responsibility to take care of wetlands.

Indian treaties. Indian tribes and their agencies and courts acting on reservations are not bound by the U.S. Constitution except to the extent the U.S. Congress has made them so through legislation. Both tribes and the U.S. government are bound by the terms of treaties negotiated between them back in the 18th and 19th centuries; the terms of treaties are in principle superior even to the Constitution. Some tribes have treaties, while others do not. Among the things that many treaties did was to reserve rights for tribes to certain things—like water and fish—and to the use of certain places or types of place, usually referred to as usual and accustomed places, to fish, hunt, or gather plants.

Admiralty law governs navigation and shipping. If your important place is a shipwreck, admiralty law may be what you use to protect it, and what others use to get access to it. Under admiralty law, a person who finds a shipwreck can file with an admiralty court (in the United States, the district court) to "arrest" it. If the arrest is awarded, the awarded party has sole jurisdiction over the wreck for a period of time, during which he can, and indeed in most cases must, try to salvage it. One can't arrest the wreck of a commissioned naval vessel, however; the Navy never gives up the ship. And in near-shore and inland waters of the United States, the Abandoned Shipwrecks Act gives states jurisdiction over abandoned wrecks. Protecting—or doing anything else with—a shipwreck can be a complicated and conflict-laden enterprise.

Agency procedures. Most federal agencies have internal procedures for dealing with the laws, regulations, and executive orders that are most relevant to them, and prescribing standardized ways of doing business. These may be called many things—procedures, guidelines, manuals. These are simply the agency's interpretations of its responsibilities, and its internal mechanisms for carrying them out. They don't have the force of law, but they can be very important to people working in the agencies, who often come to understand them—for better or worse—as the way things are "supposed to be done." Unfortunately, they're not always entirely consistent with the laws and regulations themselves.

Interagency agreements. Federal agencies sometimes have agreements with other agencies about how legal responsibilities are carried out. Sometimes these deal with situations where agencies share responsibilities—where the Forest Service manages the surface of a piece of land and the Bureau of Land Management is responsible for the underlying minerals, for example. Other times they're between an agency—say, the Forest Service with respect to managing a national forest—and a rulemaking or regulatory agency like the Advisory Council on Historic Preservation. In such cases, the agreements typically specify how the action agency will bend the requirements of the rulemaking agency's regulations a bit to accommodate its particular needs. Such agreements are perfectly legal provided they're executed in accordance with specified procedures (usually set forth in the rulemaking agency's regulations) and provided the public has had an opportunity to learn about them and influence their development. When such an agreement is in force, it—rather than the regulation it tweaks—governs how the agency complies with the relevant law. There is a good deal of mischief to be found in such agreements, as we'll see. Federal agencies also enter into agreements with state and local agencies, and with tribes; these too may legally alter the way an agency carries out its responsibilities, provided they're consistent with relevant laws and regulations.

International agreements, conventions, and recommendations can influence how places are managed, even within the boundaries of the United States. The North American Free Trade Agreement (NAFTA), for example, is a treaty among the United States and its neighbors, Canada and Mexico. It includes provision for adjudicating conflicts when the actions of one party affect the trade-related interests of another. NAFTA has been used—at this writing, unsuccessfully—by a Canadian company to try to overturn a California state law whose effect was to keep the company from mining the Trail of Dreams landscape, a place of great spiritual importance to the Quechan tribe. Conventions and recommendations are issued by United Nations bodies such as the United Nations Educational, Scientific, and Cultural Organization (UNESCO). A convention is binding on nations that become parties to it; a recommendation is simply the international organization's statement of "best practices." For example, the United States is a party to the UNESCO Convention Concerning the Protection of the World Cultural and Natural Heritage, which means it can nominate places to UNESCO as having cultural and/or natural significance to the whole world, through a complex set of procedures laid on top of those used for putting something on the National Register. UNESCO's Recommendation Concerning the Preservation of Cultural Property Endangered by Public or Private Works, on the other hand, merely advises the U.S. and other governments about how cultural places should be treated when threatened by construction projects. The government is free to ignore it, but it's not entirely without value. If nothing else, it indicates a worldwide concern for such places, and a worldwide preference for not letting construction and land-use projects muck them up.

Confused? Let it go; don't worry about it. Just hold onto the fact that the federal *laws* we'll be discussing, the *regulations* that spring from them, and the *executive orders* that surround them, govern the actions of *federal agencies*, which *carry out* projects, *help others* carry out projects, and *license others* to carry out projects. And without getting bogged down in the complexity of it all, remember that the legal requirements *are* complex, and as a result there may be a range of ways to interpret them—all of which may be more or less equally "correct," depending on where you're coming from and where you want to go. This is why people pay lawyers big bucks.

> CONTACT: You can find UNESCO conventions and related documents at http://www.icomos.org/unesco/

Federal versus State versus Local Laws

One more thing to be clear about is that different levels and kinds of authority are more or less reserved to different levels of government. Generally speaking, it's local governments that have what is sometimes referred to as *police power*—that is, the power to direct *individuals* in how to behave *on their own property*—while the federal government does not. There are exceptions, of course, where the Constitution gives the federal government authority over individuals—this is why federal courts try the killers of civil rights activists not for murder but for violating their victims' civil rights. In general, though, the local cops walk or drive the beat and make sure individuals don't rob or murder others or jaywalk or park cars in the wrong places. State police will pull you over for speeding on an interstate highway, but don't give parking tickets in town. The FBI won't give you a speeding ticket. In the same way, the federal government doesn't regulate how land is used by private property owners, except where that use involves something over which the federal government has jurisdiction—such as a national forest, land managed by the Bureau of Land Management, a river used in interstate commerce and its tributaries and wetlands, and, to some extent, the air we all breathe and the water we all drink. The federal government can't tell you what color you can paint your privately owned house, or whether you can cut down your privately owned tree. But local government can, and does; it has that local police power.

So, with respect to privately funded projects on private land, it's the local planning and zoning authority that has the power to say yes or no—within the framework of local law. The authority may be a city planning commission, a county zoning board, a board of supervisors, or a town's historic preservation commission. That authority, whatever it is, can say yes, you can build a shopping mall in X location because it's consistent with local planning and zoning, or no, you can't because it's not. Assuming, of course, that local law gives it that authority. The federal government can't say that unless the land involved is something over which the federal government has authority. So if you want to truly kill a private project on private land, you're almost certainly going to have to convince local government to do so.

You can use federal laws like Section 106 of NHPA to influence a project if the developer needs a federal grant or loan, or if the project involves something over which a federal agency has jurisdiction, like federal land, navigable waters, or (in many cases) wetlands. But even in such cases, the federal government's authority is seldom to say yes or no to the project per se; it is usually to say yes, you can use this federal assistance, or no, you can't; yes, you can fill this marsh to build your project, or no, you can't. If the project proponent can find a way to build the project without federal assistance and without filling the marsh, then the federal government is out of the picture. This obviously can affect your strategy in dealing with a threatening development. You can't expect a federal agency to do more than the law—ultimately the Constitution—allows it to do. And if you make things so difficult that the private developer gives up on using federal money or getting a federal license and designs the project to require neither, you'll no longer be able to use federal law to influence the project. In the final analysis, your best recourse may be to local authorities.

But where the development can't be done without federal involvement—on federal land, for instance, or where a private or state project really needs federal assistance or a federal permit—then skillful use of federal laws like Section 106 may be the key to success. If nothing else, you may be able to use the federal review processes to slow down the project and force consideration of alternatives, while you work on local government to kill it altogether.

The laws aren't the only complicated issues you have to deal with in trying to save your special place. Before we get into how you can actually work the system, we need to be acquainted with the groups, institutions, agencies, and organizations that participate in Section 106 review. That's what the next chapter is about.

CHAPTER THREE

The Cast of Characters

When we write about laws like Section 106, we refer to institutions such as "the agency," "the State Historic Preservation Officer," and "the environmental advocacy group." In the real world, of course, you don't deal with institutions; you deal with people. It's a mistake to stereotype—to assume that land developers are always rapacious exploiters of nature, for example—but people with particular jobs and missions do tend to behave in somewhat predictable ways, because they're subject to somewhat predictable pressures. Let's summarize some of the major types of characters you're likely to deal with.

THE PROJECT PROPONENT

The *proponent* of a project, of course, is the person or group that wants to do something, for example, to build something. The proponent may be a federal agency, or may be somebody else entirely—a state agency, a local agency, an Indian tribe, a corporation, a property owner. Generally speaking, private project proponents—land developers, pipeline companies, mining companies, for example—have more freedom to put money into planning their projects than government agencies do, and more flexibility in how they seek to advance their interests. They can and often do hire very good lawyers, planners, and environmental impact assessment firms. Government agencies—federal, state, tribal, and local—tend to be less well supported financially and less well equipped with expert assistance. Their representatives may seem frazzled, because they're trying to juggle a lot of different responsibilities. The saddest kind of project proponent is the plain-joe citizen who wants to do something like put in a boat dock or a sewer connection for which he needs a government permit. Such a citizen usually has very little money and expertise, little professional backing, and is pretty much at the mercy of those with more of both.

It's important to size up the project proponent, get an idea of who or what he or she or it is, what kind of financial and personnel and technical resources they have, and who they answer to.

One special kind of proponent that often gets tripped up by Section 106 is the state transportation agency—the (state) Department of Transportation, (state) Division of Highways, (state) Bureau of Mass Transit. These agencies get a lot of money from the U.S. Department of Transportation, through agencies such as the Federal Highway Administration (FHWA). They typically have large, well-equipped environmental review and historic preservation staffs, but their understanding of Section 106 and other laws is often narrow and stilted. FHWA and other U.S. transportation agencies delegate most of their Section 106 responsibilities to the states but remain responsible for compliance with the law. This means that on a particular project you'll find the state transportation agency in the fore, but it's often a good idea to try to bring in the state's federal partner. If nothing else, you can cause the state to sit up and take notice if you complain to the feds.

Another special case is a local government that receives grant assistance from the federal Department of Housing and Urban Development (HUD). HUD has the legal authority to delegate environmental review responsibilities to its grant applicants, so for all practical purposes the local government takes on the federal agency's role. But HUD is there in the background and can be complained to if the city shirks its responsibilities. HUD has even been known to *do something* in response to such complaints—like investigating and, if it finds that the city government really has screwed up, yanking the city's grant until it cleans up its act.

Here are some examples of common project proponents who see their projects reviewed under Section 106:

Federal agencies

- The U.S. Army Corps of Engineers, when building or maintaining dams, locks, levees, and so on
- The Bureau of Land Management, managing federal lands and projects on such lands
- The Forest Service, managing national forests and projects like timber harvesting

The Cast of Characters

- The National Park Service, managing National Parks and the historic places they contain
- The Fish and Wildlife Service, managing wildlife refuges
- The Department of Energy, managing various laboratories and test facilities, often quite large ones
- The military services—Army, Navy, Air Force, Marines—managing military bases, carrying out exercises, doing construction, closing and disposing of bases
- The General Services Administration, building and managing federal buildings, disposing of federal property

State agencies

- Highway, railroad, and airport authorities with assistance from the U.S. DOT
- State water or waste management agencies, getting financial assistance from the U.S. Environmental Protection Agency (EPA)
- State toxic waste agencies, getting financial aid from the U.S. EPA, Department of Energy (for nuclear wastes), and sometimes other agencies
- State agencies that need permits from federal agencies like the Corps of Engineers (see below)

Local agencies

- Local utility (sewer, water, electricity, etc.) agencies getting assistance from Rural Development or other Department of Agriculture agencies
- Local governments with Community Development Block Grants and other forms of assistance from the U.S. Department of HUD
- Local agencies that need permits from federal agencies like the Corps of Engineers (see below)

Non-governmental bodies

- Anyone who wants to dump fill into a wetland, if the wetland has some sort of connection with a navigable waterway, and who therefore needs a permit from the U.S. Army Corps of Engineers. Besides federal, state, and local agencies, this can include (for example):

- Mining companies
- Oil, natural gas, and other pipeline companies

Snoqualmie Falls in Washington State is an Indian tribal spiritual site managed by a public utility company (Puget Sound Energy) under a permit from a federal regulatory agency (the Federal Energy Regulatory Commission, or FERC)

The Cast of Characters

- Farmers and ranchers
- Developers of housing tracts, shopping malls, and other such developments
- Private citizens who want to stop their shorelines from eroding, or build boat docks
- Anyone who needs a permit to use federal (for instance, BLM or Forest Service) land, such as:
  - Mining companies
  - Pipeline companies
  - Suppliers of electricity and builders of transmission lines
  - Owners of recreational residences on federal land
- Anyone who needs a permit from a federal regulatory agency to do something that could change the environment—for instance:
  - Utility companies with hydroelectric projects regulated by the Federal Energy Regulatory Commission (FERC)
  - Telecommunication companies putting up things like wireless communication antennae, which require approval by the Federal Communications Commission (FCC)

So, there's always a project proponent, who may be a federal agency or may be almost anyone else, provided he or she or it has some kind of federal connection—funding, a permit, whatever.

Federal Agency Overseers

Federal agencies that provide assistance or permits to non-federal parties (or sometimes to other federal agencies) are responsible for doing Section 106 review on the projects that those other parties are trying to undertake. They aren't necessarily the proponents of the projects, but they're responsible for making sure that project planning is carried out in a manner consistent with law and regulation. Some of these agencies do nothing but provide assistance or permits; others do other things besides—such as managing land or building things themselves.

For example, the U.S. Army Corps of Engineers, besides building and maintaining levees, dams, locks, and the like, and building things for the military services, also administers a permit program under Section 404 of the Clean Water Act. Anyone who wants to discharge fill—that is, dirt, rocks, or something of the kind—into U.S. waters that are either navigable or in some plausible way connected to navigable waters must get a Section 404 permit from the Corps.

Unlike the Corps, the Federal Energy Regulatory Commission (FERC) and Nuclear Regulatory Commission (NRC) are "pure" regulatory bodies; they don't build or manage things, they simply regulate the way others build or manage hydroelectric projects or natural gas pipelines in the case of FERC, nuclear facilities in the case of NRC.

The Federal Highway Administration (FHWA) is one of the biggest federal overseers, providing assistance to, and therefore overseeing the actions of, the state departments of transportation. Other U.S. Department of Transportation agencies like the Federal Aviation Administration (FAA) do similar things, though FAA also has a variety of regulatory and standard-setting functions.

Other overseeing agencies include:

- **The U.S. Environmental Protection Agency**, which provides financial assistance to communities to improve wastewater systems and to state toxic and hazardous waste agencies to help find and clean up environmental pollutants.
- **The Department of Homeland Security (DHS)**, which gives grants to states and cities to improve security arrangements, train first responders, upgrade equipment, respond to emergencies, and so on. Some agencies of the DHS also carry out their own projects and have their own regulatory functions. For example, the Coast Guard builds and upgrades aids to navigation and regulates certain bridge projects.
- **The Federal Deposit Insurance Corporation (FDIC)**, which has to approve things like the installation of automated teller machines (ATMs) in banks.
- **The Bureau of Land Management (BLM)**, the Forest Service, or any other land management agency whenever they consider permitting someone to do something on or across land they manage—such as installing a pipeline or running an off-road vehicle race, or when they lease such resources as timber and minerals to others.

State, regional, and local agency overseers are a special case. Some state agencies, local governments, and regional intergovernmental groups are conduits for federal funds; for example, a state environmental agency may receive funds from the U.S. EPA and pass them on to Community X to put in a new sewer plant. In such a case the state, local, or regional agency is part of the project's administration and therefore plays a role in review of the project under laws like Section 106, but it's in a kind of ill-defined middleman position. Its exact role varies considerably from case to case.

Other state/local/regional bodies are delegated permitting responsibilities by federal agencies, like the U.S. EPA under the Clean Air Act, or have permit programs overseen by federal agencies, like the National Oceanic and Atmospheric Administration (NOAA) under the Coastal Zone Management Act. Permits issued by these non-federal agencies aren't subject to review under Section 106, but the federal agency programs under which they're administered *are* subject to review, so the federal agencies that oversee them—in theory—have some kind of responsibility under the law. Exactly what kind of responsibility is something that people like me argue about; it's not been very thoroughly worked out.

Government Review Agencies

Under Section 106, there are two or three critical government agencies that review projects, though usually only one is deeply involved in any given project.

The SHPO

The State Historic Preservation Officer is usually that agency. According to the law (NHPA), the SHPO is responsible simply for advising and assisting agencies, project proponents, and others as they work with the Section 106 process, but the regulations make the SHPO a sort of gatekeeper. The federal agency responsible for a project must consult with the SHPO at every step in the process. Many agencies, and quite a few SHPOs, have let this consultation requirement evolve into one in which the SHPO basically sets standards and then reviews the work of agencies, proponents, and their contractors to see if they meet them. SHPOs in such systems come to be regarded as approvers or disapprovers of projects, essentially the same as permitting agencies. That's not what the law or the regulations say they are, but that's what many have become. This can be a problem for several reasons that we'll discuss as we go along, but one big one is that SHPOs are virtually never staffed or financially supported to fill the permitting agency role, and they have lots of other things to do.

The SHPO is designated by the governor of each state, by whatever system the state wants to use. In some cases they're lodged in state historical societies, sometimes in state museums. Others are in state planning offices or environmental departments. The SHPO receives funding from the National Park Service, which has to be matched by state or other non-federal support.

People often assume that the SHPO ought to be an unblinking advocate for the preservation of historic places, but this is unrealistic. If an SHPO is to survive in state government, let alone accomplish anything, he or she has to be political, and the most successful SHPOs are just that. This of course has a downside—if the SHPO's political butter is on the project proponent's side of the bread, it may be difficult for the SHPO not to lean toward the proponent's point of view. But because the SHPO is expected, in the words of the Section 106 regulations, to "reflect the interests of the State and its citizens in the preservation of their cultural heritage," there has to be some balance; even the governor can't expect the SHPO not to pay *some* attention to historic preservation. And SHPO staff—typically archaeologists, architectural historians, and historians for the most part—tend to regard themselves as defenders of the state's historic heritage, sometimes to a fault. Unfortunately, being a vigorous defender of historic places within a state agency can be a thankless task, and a lot of SHPO staff experience burnout. When they do, if they remain in their jobs they can become the most soulless of bureaucrats, intent on making the paperwork move efficiently but with little enthusiasm left for actually preserving anything.

> CONTACT: You can find out who your State Historic Preservation Officer is at http://www.ncshpo.org/stateinfolist/fulllist.htm

The THPO

A Tribal Historic Preservation Officer performs essentially the same functions as an SHPO, but does so within an Indian tribe, on behalf of that tribe's government. The THPO can act in lieu of the SHPO if the tribe has reached an agreement with the National Park Service about how this will be done; this sort of substitution applies only to lands within the exterior boundaries of the tribe's reservation, and to "dependent Indian communities." Because much of the land originally reserved on behalf of tribes was more or less stolen by others during the 19th and 20th centuries, there may be quite a bit of land within the external boundaries of a reservation that's not owned in fee by the tribe or held in trust for it by the U.S. government. So even if you're not a member of an Indian tribe, your special place may be on what's defined in NHPA as "tribal land," and you may be dealing with the THPO instead of the SHPO. Elsewhere, you may deal with both—for instance, if the tribe has interests in areas outside the reservation (as all do). Incidentally, "Indian tribe" for NHPA purposes means a tribe that's officially recognized as such by the U.S. government—that is, by the Department of the Interior. There are over 500 federally recognized tribes, but as of 2006 fewer than 70 have THPOs.

Except in the case of giant tribes such as the Navajo, THPO offices are usually small, often only one or two people, and they usually have miniscule financial resources. Some tribes (particularly those that get some financial support from the National Park Service) have professional archaeologists or other preservation experts on staff; others don't. Besides having to do everything (more or less) that SHPOs do, the THPO has to work closely with the tribal government and with the tribe's elders, who usually hold most of the historical and cultural knowledge.

CONTACT: For information on THPOs, see www.nathpo.org

The ACHP

The Advisory Council on Historic Preservation is a tiny, tiny independent federal agency—meaning it's not inside any big executive department like Interior or Agriculture or Defense. It reports to both the president and Congress and has two major functions: advising them about historic preservation matters by commenting on proposed legislation, doing studies, and sometimes carrying out special programs; and overseeing the Section 106 process. The ACHP is the rulemaking agency for Section 106; it's the ACHP's regulations (36 CFR 800) that agencies have to follow in carrying out their 106 responsibilities.

The ACHP is based in Washington, DC. It's made up of two parts: the Council itself, and the staff. The Council is a 20-member body that meets about four times a year to ponder matters of importance and occasionally comment on a Section 106 case. It has the following members:

- A chairman and vice-chairman appointed by the president
- The Secretary of the Interior
- The Secretary of Agriculture
- The Architect of the Capital
- The chairman of the National Trust for Historic Preservation (a nationwide advocacy group)
- The president of the National Conference of State Historic Preservation Officers (the SHPOs' national organization)
- Four other agency heads appointed periodically by the president
- A governor appointed by the president
- A mayor appointed by the president
- A representative of Indian tribal or Native Hawaiian interests, appointed by the president
- Three historic preservation "experts" appointed by the president
- Three general citizen members appointed by the president

The staff does the day-to-day work of the ACHP. It's made up of about 40 people in Washington, most of them historic preservation professionals (architects, historians, archaeologists, and the like) with a sprinkling of lawyers and planners and support staff. Some of the ACHP's staff members are actually paid for by other agencies and provide liaison between the ACHP and those agencies; the potential for conflict of interest arising from this situation doesn't seem to bother anybody.

It's important to recognize that the ACHP is the Advisory Council *on* Historic Preservation, not *for* Historic Preservation. In other words, it's no more the unblemished advocate for preservation than the SHPO is; it purports to seek "the public interest," whatever that may be. It's just as susceptible to political pressure as an SHPO is, but the pressure typically has to come from a higher level—the White House, the Congress, or somebody with strings to pull in one of those two locations.

There are many government review agencies under laws other than Section 106. The Council on Environmental Quality (CEQ) and Environmental

Protection Agency (EPA) oversee aspects of compliance with the National Environmental Policy Act (NEPA). The Fish and Wildlife Service (FWS) in the Department of the Interior is one of the overseers for the Endangered Species Act (ESA), and so on. You may well need to deal with these agencies, but for Section 106 purposes it's the SHPO, THPO, and ACHP that you'll most likely be working with.

> CONTACT: To learn about the ACHP, visit www.achp.gov

INDIAN TRIBES AND NATIVE HAWAIIAN GROUPS

Federally recognized Indian tribes have special roles and rights under Section 106, whether or not they have THPOs. Although anyone's special places may be eligible for the National Register, Section 102(d)(6) of NHPA makes a point of telling agencies that places of cultural and religious significance to a tribe can be eligible. This is because back in the late 1980s a lot of agencies treated them as not eligible, and Congress was persuaded that they needed a reminder. The same section requires agencies to consult with tribes during Section 106 review about such places, wherever they may be. More generally, tribes are regarded in federal law as sovereign nations, with whom the U.S. government must relate on a "government to government" basis. Consultation with tribal governments is supposed to be carried out by "line officers" in an agency—people like regional directors or forest supervisors who are directly (if remotely) answerable to the president—and not just by staff or contractors. And the U.S. government has what's called a "trust responsibility" toward tribes. This means different things to different people in different contexts, but in a broad sense it means that federal agencies are supposed to look out for a tribe's interests, and act in ways that support—or at least don't do great damage to—those interests. Finally, many tribes have treaties with the U.S. government, and treaties are the "supreme law of the land." Exactly what that means in terms of consultation can be pretty unclear, but if nothing else, treaties can make federal agencies very nervous and complicate matters for their lawyers.

So if you're a federally recognized tribe, you have a bit more power in the Section 106 process than others do, and in some cases a lot more power. If you're not a federally recognized tribe, it means that gaining the alliance of such a tribe may be a very, very good idea.

In Hawaii, NHPA tells federal agencies to treat Native Hawaiian groups—that is, groups composed of people tracing their ancestry to the days before Captain Cook—in pretty much the same way as Indian tribes. The trouble is that Native Hawaiian groups don't have the sort of government-to-government relationship that tribes do with the U.S. government, so their power in the Section 106 process is a good deal less clear. This may change in the not too distant future; the political status of Native Hawaiian groups is in flux.

A tribe can also be a project proponent, a recipient of federal assistance and permits, or the administrator of federally delegated programs. Tribes can take over federal program responsibilities on their reservations—running timber operations, building roads, and so on—and because their work is carried out with federal supervision, they're subject to Section 106 review themselves, just as though they were state highway departments or regulated pipeline companies. In theory, Section 106 review of such a tribal project works in the same way as does review of any other project. In practice, though, the sovereign nation status of tribal governments can complicate your involvement in such review if you don't happen to be a tribal member—and sometimes even if you are.

Architect/Engineering/Planning Firms

The projects that get reviewed under Section 106 are often designed by some kind of specialist—architects where buildings are concerned, landscape architects where the action involves parks, parkways, and the like, and engineers, and planners. These specialists are typically found in private firms that compete for contracts with government agencies, public utilities, and private development firms. These are the guys who'll be at public hearings with slick plans and drawings, tabulated facts and figures, and fancy Powerpoint shows describing the project and its many benefits. And if you suggest that maybe the purpose of the project could be achieved as well or better by doing something else, they're the ones who'll assure you that it can't be done that way.

There are a lot of fine, skillful, thoughtful people in architect and engineer (A&E) firms, and they can be quite creative and responsible. But they do tend to exhibit linear thinking and to get very attached to their way, or their clients' way, of doing something. And they have no legal responsibilities under Section 106; they don't have to take effects on historic places into account except to the extent their clients tell them to. Some of them have some idea what Section 106 requires (though sometimes their ideas are pretty exotic), and some firms even have expertise in historic architecture, archaeology, and other such fields. But even the best firms are mainly (and understandably) focused on getting the job done in a manner that's acceptable to the client, which means (among other things) on time and within budget. There are times when you can make this work in your favor, but most times, if what you want is the thorough consideration of alternatives that will save your special place, it will be something you have to struggle with.

Environmental Impact Assessment Firms

Some A&E firms have branches or offices that specialize in environmental impact assessment work—doing the studies and preparing the documents necessary for compliance with such laws as the National Environmental Policy Act (NEPA), the Endangered Species Act (ESA), and Section 106. There are also freestanding environmental impact firms, independent of any A&E firm, that do impact assessment work and nothing else, and there are some firms that do nothing but "cultural resource" impact assessment. Both types of operation may be staffed and run by honest and honorable people, but the freestanding impact assessment firm is a bit less likely than the A&E firm to see itself as representing the project proponent's interests.

In theory, an impact assessment firm should perform an objective analysis of the probable effects that the project may have on the environment, including the effects of reasonable alternative ways of achieving the project's goals. The firms are usually staffed with professionally trained biologists, geologists, soil scientists, air and water quality specialists, and so on, and their "cultural resource" sections are typically made up of archaeologists, historians, and architectural historians. These are the people who'll be contracted by the project proponent to do the studies needed for compliance with Section 106.

Some environmental impact assessment firms have a clear understanding of Section 106 requirements, and others don't. You ought not assume that they're experts, no matter how many Ph.D.s their people have strung behind their names. Dr. X may be an expert archaeologist, but he or she doesn't necessarily know anything about historic buildings or landscapes or the traditional culture and history of your community, nor much about what the law and regulations require. And they can't help but be conflicted by the fact that they're being paid by the project proponent. Honestly and in some ways honorably, they feel an obligation to help the proponent advance his or her interests.

When you think about it, it's really a pretty strange way to seek an objective assessment of a project's potential effects on the environment: let the proponent hire the experts to do the assessment. But it's the way the system has evolved in the United States, and the courts and regulatory agencies have allowed it. So we're stuck with it, but there's little question that it works against the interests of the public—including your interests. Most impact assessment specialists I know—while they're entirely honest, honorable, professional people—see their job as keeping their clients' backsides covered, showing them how to get their projects built in a manner that doesn't outrage the requirements of law. A lot of these folks are very nice people, but don't think of them as your friends, or as objective analysts. They can't be.

Some oversight agencies hire "third party" contractors to do assessments, tapping the project proponents for the money to do so. This insulates the contractor from the proponent and may result in more objective analyses, but it makes the contractor subject to the agency's rules and biases, and that may not be very helpful.

CULTURAL RESOURCE MANAGEMENT FIRMS

There are also firms that do only "cultural resource management" work—by which they usually mean something they think approximates helping their clients comply with Section 106. Such firms may also do things such as preparing National Register nominations, managing artifact collections, and planning for the management of historic places on military installations. Some—particularly those whose main focus is architectural history or historic architecture—call themselves "historic preservation" firms, but most emphasize archaeology and use the acronym "CRM." They often are hired as subcontractors by A&E or environmental impact assessment firms. They're generally cut from the same cloth as the impact assessment outfits; they may be honest, honorable, good scholars, but they're inevitably compromised by their responsibilities toward their employers. They're also often very strongly influenced by the values and beliefs of their professional disciplines—usually archaeology, sometimes architectural history or historic architecture.

The Cast of Characters

PROJECT SUPPORTERS

The project that threatens your special place probably has supporters besides its proponent. Local governments, local, state, and federal elected officials, chambers of commerce, and special-interest groups whose interests will be served if the project goes forward are likely to be supporters, and you'll have to deal with them. They may become formal participants in Section 106 review, and they may have considerable economic and political power. If the project has a high profile, there may be groups that support it as a matter of principle. A controversial mining project, for example, may attract the support of people who don't believe that private land use and economic development should be constrained by federal regulation, as well as by such national industry groups as the American Mining Association. Each major industry whose members' projects are affected by things like Section 106 review has its own national organization, and in controversial cases they will line up behind their members. The supporters who typically show up at public meetings, however, and who sometimes participate actively in Section 106 review, tend to be local governments, chambers of commerce, and individuals or ad hoc organizations of people and businesses that will benefit from the project. These local groups in particular can lend a good deal of credibility to the project proponent's plans, making them look less like the work of outsiders and more like legitimate responses to local needs.

LOCAL/NEIGHBORHOOD OPPOSITION ORGANIZATIONS

Besides yourself (assuming you're trying to stop or seriously modify the project that threatens your place), there are probably others ready to oppose the project. It's usually a good idea to try to ally yourself with them. You should seek out local (and state, regional, and national) groups that may either share your point of view or have interests that are compatible with yours. Historical or archaeological societies, environmental groups, groups that support indigenous interests (if you're an indigenous group)—all these and many more may be helpful to you, for moral support if nothing else, and it may be helpful to try to bring them into the Section 106 process. And don't neglect your friends and neighbors, particularly others who value the place you're trying to save or who have other interests that are threatened by the project. You may find that many of these groups are completely unaware both of the facts surrounding the project and of laws like Section 106; you may have to help them understand what's going on and what can be done.

National Advocacy Groups

Finally, there are national and even international groups that can provide advice and sometimes technical and financial assistance, and that sometimes (though rarely) get involved directly in fighting threatening projects. Such organizations typically involve themselves deeply only in cases where they perceive the stakes to be high—cases that involve places widely regarded as significant, or that represent very important principles, or that have major legal or political implications. But even if they won't get directly involved, they may be able to provide useful advice and help you network with other interested organizations and government agencies. Some groups that tend to be knowledgeable and helpful to people in your position include the following:

The National Trust for Historic Preservation is a nationwide membership group that advocates the interests of historic preservation. The Trust has a (small and rather beleaguered) legal staff that's very knowledgeable about Section 106 and related matters, and a competent network of regional offices. You may also find that your state has a statewide historic preservation group, possibly allied with the National Trust, that can be helpful.

The Society for American Archaeology may be helpful if what you're concerned about is or can be considered an archaeological site or area. The SAA is a membership organization made up mostly of professional archaeologists, and it spends most of its time and resources on professional matters such as having meetings to talk about archaeology. But it does have a public affairs element, and does get involved in cases that pose major threats to important archaeological sites or that present challenging archaeological issues.

The Sierra Club and **Environmental Defense** (originally the Environmental Defense Fund) are probably the best-known conservation advocacy groups in the country. Neither has traditionally shown much expertise or even interest in dealing with cultural aspects of the environment, and sometimes they've been opposed to traditional (and other) cultural uses of the land, but if your special place is a natural place, you certainly ought

The Cast of Characters

to be in touch with one or both of these organizations. If your special place is in the city, you might try the **Urban Land Institute**.

EarthJustice specializes in litigation supporting conservation and preservation of land. A spin-off from the Sierra Club, EarthJustice tends to focus on natural places; they probably won't help you if your special place is an urban neighborhood. Nor will they likely be very sympathetic if what you want to preserve is your family's generations-old grazing rights on a national forest. But if your place is out in nature somewhere, and you need a lawyer, EarthJustice may be able to help.

More specialized organizations include the **Trust for Public Lands**, good if your special place is in a national forest, a wildlife refuge, or on public lands administered by the Bureau of Land Management, and **Cultural Survival** and the **Sacred Lands Film Project** if you're a tribe trying to save a spiritual place. Though it's not usually thought of as an organization that favors saving places or stopping projects, the **American Land Rights Association** and similar property rights groups could be helpful if what you're trying to save is a special place that you actually own.

CONTACT: For regulatory language pertinent to this chapter go to
http://www.achp.gov/regs-rev04.pdf and see 36 CFR 800.2

CONTACT: Some helpful organizations include:
National Trust for Historic Preservation: **www.nationaltrust.org/**
Sierra Club: **www.sierraclub.org/**
Trust for Public Lands: **www.tpl.org/**
EarthJustice: **earthjustice.org/**
Sacred Lands Film Project: **www.sacredland.org/**
American Land Rights Association: **www.landrights.org/**
Cultural Survival: **www.cs.org/**
Urban Land Institute: **www.uli.org/**
Society for American Archaeology: **www.saa.org/**

CHAPTER FOUR

How Section 106 Is Supposed to Work

And Why It Often Doesn't

SECTION 106: A THUMBNAIL SKETCH

Suppose the Mitybig Development Corporation is planning to build a shopping mall in Greenfields, your hometown. Suppose there's a federal agency involved somehow in the project. Maybe the agency is considering an economic development grant to the city government, which will put part of the money into Mitybig's project. Or maybe Mitybig wants a federal permit to fill a wetland or discharge sewage. What does Section 106 of the National Historic Preservation Act (NHPA)—and more particularly, its regulations at 36 CFR 800—require that agency to do?

The agency is supposed to look before it leaps. It's supposed to consider the impacts of its action on historic places—whether that action is doing something, assisting somebody else in doing something, or permitting somebody to do something—before it makes its decision. It's supposed to think about the impacts, talk about them with knowledgeable and affected people, and figure out what, if anything, can be done to make them less destructive than they might otherwise be. And, of course, it should consider whether it should take the action at all.

A federal agency responsibility

Notice that it's the *federal agency* that has to do those things. It's not Mitybig or the city or county or state government. This doesn't mean that Mitybig and the others won't wind up having to do things (like give up or redesign the project), or that they don't have responsibilities under state and local law, but it's the federal agency whose actions Section 106 directly controls.

Chapter Four – How Section 106 Is Supposed to Work

Does it get reviewed?

The first thing the agency has to do is decide whether the project needs to be reviewed under Section 106. This depends on the project's potential to affect historic properties—which does *not* mean whether it's going to knock down something with a historical marker on it. It's a good deal more complicated than that, as we'll see.

Consulting parties

Then the agency has to find out who may be concerned about historic properties in the area the project will affect. This will include at least the State Historic Preservation Officer (SHPO), and maybe Indian tribes, local governments, organizations, landowners, and just plain people like you and me. And it needs to start *consulting* with them, finding out their concerns. It also has to figure out how its Section 106 review will be coordinated with review under other laws, like the National Environmental Policy Act (NEPA)—which we'll touch on later.

The APE

The agency also has to establish the area within which effects may occur—usually a bigger area than the project site itself. In Mitybig's case, the *area of potential effects (APE)* may extend along highways that will feed traffic to and from the shopping mall, and maybe areas where the mall is likely to induce suburban growth.

What's out there?

Then the agency, in consultation with the other interested parties, identifies historic properties (if any) in the APE. Actually, the agency probably requires Mitybig to identify them, following standards imposed by the agency, though usually developed by the SHPO. This typically involves various kinds of studies and more consultation.

Places that have already been listed in the National Register are easy to find; you check the Register, to which every SHPO has access. What's trickier is identifying places that are *eligible* for listing but haven't been listed. Very likely, such places have never been recorded at all, but that doesn't mean they're not there. So the agency, or Mitybig, or most likely a "cultural resource" or environmental contractor working for Mitybig, has to go out and look. Then the agency and SHPO, often with others, consult about which places are and are not eligible for the Register.

What's going to happen to it?

Once that's decided, the agency has to determine what effects, if any, the project will have on the properties. That's done in consultation with the SHPO and others too, following procedures laid out in the regulations. If it's agreed that the project will not affect any historic properties at all, or that its effects won't be adverse, the agency is finished with Section 106 review and can make its decision about the project—let Mitybig go ahead, don't let it go ahead, or let it go ahead but with conditions to make sure that adverse effects don't actually occur.

Seeking agreement on resolution

If adverse effects *will* occur—if the project will bulldoze an archaeological site, knock down a historic building, mess up a culturally important landscape—

Panther Meadows, on Mt. Shasta in California, is an Indian tribal spiritual site saved from development impacts through the use of Section 106.

then everybody consults some more. In most cases they reach agreement on changes that should keep the effects under control. Maybe they're made to go away altogether; maybe they're reduced somehow; maybe they're compensated for in some way. If at least the agency and the SHPO agree—after listening to Mitybig and other concerned parties but not necessarily doing what they want—they record this in a *memorandum of agreement (MOA)*. The agency can then go on and make its decision, and if it allows Mitybig to go ahead, it must make sure the terms of the MOA are carried out.

ACHP comment

In rare cases agreement is not reached, and the matter is referred to the Advisory Council. The council then makes a *comment* to the head of the agency. The comment provides recommendations—perhaps to not let Mitybig build the project, perhaps to let it do so with changes, perhaps to let it go as is. The agency head has to document the agency's response but doesn't have to do what the Advisory Council says. Once the agency has documented the response, it's done with Section 106 and can make its decision.

Other ways of doing it

Some agencies have worked with the Advisory Council to adopt variants on the standard Section 106 process to meet their particular needs. The most common way to do this is via a *programmatic agreement (PA)* executed by the agency, the Advisory Council, and in most cases the National Conference of SHPOs on behalf of its members. An agency with a PA carries out Section 106 review differently from other agencies, and you pretty much have to learn the agency's own system if you want to influence the process.

That, in a very small nutshell, is the way Section 106 review is *supposed* to work. The way it *does* work, and the way you can make it work for you and your special places, is what the rest of this book is about.

A Quick Digression into NEPA

Before we plunge into how things really work, there's another law we need to have fixed in our minds: the National Environmental Policy Act, or NEPA.

Where Section 106 is about taking care of historic places, NEPA is about taking care of the whole "human environment"—including historic places and other places that are important for cultural reasons (libraries, for example, and recreation areas) as well as plants, animals, ecosystems, water, soil, floodplains, wetlands, air quality, aesthetic qualities, and human society itself. Enacted in 1969, the law sets out government policy favoring the environment, and then says that federal agencies must prepare "detailed statements" on the environmental impacts of "major federal actions significantly affecting the quality of the human environment."

The Council on Environmental Quality (CEQ) in the Executive Office of the President is the rulemaking agency for NEPA. Its regulations—40 CFR 1500 through 1508—focus mostly on how to prepare, review, and use those "detailed statements," called *environmental impact statements* (EIS). They also establish how agencies are to decide whether a given project will have a significant enough effect on the environment to require an EIS. Unlike the consultation-centered Section 106 regulations, the NEPA regulations focus on the conduct of scientific studies and interagency review to define impacts. Briefly, the NEPA process works like this:

In regulations that each agency issues, the agency identifies *categorical exclusions*. These are categories of projects that the agency has decided, and CEQ has agreed, don't need review because there's no chance they can have significant effects. But when an agency is deciding whether Project X—say, issuing a clean water permit to Mitybig—falls into an excluded category, it has to consider whether there are *extraordinary circumstances* that require further review. In many but not all agency procedures, impacts on historic places are listed among extraordinary circumstances.

If the project is not categorically excluded, then the agency either prepares an EIS or does an *environmental assessment* (EA) to determine the significance of its likely impacts. The EA is supposed to be a "brief but thorough" analysis—though many times it's neither—of the proposed project and any alternative ways that the agency thinks the project's purposes might be accomplished. Based on the EA, the agency either decides that the impacts may be significant, and does an EIS, or it decides that they won't be significant, and issues a *finding of no significant impact* (FONSI). Then it can make its decision about the project—do it, don't do it, do it with conditions.

If there will be a significant impact, the agency does an EIS, a detailed analysis that goes through a fairly elaborate system of agency and public reviews. Once the EIS has been completed and reviewed, the agency uses it in making its decision and issues a *record of decision* (ROD), explaining what it has decided and why.

How Section 106 Is Supposed to Work

That's NEPA in a nutshell. It's important to keep in mind because it, like Section 106, gives you opportunities to slow down, redirect, and even halt a project that threatens your special place. Explaining these opportunities in detail would take another book, but as we go along I'll try to identify places where Section 106 and NEPA intersect, and where it may be helpful to remind agencies of their NEPA responsibilities.

> CONTACT: For the NEPA regulations, see
> http://www.nepa.gov/nepa/regs /ceq/toc_ceq.htm

How Agencies Abuse Their Responsibilities: A Summary

Now let's consider how proponents and agencies perform in the real world. There's often a considerable difference between what laws and regulations tell agencies to do and what they actually do. While this is regrettable, it's often understandable, as we'll see. More importantly for the purposes of protecting your special place, deviations from legal requirements can create opportunities for project opponents and critics. Procedural flaws, if skillfully exploited, can bring a project to a screeching halt, at least for a while. Here are some common sources of procedural flaws.

Pro-forma, ho-hum review

Federal and state agency employees are overworked. You may not believe that based on your own experience, or on what you've heard or read or seen on TV, but in many cases it's true. This is not to say that they're always overworked *productively*; a lot of what they do is frustrating, tedious stuff that's evolved only to perpetuate whatever system they work in, that's carried out because "it's always been done that way," or that's done to make the political party currently in power look like it's changing things. But the fact remains that most employees of federal and state agencies don't have a lot of time to give to any particular piece of work.

If you're a conscientious public servant, this can be terribly frustrating, and a lot of people burn out, leaving government service or becoming a lot less conscientious. Of course, some aren't very conscientious to begin with.

An overworked person or group tends to develop routine ways of doing business that require devoting as little energy as possible to each piece of work. They often develop rote procedures and inflexible standards. *We require a Class II archaeological survey of the project site*, they may tell a project proponent; never mind that the project won't affect the ground—the only place where archaeological sites may occur—and *will* have visual impacts half a mile away. They may emphasize form over substance—if the right forms have been filed, the right reports submitted, they're satisfied, whatever the impacts of the project. They may become obsessed with deadlines and time frames. *We provide 30 days for public comment* (and don't give a damn what comments, if any, we get).

And they may hate to be bothered, resist being asked to give a project a second look, or look at it in a different way, or examine an alternative. They may build barriers against the outside world. "You want that report? File a Freedom of Information Act request." "I'm sorry, the deadline for comments has passed; we can't look at what you've sent us."

These strategies can create smooth, low-conflict offices where paper gets processed with little muss and fuss, but where the impacts of projects are effectively ignored.

But the practices, procedures, and policies of such offices may have little to do with what the laws require. They may in fact be diametrically opposed to what the laws require, and that can create vulnerabilities.

Shortcuts

A variant on ho-hum review is reliance on shortcuts. Reviewing dozens or hundreds of projects every month gets tedious, so people look for ways to simplify—for instance, by paying attention only to direct impacts, or by not worrying about how the public has been involved in review. A project reviewer may start off using such shortcuts only with small, routine projects with little potential for impact, but the people whose projects are reviewed may get used to them, and may be surprised and unhappy if the same procedures aren't applied in more complicated or controversial cases. After a while—particularly as old reviewers move on and new reviewers come in, learning on the job—everyone may come to believe that the shortcut process is what the law requires.

Ninety-nine times out of a hundred, the shortcut system may work just fine. But the original review system was designed the way it was for good reasons, and eventually a project is going to come along that's the kind of project that process was designed for. When this happens, the shortcut won't do the job, and the integrity of the whole project review exercise may be compromised.

Biased analyses

Pro-forma, ho-hum, and short-circuit reviews aren't necessarily biased or unfair; people are just selecting and following paths of least resistance. But the analyses performed by agency reviewers, and particularly by the employees or contractors of a project proponent, may be very definitely biased, and usually the bias is unconscious. A biased person who doesn't know he's biased tends to resent having his bias pointed out to him.

One obvious kind of bias is in favor of development. You can expect such a bias on the part of a project proponent and her immediate associates, whether the proponent is an agency official or a private developer. It's natural for a project proponent to seek people to help him—as associates, employees or contractors—who accept the goodness of his project and will help advance its goals. That's fine as long as the proponent is assembling engineers and architects and project planners and administrative assistants, but it's not at all fine when it comes to hiring environmental impact assessment experts. Such an expert ought to look critically at the proposed project and its potential impacts, and provide an objective assessment to the project proponent, to the agencies involved, to other stakeholders, and to the public. Of course, it's probably the case that no assessment can be entirely objective, but objectivity, or at least balance, ought to be what the analyst tries to achieve. This isn't always what happens. Often the impact assessment group—which may be an arm of an architect and engineer company, quite possibly one involved in designing or building the project—carries out its work under contract with the project proponent, and there's an unstated assumption that the firm will support and try to advance the proponent's interests. This may or may not be understood to extend to the point of lying about a project's impacts, but even where it doesn't require deliberately slanting the results of one's studies, it's likely to color the results in subtle, often hard-to-detect ways. And the firm's contract almost always calls for the results of the analysis to be turned in to the project proponent—who has, after all, paid for them—for the proponent to share with the regulatory agencies and with the public. In such a system there is a very strong motivation for the environmental impact firm to tell the project proponent what he or she wants to hear.

Pro-development bias can also be found in the agencies responsible for reviewing the impacts of a project. Some such agencies—the Corps of Engineers, for example—are run by engineers and planners who come to the agency through a revolving door from the development community and who may expect to go back. Even if they don't feel that the butter is on the development side of their professional bread, they are likely to share with their developer colleagues a general feeling that the highest and best use for a place is the one that involves maximum profit-producing development. This is certainly not always the case, but it's an inevitable possibility. This sort of bias can permeate the agency, affecting not only those whose professional training makes them lean toward building things—the engineers, the architects, some planners—but those who aren't so development-oriented. Before long the agency's biologists, archaeologists, and air quality experts may start seeing it as their duty to advance development—while trying, of course, to keep it from doing *too* much damage to the environment.

A bias *against* development can be just as big a problem as a bias in favor of it—even for people who are opposed to a project. You often find anti-development biases among impact reviewers in pro-preservation agencies like the National Park Service, the Fish and Wildlife Service, and some parts of the Environmental Protection Agency, but it turns up with surprising frequency in development-oriented agencies like the Corps of Engineers too. The attitude is that no development is good, no project proponent is to be trusted; whatever they say, they *must* be out to screw the environment. Skepticism about a proponent's promises is healthy, but it's not very conducive to productive negotiations when one automatically assumes that the project under review is a bad one, that the effects it may have are unjustified, that the project proponent is a rotter. The problem with this from the standpoint of a project opponent is that it can taint the objectivity of the review process and tempt the ultimate decision-maker—who almost never is the person with the anti-development bias—to dismiss all objections as the products of bias and decide in favor of the project.

More common, perhaps, than pro- or anti-development bias is the bias that comes from wearing professional blinders—looking at the world through your own profession's particular lenses and neglecting other perspectives. This is common in the world of what many of its practitioners call *cultural resource management (CRM)*. One would think that the practice of CRM as applied to impact assessment would involve evaluating the effects of a project on whatever is of cultural importance in the environment—including the local opera house, a vibrant neighborhood, or the local swimming hole, as well as old buildings and archaeological sites. But most people who call themselves cultural resource managers are trained as archaeologists and think of cultural resources in wholly archaeological terms. They may talk about being concerned with all kinds of cultural resources, but the decisions they make are often decisions that are sensible only if archaeology is all you're concerned about. Where will we do studies of impacts on cultural resources? Where the ground will be disturbed. How will we look for cultural resources that might be affected? Hire archaeologists to survey the ground. This is a very common flaw in impact analyses, and as we'll see, it's easy to exploit.

Archaeologists are not the only ones who can fall victim to professional bias. Biologists may define the environment wholly in terms of plants and animals. Architectural historians may walk through a neighborhood recording the building styles they see, without ever talking with the people who live there. Environmental engineers, concerned with controlling the discharge of toxins into the air and water, often have trouble understanding that there is anything to environmental impact analysis *other than* the control of such discharges. Professional biases can produce huge holes in the way a project is planned and the way its impacts are considered.

Footprint fetishism

When identifying and dealing with historic properties, project proponents and review agencies regularly try to restrict their responsibilities to the precise "footprint" of the project. In other words, when seeking historic properties that might be affected, the only areas they'll look at are the places where the project will knock down buildings or churn up soil. The project may have visual, auditory, socioeconomic, and other effects at various distances from the project site, but they'll still focus only on the footprint. But the regulations call for attention to all kinds of effects—physical, visual, auditory, economic, traffic; direct, indirect, and cumulative. Any plausible effect on historic properties is supposed to be considered. If they're not fully considered, the agency may have a hole in its Section 106 compliance.

Document and destroy

It's widely understood that Section 106 seldom stops projects—in most cases the consulting parties work out a mutually acceptable way for the project to go forward while something is done to take care of historic properties. In many cases there's really no way to save a property physically, and there's often no reason to do so. An old building may be termite ridden, falling off its foundations, and of no interest to anyone, but still have some historic or architectural value, perhaps as an example of its type, or because something special happened in it. An archaeological site may contain some interesting information, but nothing *so* interesting that it needs to be left in the ground for future research. In such a case we often can agree to document and destroy the place—make a record of its characteristics, do research on it, and let it go. Unfortunately, some agencies get so used to the *document and destroy* (D&D) strategy that they think it can be applied in every case—that it's the only thing one *ever* needs to do with a historic property. And since it's the only thing they can imagine, why should they go through a lot of analyses and consultation to consider alternatives to D&D? Why not just get on with the program? So they do, assuming that D&D has taken care of their 106 responsibilities, or expecting all the other parties in 106 review to agree with them. People who want to save a place then find themselves fighting a last-ditch battle against a project whose design is based on the assumption that the place can and should be documented and destroyed.

Flag and avoid

A simple way to deal with some kinds of impact is to adjust the project so that (in theory) they don't happen. Don't knock down the old building; put the new building next to it. Don't bulldoze through the archaeological site, route the pipeline around it. This strategy is often known as *flag and avoid*, because it typically involves "flagging" a property somehow and keeping project activities away from it. Often this is perfectly fine and is agreed to through the 106 process. But as with D&D, agencies sometimes come to believe that it's the only, or always the preferable, way of dealing with impacts. And then, they reason, since we're avoiding impacts by putting flags up and keeping the bulldozers away, why go through that tedious Section 106 review? So they don't.

The trouble is that flag and avoid doesn't always work, and it's often irrelevant to the issues at hand. For instance, if the place is one whose quiet character people appreciate, the issues may be visual or auditory impact, and these aren't avoided by physically missing the place. If you're concerned about a new project cheek-by-jowl with your special place, and the agency you have to deal with is one that habitually flags and avoids, you may find that the agency has gotten well along toward a decision to go forward—and even completed what it thinks is Section 106 review—without addressing your concerns or even talking with you.

Obsession with the SHPO

The State Historic Preservation Officer (SHPO) is a very important person in Section 106 review; the responsible federal agency has to consult her at each step—when initiating review, when scoping identification work, when determining the significance of properties and the nature of effects, and when looking for ways to resolve adverse effects. This has encouraged many agencies to think of the SHPO as having approval authority, and to believe that the SHPO is the *only* person they have to consult. Rather than looking for consulting parties, bringing them in and beginning to consult with them, the agency just does whatever identification work it's used to doing (usually an archaeological survey) and files a report with the SHPO. If the SHPO approves it, they figure they're done. Sometimes agencies consult only with the SHPO to reach a memorandum of agreement (MOA) about how to resolve adverse effects. This is not what the regulations provide for, but quite a few SHPOs kind of like the power it gives them and act as though it's the way the system really works. What this does is to shut out other consulting parties, other voices and ideas, other alternatives, and it's entirely inconsistent with the regulations. You can tell whether this kind of thing is happening by examining the records of Section 106 consultations carried out by an agency, or participated in by an SHPO. If the files contain correspondence just between the agency and the SHPO, with little or nothing documenting participation by other people, and perhaps MOAs with signature lines only for the agency, perhaps a non-federal project proponent, and the SHPO, then the agency and SHPO are probably a lot cozier together than the regulations allow.

Shutting out the public

The Section 106 regulations require that people who may care about a place be involved in reviewing project impacts on it, though this requirement is not as clear as it might be. But on many projects, particularly routine ones like small-scale highway improvements and the maintenance of federal installations, the interested public often may not get involved, because there just aren't that many people interested. As a result, some of the commonest short-cut Section 106 strategies are those that curtail public participation. "Public participation" may come to be thought of as simply putting out a public notice and giving people 30 days to "comment"—leaving it entirely up to the agency to decide whether to give such comments any weight at all. Or it may come to be thought of as holding a public hearing, explaining the project, taking some comments, and then going off and making a decision. Or the actual public may be ignored completely in favor of consultation only with the SHPO.

Another reason that the public may be cut out is the perception that review of a project's impacts is a technical, scientific, or bureaucratic matter that only experts can understand. If you believe this—and quite a few people in agencies and consulting firms do, or act as if they do—then public participation is just a pesky intrusion into the process of expert analysis, and the only people who *really* need to have a crack at the project are the experts, like the archaeologists and historians in the State Historic Preservation Office.

Because the Section 106 regulations are not as directive as they might be about public participation, it may be hard to turn poor public involvement into a fatal flaw in a project's review. But it's a flaw nonetheless, and it is a very common indicator of a review that's been poorly done.

Arbitrary decisions

Another way agencies simplify their lives is to establish arbitrary standards and criteria. These simplify by reducing the need to think. For example, an agency may decide, and advise the rest of the world, that it will examine the impacts of a given project or type of project within X feet of the project construction right-of way. In some cases, arbitrary decisions may be necessary. If you have a pipeline going 700 miles across flat country, you're probably going to have to establish some kind of more or less arbitrary corridor within which you'll analyze a given kind of impact. But the more arbitrary the decision is, and the more mindless the adherence to it, the more it corrupts the analysis. An arbitrary corridor that makes sense for archaeology doesn't necessarily make sense for visual impacts. An arbitrarily bounded study area is a problem if its boundaries can't be flexed to accommodate an impact that wasn't considered when the area was established. Section 106 requires that project effects be taken into account, not just those effects that will take place within X feet of the right-of-way or within Y-acre land areas.

Ignoring some requirements in favor of others

NEPA is probably the best known of the laws that require project review, and some agencies act as though it's the only one. Quite a few agency environmental review offices know a lot about NEPA but very little about Section 106. On the other hand, quite a few agency historic preservation or CRM offices know a lot about Section 106 but very little about NEPA or any other environmental or cultural resource law. Some think that they can satisfy Section 106 by complying with NEPA, or take care of the Native American Graves Protection and Repatriation Act by doing Section 106 review. An obscure but quite real project review law, the Archaeological Data Preservation Act, is routinely ignored by all agencies.

Agencies also sometimes favor one part of a regulatory system over others. Most agencies—including the rulemaking Council on Environmental Quality—have NEPA regulations that go on for page after page about how to do environmental impact statements (EISs), but dispense with environmental assessments (EAs) in a paragraph or two. This is a problem because every agency prepares EAs a lot more often than they produce EISs, and their regulations leave them floundering around for guidance—which they often make up or grab from other agencies without much thought about their applicability.

The result of all this is that an agency's environmental review staff may honestly think they're complying with all the relevant laws in a manner consistent with all the relevant regulations, when in fact they're doing nothing of the kind. Their confusion may make it easy for projects to slip through the review process without much exposure of their impacts, but their confusion can also create flaws that project opponents can use to good advantage.

Low bid and flawed scopes of work

Finally, most agencies and non-governmental project proponents get most of their professional services by contracting with architect and engineer or environmental impact assessment firms. (This is referred to as "procurement," just as is the purchase of paper clips.) The contractor is typically expected to perform according to a "scope of work" that lays out the work that's supposed to be done. Unfortunately, these scopes are not always very good. They may be incomplete—directing the contractor to do an archaeological survey, for example, when there are all kinds of non-archaeological historic places subject to effect. They may direct the contractor to produce standardized results that don't have anything to do with the regulatory requirements. As in so many other cases, the result can be that the experts responsible for helping the agency comply with the law are actually spending their time doing things that don't contribute to the agency's fulfillment of legal responsibilities, while the things that need to be done don't get done.

And although they're not required to, many agencies and a lot of non-governmental groups have the policy of hiring whatever company comes in with the lowest bid on the job. This is a fine, efficient practice when you're procuring a standard item—7,000 widgets as described in minute detail in specification 17B32X. But when procuring something as soft and subjective as an analysis of a project's impacts on historic places, it simply makes no sense. And it selects for the companies that are least able to do the work well, either because they've deliberately lowballed the contract with the expectation of cutting corners, or because they honestly but misguidedly thought they could do the work more cheaply than anybody else thought feasible.

These factors—and undoubtedly others I've forgotten—make Section 106 review a very chancy business for all concerned. With the best of intentions an agency can easily drift into noncompliance with the regulations and, if their intentions are less than pure, there are all kinds of ways to twist the process to their will. But if you're alert, you can catch them in the act, and use their slips and shenanigans to slow them down, get them to pay attention, and perhaps save your special place. In the next chapter we'll start looking at how you can do this.

A Case Study: How the BPS Did It

It would be good if I could illustrate Section 106 strategy with a lot of real-world case examples, but that's hard to do. Every case is unique, and each one has so many peculiarities, so many twists and turns, that it would take a whole book to explain any one of them. I've been involved in a case recently, though, that I think I can use to illustrate—briefly and in far less detail than I'd like—how a group of concerned citizens can use the Section 106 process.

The Broad Run Bridge

U.S. Routes 15 and 29 come together just northeast of Broad Run in Prince William County, Virginia, and continue together southwest across the stream and through the village of Buckland. The road crosses Broad Run on a pair of bridges built in 1953 and 1980, near but not on the site of an 1807 stone bridge rebuilt in 1823 by Claudius Crozet, Napoleon Bonaparte's bridge engineer. The road today is four lanes wide, but back in the 1950s the Virginia Department of Transportation (VDOT) acquired right-of-way from Broad Run on to the southwest sufficient to allow widening the road to six or more lanes. A plan developed by the Northern Virginia Transportation Coordinating Council[1] and adopted by the Prince William County Board of Supervisors in 1999—the Northern Virginia 2020 Plan[2]—proposes expansion to six lanes by 2020.

The relationship between highways and suburban sprawl is pretty well established and is nowhere better exemplified than in northern Virginia. In simplest terms, it's a matter of "build it (the highway) and they (shopping malls, light industry, residential tracts) will come." In reality the relationship is somewhat more complex and less linear—a swirl of positive feedback loops in which development begets highways which beget more development. At present in Prince William County, sprawl is chewing up the countryside on the northeast side of Broad Run. To consume the area south of the run, it needs more traffic lanes across the stream and on to the southwest.

More traffic lanes, that is, through Buckland, a remarkably well-preserved 18th- and 19th-century mill village and its associated cultural landscape, where a group of dedicated property owners is putting together a plan to preserve the town and make it a center for historical studies and education. And through the Buckland Mills Battlefield, a relatively intact Civil War landscape where J. E. B. Stuart sent George Armstrong Custer fleeing in a battle sometimes called "Custer's First Stand," though Custer didn't stand long.

The project that was the subject of Section 106 review was the replacement of the deck on the 1953 bridge, which carries southbound traffic across Broad Run. The bridge is old and deficient, and there's no argument over whether it needs fixing. It does. The controversy has been over how to fix it. VDOT proposed to replace the existing bridge deck with a new one that would be some 25 feet wider. The Buckland Preservation Society (BPS) saw this as a stealthy first step toward widening the highway through the village.

At the end of each of the following chapters, we'll look at how the BPS addressed the problems and pursued the opportunities each chapter discusses, to fight a project that its members feared would open the floodgates for sprawl-induced destruction of their community and its surroundings.

CONTACT: For the Section 106 regulations' statement of purpose, go to http://www.achp.gov/regs-rev04.pdf and see 36 CFR 800.1

– NOTES –

1. A consortium of northern Virginia counties and cities. See *www.virginiadot.org/projects/nova/nv2020/overview.htm*.
2. See *www.virginiadot.org/projects/nova/nv2020/*.

CHAPTER FIVE

Place-Saving Strategies

Getting Into the Action

So far we've discussed what Section 106 of the National Historic Preservation Act (NHPA) requires and how an agency's interpretations of the law can deprive your important place of the consideration it's entitled to. Now, what can you do about it?

We'll begin with some things you need to think about in formulating strategy to save a place. Then we'll walk through how Section 106 review is supposed to get started, highlighting ways that you can make sure that review *does* start on a project you're concerned about. In the next several chapters we'll go into how the Section 106 process proceeds, how impacts on valued places are often missed, ignored, or covered up, and ways to bring them out and force them to be considered.

STRATEGICS

Here are some general things to think about as you plot your strategy for making Section 106 work for you.

Timing, timing, timing

A gentleman called me the other day wanting help in saving his family farm—it's been in the family for five generations—from a highway interchange. He'd just received a preliminary eviction notice. The final environmental impact statement has been filed, along with the record of decision; there's a Section 106 memorandum of agreement on the project. The bulldozers are about ready to roll. I'll try to help him, but we don't have many tools left to work with. He's waited until way, way too late.

The first, most basic thing I can think of that you should do in trying to save a place is *start early*. As soon as you learn that the project is a twinkle in some planner's or developer's eye, get to work doing the things we'll talk about in the rest of this book. *Don't wait.*

There will be times, as things go along, when you *have* to wait—while studies are being done, or decisions are being made that you can challenge. There are times when you'll have to be patient. And there's no need to panic; if you *do* start early in the project planning process, you should have plenty of time to give it your best shot. If you don't start early, you're likely to be in trouble no matter how good a case you make.

Find the federal connection

This is absolutely critical. If there's no federal connection—no federal money, no federal permit, no federal land—there isn't going to be any federal review process. So if you want to use Section 106 or most other federal project review laws, *you must find the federal connection.*

Sometimes it will be obvious—a federal agency will be the project proponent, or you'll see a public notice that a federal agency is considering a permit application, or issuing a grant. Other times it won't be obvious at all. Though the connections are often hidden, the federal government is entwined in all our lives in many ways. The Federal Communications Commission licenses wireless phone antenna towers; the Federal Deposit Insurance Corporation licenses automated teller machines. The Department of Housing and Urban Development (HUD) gives Community Development Block Grants to local governments, which then use the money for all kinds of things.

How do you find the federal connection? You inquire. Ask the project proponent (who may, of course, lie, or honestly not know the answer to your question). Ask the local planning department. Ask any federal agency that you suspect is involved. Ask people who deal with the federal review process all the time—the State Historic Preservation Officer, for example. Check public notices about the project, and any not-so-public documents you can get your hands on.

Sometimes the federal connection isn't very tight. In the case of Community Development Block Grants, for instance, Congress has allowed the local governments to act for HUD in carrying out the federal review process. HUD is kind of hovering in the background, but it's the city or county government that's actually managing the review, just as though *it*—the local government—were a federal agency. The Federal Highway Administration (FHWA) lets state departments of transportation manage most of the review process, though its oversight is a good deal more hands-on than HUD's. You can usually get FHWA involved if you make enough noise about a state DOT project that's using federal funds; it's a lot harder to get HUD to take a hand in a Block Grant case. But even in the case of a Block Grant, if it's from the federal government, then somebody has to go through, and manage, the federal environmental review process, including Section 106 review.

Do you need a lawyer?

Yes and no. You're dealing with legal requirements, and hence laws, so it's very good to have a lawyer's advice and assistance. But not just any lawyer's. And there's a lot you can do without a lawyer.

Of course, there are many kinds of lawyers—divorce lawyers, insurance lawyers, tax lawyers. You want a lawyer who knows about environmental laws, and preferably about Section 106. An environmental lawyer who knows only the toxic waste laws may not do you much good. If you can find a lawyer who knows about Section 106, he or she will definitely be helpful. But also, probably, expensive, and there aren't too many of them around.

Section 106 and its regulations aren't so complex or esoteric that you can't understand them yourself. So get a lawyer if you can, but don't despair if you can't. And don't hesitate to insist that your lawyer make sense when he or she talks about the laws, and that he or she make things understandable to you.

Of course, if you go to court, you'll definitely need a lawyer. Which raises the question . . .

To court or not to court

As you think about challenging a project, you need to consider whether you're prepared to take your challenge to court. There's a lot you can do *without* taking it to court, and there's a reasonable chance you can be successful, but if the project's proponents dig in their heels, if the federal agencies involved aren't responsive to you, the time is going to come when you have to decide: am I going to put up the money, time, and trouble to put my issues before a judge, or am I not?

I'm not suggesting that you need to decide your answer to this question before you take any action at all, but at some point you ought to think through how far you're prepared to go, and plan accordingly. Litigation is a fairly complicated and expensive proposition. You'll need a lawyer, who'll need to pull together a lot of information to prepare the necessary pleadings, and he or she will need a lot of help from you—besides paying his or her fees and expenses. If you're not prepared to bear the expense and take the time, that doesn't mean you should give up, but you *should* think through your options. Maybe you can find help in funding and carrying out litigation, or maybe you'll have to acknowledge—to yourself; you certainly don't want the opposition to find out—that there's a point at which, if you haven't won, you're going to have to cut the best deal you can and quit.

Although you ought to be prepared for it, there's a good chance that you won't have to go to court. There are quite a few ways to get attention paid to your concerns without it. In fact, you won't be *able* to go to court until you've exhausted all your "administrative remedies"—for example, using an agency's internal appeals process. And it won't be appropriate to take it to court until some action has happened that arguably can't be reversed without the court's intervention—for example, a government decision that allows a project to move forward, a spurious determination that a project won't adversely affect a historic property, or a decision not to prepare an environmental impact statement under NEPA where significant environmental effects will occur. Jumping the gun, trying to file a case before it's "ripe," will just waste your time and money as well as the court's patience.

What about pro bono help?

Most lawyers do a certain amount of *pro bono*—that is, free—work for people with special problems (like being really poor) and/or important cases. And there are helpful organizations with lawyers who can take on environmental and historic preservation litigation; EarthJustice is one, the National Trust for Historic Preservation is another. Such organizations usually take only cases where they think a favorable decision will set good precedents for use in other litigation—in other words, where their efforts can produce "good law." You may think that your case is easily important enough to merit help from such an organization, and it may be, but there are an awful lot of good litigation targets out in the world and (believe it or not) only so many attorneys to pursue them. You shouldn't count on getting free assistance.

Non-lawyer consultants

People like me—I'm generally thought of as a "cultural resource consultant"—are sometimes accused of practicing law without licenses, and there's some truth in that. There are lots of consultants and consulting firms to which you can turn for help with Section 106, and we're usually a good deal less expensive than lawyers. But we can't take a case to court, and we're not bound by the same standards lawyers are. We don't know the ins and outs of legal practice like lawyers do. And a lot of consultants have only vague, limited, or downright incorrect notions about how the laws work. Finally, most consultants work most of the time for project proponents. That doesn't mean they can't or won't help you, or that they're not sympathetic to your interests. Quite the opposite; they may be raring to go, happy to do something other than helping some change agent build things that they, personally, don't much like. Still, though, their experience is likely to be mostly with helping proponents, and that necessarily influences their knowledge and world view. So be careful in choosing a consultant, take anything they say with a grain of salt, and always, always ask questions. Of course, this goes for your relationships with lawyers too.

Learn about the law

Even if you get a lawyer or a consultant, that doesn't relieve you of the need to know what the laws are about or what options you have. You need to get acquainted with the laws and regulations that you, your lawyer, or others think may be helpful in fighting your battle, if for no other reason than to be able to ask good questions. The laws are all available on the World-Wide Web, along with their regulations and lots of guidelines for applying them (see the "Resources" appendix at the end of the book). There are lots of sneaky little tricks to the trade of applying the laws, but as a general matter they're not terribly complicated. Of course, this book is designed to help you with them. There are also short training courses you can take; I provide some,[1] and so do the ACHP and others.[2]

And not just Section 106

Although this book is about Section 106 review, it's important to keep track of all the other laws that may be relevant and can both help and hurt you. It's especially important to stay on top of how local law, and local decision-making, may affect you, the place you're trying to protect, and the project(s) you're trying to protect it from. The project may be a federal one, or federally funded or licensed, but it probably needs local approvals too, and a project proponent can play one level of government off against another. "We have our local approvals, so why should the big, remote, bureaucratic feds get in our way? Surely locals know best"—and—"All we need is the Board of Supervisors' approval in order to open up this big pot of federal money." If you don't stay abreast of all the reviews the project is going through, you may find yourself blindsided by a decision made without your knowing, by a poorly informed decision-maker. And once a decision has been made—such as a local zoning change—it's awfully hard to get the decision-makers to reconsider.

Don't be the Lone Ranger

Make, welcome, seek alliances with others. Allies can be useful even if they don't share your precise interests. Perhaps you're interested in saving Grandpa's homestead and the local Audubon Society wants to save the grey bearded owl, which roosts in the trees along the adjacent creek. They may not care about Grandpa and you may not give a hoot for the owl, but your interests coincide in keeping the area from being overwhelmed by a highway or shopping mall. Even if you don't speak to each other under other circumstances, recognizing the coincidence of interests and working together on this area of common concern may help you both.

Right is not necessarily might

The fact that the place you want to save really *is* important—the oldest house in the county, the neighborhood where the Polish American community has been centered for a hundred years, the burial place of the ancestors—will take you only so far. You don't want to be *wrong*, of course; that would definitely undermine your credibility. But being right isn't necessarily going to save your place. You have to be able to demonstrate your rightness, and use your rightness, at the right times in the right ways to make a difference. Your strategy, your ability to play the project review system, may be as important as, or even more important than, your facts.

Be particularly cautious if you find yourself relying on moral, ethical arguments—what you think is the morally right thing to do. If you're quite sure where the boundary is between good and bad, you certainly want to be on the good side, but being there isn't necessarily going to help you much, even in the (rather unlikely) event that everybody agrees with you about where that line is. However much you may think yourself to be on the side of truth and virtue, you still need to know how to work the system. There's a management mantra that urges executives not only to "do the right thing" but to "do the thing right." It applies to people in your position too.

Eschew emotion—except when it's useful

You feel passionate about saving your place, and that's fine, but don't expect passion to win the day. Weeping, shouting, swearing, even raising your voice is usually not helpful. Don't think you can shame people into agreeing with you, or bludgeon them into doing so—no matter how righteous your cause is. It probably won't work, and it may be counterproductive. You may just drive them to avoid talking with you, and hence listening to you.

That said, there are certainly times and places where a display of emotion *is* useful. Tribal elders getting emotional about destruction of the ancestors' graves can convince people that there's a serious problem that they should pay attention to; a bunch of kids pleading for the preservation of their neighborhood can twang heartstrings. There are strategic times to use such displays of emotion, but there are other times when it just gets in the way, even turns people against you. It may seem terribly cold and calculating, but you'll get farther if you use emotion sparingly and strategically. Have the elders or the kids emote, but then let them fade into the background while the hardheaded realists negotiate.

Keeping these general ideas in mind, let's consider the things that happen—or are supposed to happen—during the early stages of Section 106 review. Let's also look at how project proponents and review agencies cut corners, bend required procedures, and simply screw up. And let's consider what you can do to make the most of their mistakes.

We'll start with the first steps in review under Section 106, not only because it's commonsense to discuss things in sequence, but because it's important for you to get engaged in the review process as early as possible. To start early you need to do two things: find out that a threatening project is planned, and prevail upon people in positions of authority to pay attention to you.

How Section 106 Review Gets Started

Somebody has an idea—for a highway, a housing development, an oil tanker port, or whatever. Suppose that somebody, that project proponent, either is a federal agency or needs a federal agency's assistance or permit. What happens then?

Although Section 106 applies in essentially the same way both to the projects of federal agencies and to projects that require federal assistance or permits, there are important practical differences. When a federal agency comes up with a proposal, the agency obviously knows about the proposal from the get-go. But if the proponent is somebody other than a federal agency—a land developer, for instance—he may be pretty far advanced in planning his project before the agency that's going to be involved even knows about it. He may march in the agency's door, drop a bunch of completed project plans on the desk, and ask how soon he can get his permit or assistance. He may already have approvals from local government; he may own the land; he may have assembled his financing. He may have lined up his elected representatives to lean on the agency.

Agency people hate this, and it's often a poor strategy for a proponent. When people feel that they're being railroaded, they're likely to be suspicious of the railroader's motives, and if they're responsible public servants they're likely to feel that the public interest is getting shafted. Smart non-federal proponents get together early with the agencies they're going to have to work with, when they're just starting to develop conceptual plans. Even though the agency may then say they don't have enough information to review, so please come back when you're further advanced, early consultation at least makes the agency people feel that they're being respected, and that makes later consultation easier.

But many project proponents aren't smart enough, or humble enough, to realize this, and a fair number respect neither agency employees nor the public the agencies are supposed to serve. These are the guys who plop the plans down on the desk and say, "I need my permit in 30 days."

If the proponent of a project that's dangerous to your valued place acts like this, it's obviously a problem for you. If the agency from which the guy needs his assistance or permit doesn't know about the plan, you probably don't either. When you *do* learn about it, you're both going to have to scramble to respond. *But attempts to railroad a project through also create huge vulnerabilities for the proponent, and you may be able to exploit them.*

What are those vulnerabilities? For one thing, a basic principle of Section 106 and NEPA is that you look at the impacts *before* you decide to have them. The agency is supposed to look *before* it leaps, not when it's in the air. If the proponent has decided what he's going to do and expects the agency to rubber-stamp it, he's asking the agency to ignore that basic principle. Responsible agencies don't like that, and neither do courts. For another thing, the very fact that the proponent thinks he can blast his way through the review process suggests that he isn't very knowledgeable about how it works, so he's likely to make mistakes.

Perhaps most importantly, he's almost certainly invested heavily in his project. His plans are drawn up; he's probably got bankers or investors or both all lined up in support of his plan, and he's promised them it's a done deal. He's paying interest on whatever loans he's taken out. He's got his lawyers on retainer, his engineers and architects under contract, maybe even his construction team mobilized. He can't afford delay; in fact, delay may kill his project stone cold dead.

So you want to find every possible way to delay him.

Where a federal agency is itself the proponent, it's likely to go through project review in a more orderly, deliberate manner. But not always. Sometimes political pressures or even just the ego of a regional office head can cause an agency to behave as badly as the most unruly of private developers—and become subject to roughly the same vulnerabilities. They don't have investors holding their purse strings, but they do have higher-ups in the agency, and the agency's budget people, and they're subject to the tyranny of the federal (or state) budget cycle. In most cases, funds budgeted for a project expire after awhile, or have to be reauthorized; the agency may have to go back to Congress for more money if the project gets delayed. So delay is something that agencies hate too.

Is it the best idea, then, to lie low while the project proponent shapes up her plans, develops her funding, and crawls out on a financial limb, and then spring out to cut it off? Maybe sometimes, but it's a chancy proposition, and I'd not usually recommend it. As soon as you hear about a project, you ought to start figuring out what to do about it, and encouraging everyone concerned to get started doing what the law requires.

Which is? Let's look.

First steps

The Section 106 regulations are very explicit about the first steps in the process and the necessity to take them. But those first steps are pretty much in the hands of the agency, and you may not have a good way of knowing whether and how they're happening.

Triggering review under Section 106

> *(a) Establish undertaking. The agency official shall determine whether the proposed Federal action is an undertaking as defined in §800.16(y) and, if so, whether it is a type of activity that has the potential to cause effects on historic properties (36 CFR 800.3(a)).*
>
> *(1) No potential to cause effects. If the undertaking is a type of activity that does not have the potential to cause effects on historic properties, assuming such historic properties were present, the agency official has no further obligations under section 106 or this part (36 CFR 800.3(a)(1)).*

The agency first decides whether the project is an "undertaking"—which it is, with a few narrow exceptions, if the federal government is somehow involved in it, so that's pretty straightforward. It then decides whether it needs review under Section 106. Since Section 106 is about dealing with effects on *historic properties*, the question the agency has to ask itself is, "Is this the type of project that has the potential to affect historic properties, if any are out there?"

And here is where a lot of agencies and project proponents mess up. Unfortunately, project opponents often do the same.

Critical point: The project requires review if it's the *type* of project that *has the potential* to affect historic properties. We may not have any idea whether there are historic properties out there in the world where the project may do damage. If it's the *type* of thing that *could* affect them, *if* they turn out to be there when somebody studies the area, then it has to be reviewed.

People trying to save places often think that they have to nominate the place to the National Register of Historic Places, or somehow otherwise get it "designated historic"—before Section 106 applies. *Not true!* If the project will mess up buildings, dig up soil, or otherwise change the landscape, it has the *potential* to affect historic places, including places that haven't even been found yet. The fact that nothing's been found, recorded, documented, and formally designated doesn't mean there's nothing there—it just means nothing's been found, recorded, documented, and designated.

And the effects don't necessarily have to be direct, physical, knock-em-down or dig-em-up kinds of effects. Visual effects count too, and auditory effects; changes in land use, changes in traffic patterns. Sometimes it's a trick to demonstrate such effects, and there are some fine angels-on-pinhead arguments that people can have about them—we'll go into some of these in the next chapter—but the bottom line is that all reasonably foreseeable effects are supposed to be considered.

So what do you do if the project proponent or agency official says, "We don't have to do Section 106 review, because there aren't any National Register properties there"? Direct their attention to 36 CFR 800.3(a)(1)—the section of the regulations on how to decide whether a project requires review. Note that it says that an agency "undertaking" (anything an agency does, assists, or permits) need *not* be reviewed under Section 106 only if it is:

> the type of activity that does not have the potential to cause effects on historic properties, assuming such properties were present (36 CFR 800.3(a)(1)).

Which means that if it *does* have such potential, then it *does* need to be reviewed.

Then ask them some questions, like:

- Is this not the type of undertaking that has the potential to affect historic properties? If not, why not?
- Do you actually know that there aren't any historic properties present? If so, how do you know it?
- Do you understand that there are lots of historic properties that haven't yet been found or recorded?

And put them in touch with your State Historic Preservation Officer, who—assuming he or she is alert, knowledgeable, and willing—ought to be able to set them straight.

Of course, when I say to tell an agency this and ask them that, I'm assuming that you're able to communicate with them somehow. Luckily, the Section 106 process is set up to make that happen, though it doesn't always work very well.

Consultation

> Consultation means the process of seeking, discussing, and considering the views of other participants, and, where feasible, seeking agreement with them regarding matters arising in the section 106 process. The Secretary's "Standards and Guidelines for Federal Agency Preservation Programs pursuant to the National Historic Preservation Act" provide further guidance on consultation (36 CFR 800.16(f)).

Consultation is at the heart of Section 106 review. The responsible agency—the one proposing, or assisting, or considering permitting the project—is required to consult with the State Historic Preservation Officer, the project proponent, local governments, and Indian tribes, and it's also *supposed* to consult with other interested groups and individuals—in other words, you. One of the first things an agency is supposed to do once it's decided it needs to do Section 106 review is to *identify consulting parties*. Then it's supposed to consult them, starting as early as possible and continuing throughout the review process. And consultation is defined in the Section 106 regulations as actually discussing, considering, sitting down and talking with one another, trying to work things out and come to an agreement—not just filing notices and holding public hearings.

> *(c) Identify the appropriate SHPO and/or THPO. As part of its initial planning, the agency official shall determine the appropriate SHPO or SHPOs to be involved in the section 106 process. The agency official shall also determine whether the undertaking may occur on or affect historic properties on any tribal lands and, if so, whether a THPO has assumed the duties of the SHPO. The agency official shall then initiate consultation with the appropriate officer or officers (36 CFR 800.3(b))*
>
> *(f) Identify other consulting parties. In consultation with the SHPO/THPO, the agency official shall identify any other parties entitled to be consulting parties and invite them to participate as such in the section 106 process. The agency official may invite others to participate as consulting parties as the section 106 process moves forward (36 CFR 800.3(c))*.

But consultation is not something that either agencies or non-governmental project proponents necessarily do very well; it's not something most agency people, engineers, and lawyers are trained very well to do. As a result, there are several ways that consultation tends *not* to get started, or tends to devolve into meaningless exercises in paper-passing or public relations.

NEPA-think. Agency environmental review people tend to be more familiar with NEPA than with Section 106, and NEPA doesn't require the intensive consultation that Section 106 does. It's often difficult for NEPA experts to understand that Section 106 does require consultation, or to fathom what consultation means. An extreme but not uncommon example

Place-Saving Strategies – Getting Into the Action

is for the agency to figure that if a project is categorically excluded from NEPA review, it must be categorically excluded from Section 106 as well. That's not at all true; the two statutes are entirely separate (though it's fine, indeed recommended, that compliance with them be coordinated). But if the agency thinks it's true, it may not get started doing any sort of 106 review on a categorically excluded project, which means it won't consult anyone, which means you may not know the project is being planned, so you're not in a position to insist on consultation.

Consulting only with those they must consult. The only specific person the regulations insist that an agency always consult is the State Historic Preservation Officer (SHPO). Others must be consulted under particular circumstances—for example, Indian tribes and Native Hawaiian groups must be consulted if places of cultural importance to them may be affected by a project, and local governments are entitled to be consulted if effects will take place within their jurisdiction. If you're just an ordinary concerned citizen, or even an affected property owner, the regulations allow an agency the discretion to consult or not consult. Often enough, an agency will decide it doesn't want to consult with people or groups it finds troublesome.

Confusing consultation with public notice. The agency may figure that if it publishes a legal notice in the newspaper saying it's reviewing a project under Section 106, it's initiated consultation. That may not be an entirely unreasonable assumption in the case of a little project with low potential for doing damage to anything, but it's certainly not reasonable, not sufficient, where the project is bigger or otherwise more likely to cause injury. Unfortunately, agencies tend to want to do things the same way every time; it's hard to build flexibility and a recognition of variable circumstances into agency procedures. An agency that's used to dealing with little, unproblematic projects may try to deal with a big, dangerous one in the same way, and be terribly surprised when it doesn't work.

Confusing consultation with review and comment. The idea of consultation as a back and forth discussion, aimed at solving problems, is not one that all agency people are ready or willing to embrace. To some, it is downright scary; it involves surrendering a degree of control. Few agencies train their people in consultation methods, and such training is pretty rare in law schools too (though more and more of them, to their credit, are offering classes and programs in "alternative dispute resolution," involving methods of consultation, mediation, and negotiation). So the knee-jerk agency response, when somebody mentions consultation, may be to say, "OK, we'll send out our proposal/notice/plan for 30-day review and comment." Which reads as: Tell us what you think, folks, and we in our wisdom will take a look at what you say and then make our decision. It's deeply insulting to the interested public, or ought to be—though it surprises me how often concerned citizens are willing to accept it—but it's very, very common.

Public hearing. It's also not unusual for agencies to think—or act like—they've done consultation if they've held a public hearing. Possibly one of the most useless, time-and-money-wasting enterprises there is, but deeply embedded in the psyches of the American public and the U.S. government, a public hearing is a set-piece exercise in "let's pretend." Let's pretend that the agency is really interested in what the public has to say, will really consider, really think about it. So we give the public an opportunity to speak. We hire a hall, invite everybody to come in and say their piece. We line our people up on a stage or behind a podium, and we make a bunch of presentations about the project. Then—protocol being protocol, after all—we invite elected local officials to speak, and they do, on and on. Then maybe there are state or federal legislators or their staffs; they get to speak. Then finally members of the public get up, usually with strict time limits, and by this time everybody's bored and angry anyhow. So people speak, often angry to the point of incoherence, and in any event so constrained by time that they can't do more than lob rhetorical grenades. Then the meeting's over and the agency goes solemnly off to consider the public's comments. Which by and large it rejects—after all, they're mostly incomprehensible and emotional.

The public hearing is an institution that made sense when practiced by small communities in colonial New England, and maybe it still works in small communities now, but it makes no sense whatever when practiced by a federal agency dealing with a large project with complicated environmental impacts. It is an institution so deeply embedded in our political systems, however, that it's taken for granted as a Good Thing To Do. I've seen project opponents rant and rave about the fact that an agency has failed to hold a public hearing, and therefore hasn't done a proper job of involving the public in its project. Bad strategy; all the agency has to do is hold a hearing and (as usual) ignore the results, and it's taken the wind right out of its opponents' sails.

Place-Saving Strategies – Getting Into the Action

So, what to do? You need to convince the agency that it's got to do real consultation—really talk with you, listen to you, give thoughtful consideration to what you say. Pay attention and either do what you say it ought to do, or explain why it does something else. The place to start is with the letter of the regulations. The Section 106 regulations include a definition of "consultation" that goes like this:

> *Consultation means the process of seeking, discussing, and considering the views of other participants, and, where feasible, seeking agreement with them regarding matters arising in the section 106 process. The Secretary's "Standards and Guidelines for Federal Agency Preservation Programs pursuant to the National Historic Preservation Act" provide further guidance on consultation (36 CFR 800.16(f).*

Those *Secretary's Standards*—"Secretary," in the Section 106 regulations, always meaning Secretary of the Interior—can be found on the World-Wide Web at *http://www.cr.nps.gov/hps/pad/sec110.htm*. They elaborate on what's laid out in the regulations, and though they don't themselves have the force of law—in other words, agencies don't *have* to follow them—the fact that they're referenced in the regulations means that agencies really ought to follow them unless they have some good reason to do otherwise.

The key words and phrases to emphasize in the definition are:

- **Process:** Consultation isn't simply an action—sending out a letter, holding a hearing, posting a notice; it's a process. A process is something that develops over time and that involves interactions among whatever entities are involved in it.

- **Seeking:** The agency needs to reach out and try to find out what people think.

- **Discussing:** The agency is supposed to talk with people about what they think.

- **Considering:** The agency is supposed to think about what people tell it. And who is it supposed to be interacting with?

- **Other participants:** Not just the State Historic Preservation Officer, or the technical experts, but whoever's involved.

Finally, what is the purpose of the interaction?

- ▣ **Seeking agreement:** A key phrase. The agency is supposed to negotiate, to try to reach agreement with the other participants about whatever it's considering—like how to identify historic places, whether a given place is significant, what effects a project will have on a significant place, and what to do about such effects.

So you need to argue for real consultation and quite possibly educate the agency about what the regulations say. For some excellent guidance on how consultation *should* work, see Nicholas Dorochoff's recently published *Negotiation Basics for Cultural Resource Managers* (Left Coast Press, 2007).

BECOMING A CONSULTING PARTY

Getting the agency to consult isn't enough, of course; you want to make sure it consults *you*. In the jargon of the Section 106 regulations, you want the agency to regard you as a *consulting party*.

Luis Rosas, a New Mexico rancher, is a consulting party in Section 106 review of a proposed permit for railroad construction through Dripping Springs Ranch. Photo by the author.

Place-Saving Strategies – Getting Into the Action

So why should the agency consult with you? You need to think of all the reasons, so you can use them as ammunition if you need to. Are you an Indian tribe or a local government? If so, you have special rights to be consulted. Are you a property owner? A local or national environmental or historic preservation group? Simply a concerned citizen? Then the regulations aren't terribly directive. However, they do say that:

> *Certain individuals and organizations with a demonstrated interest in the undertaking may participate as consulting parties due to the nature of their legal or economic relation to the undertaking or affected properties, or their concern with the undertaking's effects on historic properties (36 CFR 800.2(c)(5)).*

So you need to *demonstrate* to the agency and to anyone else who'll pay attention (like the State Historic Preservation Officer) that you have an *interest*—that is, that you'll be affected somehow by the project and/or you're concerned about how historic properties may be affected.

Asserting your interest

In asserting such an interest, I usually recommend being polite but not subservient. Act like you respect the agency and its work, and understand that it wants as simple and straightforward a process as it can get. Request consulting party status, respectfully but forcefully. Never forget that agency officials are public servants, and you're part of the public (see Mr. Sanchez's letter on page 90). They have no business mounting high horses.

And they may well mount them. For instance, the agency people may tell you that you don't have the right to be a consulting party, making up "requirements" that such a party must meet in order to be qualified (see the example of agency obfuscation on page 91). Such requirements almost always are made up; the regulations allow anyone with an interest to become a consulting party.

Another angle is to say that you can't be a consulting party unless you write the agency a letter that says just the right things, citing just the right regulations just the right ways. Nonsense; this is supposed to be a government of, by, and for the people, not just the people who can write the "right" kind of letter. Sure, you need to write them a letter—otherwise there would be no record of what you said—but it doesn't' have to use precisely the words the agency wants used.

SAVING PLACES THAT MATTER

Or they may tell you that if they let you be a consulting party, they'll have to give every other Tom, Dick, and Harriett a seat at the table too. This is probably a bluff, but even if it isn't, who cares? Other people have the right to be consulting parties too, and if they don't have anything to contribute to the consultation, they'll soon enough get bored and drop out. You'll seldom go wrong promoting an open door policy.

Lt.Col. Bruce Estok
District Manager
Department of the Army
Albuquerque District, Corps of Engineers
4101 Jefferson Plaza NE
Albuquerque, NM 87109-3435

RECEIVED
31 Jan 07
REGULATORY BR.
CORPS OF ENGINEERS

Re: BNSF Proposed Second Track Project through Abo Canyon, NM;
Application No. 2005 00269

Dear Lt. Col. Estok   01/29/07

My name is Juan Sanchez and I own a ranch of 5500 acres near Abo Pass. Much of the land of this ranch has been in my family for 3 generations; the home in which I live was built by my grandfather in 1883. I have lived on this ranch and ridden the lands of the pass and canyon for my entire life, as did my father before me.

I am very concerned about what BNSF Railway has done to Abo Canyon over the last century, and what they propose to do now with their "Second Track" project. I understand that you will soon be consulting with the New Mexico State Historic Preservation Officer and others about the impacts of the BNSF project, and the alternative of placing the track in a tunnel to preserve Abo Pass's historical landscape. Because of my concern with the impacts of the project on this historic place, I request the opportunity to participate in your consultation as a consulting party. I am advised that the federal regulations for compliance with Section 106 of the National Historic Preservation Act authorize people like me to participate in this manner. I understand that my name was given to you over a year ago by my neighbors, the Rosas, so that I could be contacted as a possible consulting party and so that I could share information on the history of the area, but I have not as yet been contacted for these purposes.

Please advise me of your decision as to whether I can participate.

Respectfully,

Juan Sanchez
Juan Sanchez

Cc: Katherine Slick - New Mexico SHPO, Santa Fe
      John Eddins - Advisory Council on Historic Preservation
      Ti Hays- National Trust for Hisroric Preservation
      Randall Vicente, 2nd Lt. Gov. – Acoma Pueblo
      Governor Ed Roybal, II –Piro/Manso Tiwa Indian Tribe
      Lewis Ruder, BNSF

An example of a request for consulting party status. Mr. Sanchez was successful with this request.

Another high-horse strategy is simply to ignore you, hoping you'll go away. If called on this, the agency people will probably say that, gee, they lost

United States Department of Agriculture — Forest Service — Land Between The Lakes National Recreation Area — 100 Van Morgan Drive, Golden Pond, KY 42211

File Code: 2360-1
Date: December 13, 2006

Mr. Harold Dixon
695 Irvin Cobb Road
Murray, KY 42071

Dear Mr. Dixon:

Thank you for your continued interest in the heritage resources at Land Between The Lakes (LBL) National Recreation Area (LBL). We are very interested in working with you.

Land Between The Lakes has received numerous requests for consulting party status during the past six months as the revised regulations covering Section 106 have been issued. In the interest of ensuring that I have been fair and consistent as well as legally compliant, I have taken the opportunity to review again the regulations and policies. I have also conferred with the Kentucky and Tennessee heritage councils, the Advisory Council on Historic Preservation, and Forest Service staff to discuss how LBL is interpreting the new regulations and applying them to local concerns.

The Section 106 process is intended to involve all persons that can help the decision maker identify, consider, and avoid harmful effects to historic properties. As I interpret the regulation, the formal consulting party status seems to be intended for those with rights in LBL that are similar to local governments, American Indian tribes, as well as directly affected permittees or landowners. A potential consulting party has standing only if there is clear evidence that implementation of a specific undertaking would cause direct injury. Granting of consulting party status gives that individual added influence in the decision related to the undertaking, and in effect, grants special rights above and beyond those of the general public. As the local official, serving the interests of all members of the public, I am responsible to only do so when clearly justified.

I have noted your interest in the designation for consulting party status. Your letter indicates very clearly that you are interested in working with the Forest Service on matters of heritage resources and specifically, related to the listed cemeteries that are part of your family history. We have recorded the information you provided in our heritage resources contact list and will keep you informed of undertakings and projects within your area of interest. This means that we will be contacting you to make you aware of projects underway and invite you to participate and provide input on them. In some cases, we may ask to meet with you or invite you to a meeting where discussions on these issues are planned. My sincere hope is that we can work together to care for the heritage resources of LBL. I am not granting you the status of consulting party at this time, however, in the event that an assessment related to an undertaking at LBL indicates that there is potential injury to your rights related to a historic property, I will reconsider your request at that time.

   Caring for the Land and Serving People   Printed on Recycled Paper

Example of agency obfuscation. The "interpretation" of the Section 106 regulations in the third paragraph is fanciful at best; the writer has simply made it up to support rejecting Mr. Dixon's request. But to anyone unfamiliar with the regulations, such as the letter writer's superiors, it doubtless looks persuasive.

your letter. So send letters with return receipt requested, or get some other record of receipt, and keep bugging them.

Seek allies, especially the State Historic Preservation Officer. But don't ask the SHPO to take your side unless it's obvious that he or she agrees with you. Just ask him or her to help you get a seat at the consultation table so your voice can be heard.

Bring up legal authorities *other than* Section 106 to bolster your argument. Are you a member of a minority group, or is your income low relative to that of other people in the area? If so, Executive Order 12898 pushes agencies to consult with you. Are you a property owner? Then Executive Order 13352 tells agencies to engage you in a collaborative manner. The Administrative Procedures Act (APA) encourages transparent agency decision-making, and consultation is one way to achieve transparency. The Federal Advisory Committees Act (FACA) discourages closed-door meetings with select groups of people unless they're formally established according to FACA's regulations. You shouldn't have to throw all these authorities at the agency, but if you have to, they're there to be thrown.

If you make enough noise, convince the agency that you're not going to go away, but avoid looking like a nutcase, you ought to get recognized as a consulting party. This will entitle you to get copies of correspondence, study reports, and other documents that get generated as the 106 process continues, and will give you a "seat at the table" (though there isn't necessarily a real table) in negotiating how the process will be carried out and what its outcome will be.

If you don't get recognized as a consulting party, you're not completely out of the loop. The agency is required to involve the public throughout the process, and you're clearly a member of the public. You'll just have to work harder to keep track of what's going on. You'll have to ask—repeatedly.

A useful court finding to cite—though it's unambiguously binding only in the district where it was handed down (Oregon)—is in *Bonnichsen v. United States* (217 F. Supp. 2d 1116 (D. Or. 2002)). *Bonnichsen* dealt mostly with the Native American Graves Protection and Repatriation Act (NAGPRA)—it was a fight between Indian tribes and various non-Indian scientists over a 9,000-year-old skeleton that washed out of the bank of the Columbia River. But a tiny part of the case was about Section 106. The Corps of Engineers had dumped fill on top of the site where the skeleton washed out, and had to do Section 106 review before dumping. The Corps had consulted with the State Historic Preservation Officer, the National Park Service, and various tribes. The scientists argued that they should have been consulted too. The defendants said no, the regulations gave the Corps discretion to let the scientists consult or leave them in the cold, and the Corps had decided quite legally to do the latter. The Court found for the scientists, saying:

> In sum, I conclude that the Corps violated the NHPA requirements that the views of "interested parties" be considered.

So that particular court seems to have concluded that interested parties—such as the scientists, and you—had a sort of right to be consulted, though one could probably argue that there are other ways their "views" could have been "considered."

So, you muster your best argument for consulting-party status; you recruit allies who will support you, particularly among groups that are already consulting parties, such as tribes and the State Historic Preservation Officer; and you either get to the table or you don't. No guarantees, but not being a consulting party doesn't knock you out of the game.

How the BPS Did It

In the case of the Broad Run Bridge, the project proponent was the Virginia Department of Transportation (VDOT), but VDOT would need funding assistance from the Federal Highway Administration (FHWA). Though FHWA delegates the "legwork" of Section 106 review to the state, it would have been a grave mistake for the Buckland Preservation Society (BPS) to deal only with VDOT, which could be expected to be pretty bullish about the project. BPS needed to make sure the feds paid attention to the project, which they did through FHWA's Federal Preservation Officer (FPO). FPOs can be found through the website of the Advisory Council on Historic Preservation (*www.achp.gov*).

The BPS wrote to FHWA and VDOT, as well as to the SHPO, outlining their interests in the project and requesting consulting-party status. They sent copies of their letters to the ACHP and to others who might be interested, and at the end of their letters listed everyone they had sent copies to. This put the agencies on notice that questions were likely to be raised if they tried to ignore the letters. As it turned out, FHWA and VDOT fairly readily acknowledged the BPS as a consulting party.

The BPS also sought the involvement of the ACHP which, despite the small scale and seemingly simple character of the project, agreed to participate. The BPS also approached the National Trust for Historic Preservation. Buckland is part of the "Journey through Hallowed Ground Corridor," which recognizes all the American history that has played out between Monticello in Virginia and Gettysburg in Pennsylvania (see *http://www.cr.nps.gov/nrtravel/ journey/intro.htm*), and the Trust had just identified the corridor as one of its annual 11 most endangered historic places, so it was pretty easy to sell the Trust on participating. The American Battlefield Preservation Program in the National Park Service also joined the consultation, concerned about effects on the battlefield.

CONTACT: For regulatory language pertinent to this chapter, go to **http://www.achp.gov/regs-rev04.pdf** and see 36 CFR 800.3

– NOTES –

1. See *www.swca.com/training*.
2. For example, the National Preservation Institute at *www.npi.org*, the SRI foundation at *http://www.srifoundation.org/continuing_ed.html*, and ETCI at *http://www. envirotrain.com/training.html*. For the Advisory Council's classes, see *www.achp.gov*.

CHAPTER SIX

Place-Saving Strategies

Getting Your Place Noticed

STRATEGICS

In the last chapter, we talked about how the Section 106 process begins: with the federal agency responsible for the project deciding whether it's the kind of project that has the potential to affect historic places—that is, places eligible for inclusion in the National Register of Historic Places. If it is that kind of project—and just about anything that changes the physical environment is—then the agency figures out who it (the agency) ought to consult with. Then in consultation with those parties (strangely enough called "consulting parties"), it gets the process underway. We also discussed how to promote yourself as a consulting party, and what it means to be and not be one.

Once the agency has gotten the Section 106 process started, the major thing it needs to do is find out whether the project will damage or otherwise affect any historic properties. This involves two operations: *finding* historic properties, and figuring out whether and how the project will *affect* them. The "finding" part itself is also usually divided into two parts: finding places that *may be* eligible for the National Register, and deciding whether they *are* eligible. In this chapter we'll discuss the first part of the first part: finding places that may be eligible for the Register. It's one of the most complicated and slippery parts of the Section 106 process, and one that often goes awry.

The project proponent, if he or she is thinking about the matter at all, probably has one simple goal: not finding any historic properties that will be affected. Failing that, the proponent wants to find as few properties as possible, of kinds that can be easily documented and destroyed, or flagged and avoided (see Chapter Four).

You, on the other hand, probably have three things you need to do. First and most fundamentally, you need to make sure that your special place is identified as a historic property—that is, eligible for the Register. Second, you need to be alert to other places that may be eligible, and that may be of concern to other people; such other people can be helpful allies. Third, you need to try to make sure that the responsible agency and others fully appreciate what makes your place and others significant. This is because being eligible for the Register doesn't give your place much protection if everyone but you thinks it's only significant enough to document it before destroying it, or that it's suitable to flag and avoid it.

Agencies and project proponents make a lot of mistakes during the historic property identification process. Those mistakes can result in the loss of very important historic places, and they can cost agencies, proponents, taxpayers, ratepayers, and others a lot of unnecessary money. They can also create opportunities for anyone trying to slow down or stop a project. Let's see where the soft spots in the identification system are, and how they can be exploited.

"Historic Properties" and the "Identification Effort"

Remember that "historic properties" are districts, sites, buildings, structures, and objects included in or eligible for the National Register of Historic Places. Specialists in the field can argue endlessly about whether a given thing is a site, a structure, an object, or whatever, but it really doesn't matter; all those terms just refer to examples of the kinds of real estate (and other stuff) that can be eligible for the Register. Kinds of things that have been included in or found to be eligible for the Register include:

- Houses, office buildings, apartment buildings, warehouses, churches
- Bridges, airports, sewers, missile launch pads, ships, airplanes, canoes
- Residential neighborhoods, commercial strips, industrial complexes, military bases
- Rural villages, farms, ranches, communities of any kind
- Parks, parkways, wildlife refuges
- Lampposts, gates, signposts, totem poles
- Trees, rock outcrops, mountains, lakes, rivers, ponds

Place-Saving Strategies — Getting Your Place Noticed

- Ancient burial sites, campsites, village sites, hunting areas
- The habitats of culturally important animals and plants
- Trails, roads, railroads, pipelines, highways, expressways, ferry crossings
- Designed landscapes like parks and parkways, farming landscapes, natural landscapes with some kind of cultural significance
- Battlefields and military encampments, the routes of exploring parties, places where treaties were signed, the sites of disasters

Quite a few such places have been entered in the Register, through the elaborate process of nomination. It's fairly simple for an agency to find these; they're on file with the National Park Service and the State Historic Preservation Officer, and some data on them can be found on a World-Wide Web site maintained by the National Register (*http://www.nr.nps.gov/*). The tricky, and creative, part of identification involves finding properties that aren't yet on the Register but are eligible for it. To be eligible, a place has to meet broad criteria found in the National Register's regulations (36 CFR 60.4). We'll discuss these criteria later. All we have to know right now is that there are lots and lots of places that meet the criteria, and hence are eligible, that no one has gone to the trouble, taken the time, spent the money, to nominate. There are various reasons or this, not the least being that the average nomination requires many hours of work by, or under the supervision of, a relevant historic preservation professional—maybe a historian, an architectural historian, a landscape historian, an archaeologist—who usually has to be paid, so the nomination winds up costing several thousand dollars.

So there are lots of unevaluated places out there that meet the National Register's criteria, and of course there are lots

Archaeological survey is often an important part of the Section 106 identification effort. Unfortunately, often it's also the only thing that's done.

more that don't, and a quite a few that honorable or not-so-honorable people can argue about. Unless it's already on the Register, your special place falls into one of these categories. Your job is to make sure it's determined to be eligible for the Register. At the same time, if your goal is to delay and complicate the project in the hope that it will die a slow and agonizing death, you're going to want to make sure that as many *other* places as possible are also found to be eligible.

The agency finds out what's eligible by conducting some kind of an "identification effort." That's a pretty bland, nondescriptive term, but it kind of has to be, because it embraces a wide range of activities. It's common for people to talk about identifying historic properties by "conducting a survey," but that doesn't really describe the range of things that may be done. A "survey" typically involves getting out on the ground and looking around in some kind of systematic way. That's often necessary, but not always, and it may not be the only thing that's needed. There may need to be background research, maybe interviews with local people, consultation with tribal or community elders, maybe various kinds of specialist studies. Conversely, in some cases so much is already known about an area that little or no study is needed. The vanilla term "identification effort" covers all these possibilities.

Scoping

Having decided that the project is subject to 106 review, and having decided who it's going to consult about it, the agency is supposed to start *scoping* its identification effort—that is, figuring out what it's actually going to have to do to identify affected historic properties and establish how they'll be affected. This involves establishing the area of potential effects (APE), reviewing what's known about this area, consulting with people about it, highlighting any special issues that will have to be addressed, and then coming up with a plan.

The regulations don't spell out any standard system for identification; it would be ridiculous if they did. What's appropriate for one kind of project, with its own kinds of effects, in a particular part of the country, isn't appropriate for some other kind of project, with different effects, someplace else. This variability is why scoping is so important.

But it's something that agencies and project proponents often fail to do, or do in a rote, thoughtless way. That can be a big problem both for you and for the project proponent. It's a problem for you because important places and impacts may be missed—including impacts on your special place—if the scope of the identification effort is misdefined. It's a problem for the proponent because it may present you or others with opportunities to complicate, impede, and even halt the course of project planning.

How agencies mess up scoping

Some common errors in scoping include the following:

- **Not doing it**, instead relying on some sort of standard procedure. One agency I know, for example, always does archaeological surveys but very little else, and when it's looking at something "linear" like a proposed road, pipeline, or power line, it looks only within 50 feet of the centerline. Never mind that there may be historic properties that archaeologists have no idea how to find or recognize, or that the project may have effects hundreds or thousands of feet away from the right-of-way; archaeological survey of a 100-foot corridor is their standard and that's what they're going to do, period. If you're dealing with this agency, and your special place, say, is subject to visual impacts and sits half a mile off the right-of-way, you're going to need to get the agency to rethink its approach.

- **Paying attention only to the preferred alternative**. It's not uncommon for a historic property identification effort to focus only on the *preferred alternative*—that is, the alternative that the agency or project proponent prefers. Why? Because the proponent is convinced that this is the alternative he'll pursue; examining the others is a sham exercise designed just to satisfy the regulatory agencies, and the less money he can spend on them, the better. And he may think that identifying historic properties is a frightfully costly affair; in a moment we'll see why.

- **Just doing what someone says to do**. Agencies are required by the regulations to consult with the State and/or Tribal Historic Preservation Officer (SHPO, THPO) during scoping, and many of them do so by just asking what the SHPO/THPO wants them to do and then doing it. Some SHPOs and THPOs won't play this game, recognizing that it's not their business to do the agency's thinking for it, but many feel that it's their responsibility to give the agency quite specific direction, and insist as strongly as they can that their direction be followed. Often the direction isn't very good, particularly because SHPOs and THPOs are overworked and can't devote much time to thinking about any given project. They're likely to give off-the-cuff direction to do more or less than is really necessary, or to do the wrong kind of thing to identify the kinds of properties the project may affect. They may insist that standard procedures be employed, even where they're not really relevant to the project and its likely effects. And they may fail to recommend things that the agency or proponent really should do to make the identification effort an adequate one. SHPOs and THPOs aren't the only ones who provide this kind of direction. Agency environmental and "cultural resource management" offices may do the same thing, and so may the consultants a proponent hires. It's never a good idea to just do what somebody says to do without thinking about it, but that's exactly what agencies and project proponents often do.

Why Your Place May Not Be Noticed

Below is a typical (and entirely real) "scope of work" for contract services to help a state agency comply with Section 106 when it seeks federal assistance.

The (state) Department of Conservation annually conducts a wide variety of construction projects across the state on lands owned or managed by the agency. Before initiating projects, determination must be made as to whether or not construction activities are likely to impact cultural resources and if an archaeological survey is needed. Archaeological surveys are conducted in order to meet National Historic Preservation Act (NHPA) Section 106 requirements to consider the effect of our actions on historic properties.

As you can see, the agency thinks that "archaeological survey" is what it needs. So the state Department of Conservation will get an archaeologist, who only by sheer chance may know that anything other than archaeological sites can be historically or culturally significant for any reasons other than those of archaeological research. There is no reason to expect the contractor to know anything about consulting interested parties, defining APEs, or evaluating places like landscapes, traditional cultural properties, and historic buildings and structures. The department doesn't even demand that its contractor know anything about Section 106—which the department itself shows no evidence of understanding. So the contractor will do an archaeological survey of the department's project, the department will assume it's got Section 106 covered, and if your special place doesn't happen to be an archaeological site that's special because of its research value, it—and you—may be out of luck.

- **Talking with too few people, or a too-narrow range of people.** Some agencies don't really talk with anybody on the outside during scoping, except the outside project proponent if there is one, or perhaps other federal agencies with regulatory functions. Some contact only the SHPO or THPO, or send out form letters (often incomprehensible) to tribes and local governments. If they don't talk with you and your neighbors, they're depriving you of an opportunity you ought to have to influence how the identification is done, and what's identified.

- **Just having a hearing.** If the agency does talk with people during scoping, it often does so only in the context of a formal public meeting or hearing. Some agencies, in fact, act as if having a hearing *is* scoping. Some agencies and project proponents think this is what the law requires, but it's not. The law—the regulations, that is, for both Section 106 and NEPA—require figuring out what the scope of identification ought to be; if a public meeting is useful, fine, but it's neither always necessary nor often helpful.

    Unfortunately, as mentioned in the last chapter, project opponents fall into the "public hearing" trap too. Protesting the inadequacy of an agency's public involvement program, they'll point to the lack of a public hearing as evidence that the agency hasn't done its job. It's questionable whether holding a public hearing would improve the review process much, but the big problem with this kind of complaint is that it's very easy for the agency to take care of—just hold a hearing, stroke one's corporate or bureaucratic chin solemnly, and get on with the project. Strong recommendation: Don't get fixated on public hearings, and don't let your lawyer do it either. Lawyers are often bullish about public hearings because they're sort of court-like, they have a long, distinguished tradition in American governance, and they're what legislatures do all the time. But that doesn't make them always useful, and they should never be allowed to become the be-all and end-all of scoping—or any other form of public involvement in decision-making.

What you can do about it

What you can do about an agency's failure to perform proper scoping is—as usual—to direct the agency's attention to the specific regulatory requirements (36 CFR 800.4(a)) and ask how they're going to attend to them. Such questions should be put in writing, with copies to the SHPO, Advisory Council on Historic Preservation, and any other interested parties. If possible, outline the relationship between the regulatory requirement and the situation on the ground: "36 CFR 800.4(a)(1) requires that as part of scoping you define the area of potential effects (APE). This is particularly critical in this case because...."

As usual, the agency may ignore you. But it may not, and in any event you're building up a documentary record that can be useful in court if you wind up having to go there.

Real Scoping

The Section 106 regulations require that an agency do five things as parts of scoping:

- Establish the area of potential effects
- Review existing information
- Seek more information from others
- Identify issues that may have to be addressed
- Make special efforts to figure out what concerns Indian tribes or Native Hawaiian groups (in Hawaii) may have

Let's look at each of these.

APEs great and small

The area of potential effects, or APE, is the area or areas where the proposed project may have effects on historic properties, if any are there. *May* is the word the regulations use, not *will*. That's important. At this point in the process, most likely nobody really knows whether there are historic properties in the area to be affected, so defining the APE is necessarily hypothetical. Over here, the project will involve building a road, which will require bulldozing, so whatever's there will be churned up. Over there there's no construction planned, but the project site will be very visible, so if there's anything there that people like to look at, or look out from, it will be affected. Downstream the project's likely to cause erosion; upstream it may cause headcutting. On the shore of the planned new reservoir, someone's sure to want to build vacation cabins, and that will require more churning up of the ground. If you put in that interchange, there'll definitely be fast-food places that spring up next to it, involving more ground disturbance and changes in the visual environment.

It's in APE definition that agencies often get in trouble by being too narrow-minded. Particularly if their "cultural resource" people are archaeologists, they're likely to focus only on the places where the bulldozers will roam—where archaeological sites are likely to be churned up. Here too they may rely on standard, arbitrary rules: the APE extends 50 feet on either side of the right-of-way, or includes a half-mile buffer zone. Don't let them get away with it, because if you do, it's likely to be hard to fix later on.

You probably want them to acknowledge as large an APE as possible. You certainly want them to acknowledge an APE that includes your special place. If you're out to stop or seriously redirect the project, you also need to be sure that all its effects are tallied up, whether they have to do with your place or not—so you should try to make sure that the APE includes all the areas that might be affected. Affected, that is, in any way—bulldozed, eroded, intruded upon visually, made more noisy or smelly, subjected to development that wouldn't otherwise occur; opened up to inappropriate uses—by intentional vandals, for example, or unwary hikers. There are lots of possibilities; use your imagination.

But not too much imagination; if the impacts you predict are too far out in the stratosphere, you're going to lose credibility. It's arguable, for example, that a power plant in New Mexico will have adverse effects on historic buildings in Los Angeles because it will make continuing development possible there, but the kinds of adverse effects it might have are so speculative that it's unlikely a court would insist that an agency consider them. If the agency figures that a court will never require it to take a given kind of effect into account, it's unlikely to do so, however convincing you may be.

If the project proponents are smart (or honorable, but we needn't count on that), they'll propose a great APE—a large, inclusive one. This reduces the likelihood that the opposition (you) will blindside them with some kind of effect they didn't expect, and it generally helps prevent surprises—any plan's worst enemies. But project proponents aren't always (or even often) very smart about this kind of thing, and they're not always well advised. They may have consultants who honestly believe that the best or only conceivable APE is a skinny APE, embracing only the land that will be physically disrupted. They may even think that you can't have an APE if you don't know there's a historic property present—an easy impression to attack because it's so circular. We don't know what's there so we don't have an APE in which to identify things so we won't find out what's there, and . . . . They may also get bad advice from the SHPO; not every SHPO is the brightest bulb in a state's basket of bureaucrats.

A Multitude of APEs

Agencies and project proponents often make mistakes in establishing a project's "area of potential effects" (APE)—typically underestimating its extent and character. In fact, there are usually multiple APEs, related to different kinds of effects.

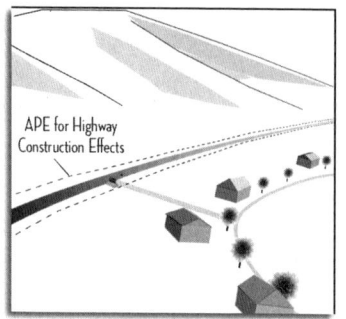

In this hypothetical example, the APE for direct construction effects—likely to be defined as a corridor of some arbitrary width—may be the only APE to which the proponent pays any attention.

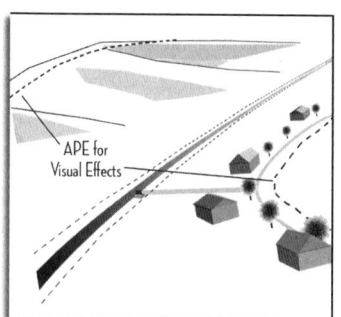

But the APE for visual effects, which may be your primary concern, is much wider.

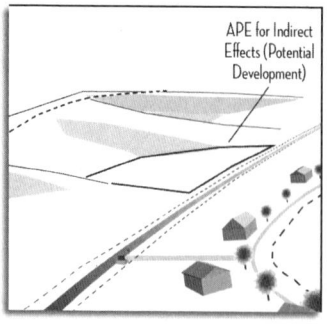

The APE for the indirect effects of, say, residential development induced by the new highway may be larger still, or include different areas. And the APE for cumulative effects would have to include already existing development as well as whatever future development is reasonably foreseeable.

Place-Saving Strategies – Getting Your Place Noticed

One reason project proponents, "CRM" contractors, SHPOs, and oversight agencies often think they need to keep the APE on a diet is that they equate "APE" with "area to be surveyed by archaeologists." This is because historically, most CRM contractors have been archaeologists, and to most archaeologists, the way you find sites is to do a "survey." A survey typically involves placing archaeologists on the ground some standard number of meters apart, where the pieces of ground they can scan overlap, and then walking over the ground, looking at it very carefully. In some areas it's standard procedure to dig a hole every X number of meters—maybe 10, maybe 20—and pass the dirt from it through a sieve with mesh usually twice to four times bigger than window screen. Detailed records are kept of everything done, seen, and picked up. Of course, this takes a lot of time, and as a result, costs a lot of money. It's also complicated by the fact that the archaeologists need access to the land, permission to walk all over whatever crops are growing there, and other perks that landowners may not be very ready to give. Understandably, project proponents are skittish about incurring the costs and complexities of extensive archaeological survey, and if they—or their CRM contractors, or an oversight agency, or the SHPO—equate "APE" with "archaeological survey area," they're going to want a small APE, not a great one.

The regulations, however, don't even suggest that anyone has to do archaeological surveys of the whole APE. The agency or proponent needs to do archaeological surveys where it's important to find archaeological sites—in the areas whose ground is likely to get churned up as a direct or indirect result of the project, for example. The project construction site, the access roads, the sewerline right-of-way, the creek banks that are likely to erode, the immediate vicinity of the interchange where the fast-food places and gas stations are likely to go. In the areas where visual impacts are likely, a different kind of identification is needed: look for the places that might be eligible for the National Register and whose residents, users, or viewers might have their views messed up by the project. Is there a nice old residence or residential neighborhood or apartment building looking out toward the project site? An old fort managed by the local historical society, whose visitors like to envision what the surroundings were like in the old days? A hill where members of an Indian tribe (or anyone else, for that matter) go to carry out rituals? Or is there something that people look at across the project site? The rock crag shaped like a Wookie's head; the only skyscraper in town; the monument to Korean War casualties? The project proponent would be dumb to do archaeological surveys of such places, but he'd certainly better talk with people about whether and how they value their views, and about what his project may do to them. The same kind of thing goes for areas where there may be auditory impacts, olfactory impacts, traffic impacts, or changes in the socioeconomic structure of the community. A lot of these kinds of impacts need to be considered under NEPA even if there are no historic properties involved, but one thing the proponent or agency ought to find out is whether historic properties are involved, so these areas should be part of the APE.

Or APEs. It's perfectly all right to have multiple APEs with different boundaries—a whole troop of APEs. There may be an archaeological APE that's pretty skinny and a visual effects APE that's fat. And since an impact analysis should give more or less equal consideration to all reasonable alternatives, there almost has to be a more or less separate APE for each one. The APE doesn't have to be very firmly delineated; it can be soft and squishy—as is likely, for example, if it's an APE for the secondary effects of general change in land use or property values resulting indirectly from the project. And APEs can evolve—change as the project plans change. We start off with a visual

Test excavation is often part of archaeological survey. TIGHAR test excavation at College Park Airport. Photo by author.

APE to the southeast of the project site, and when the design changes the visual effects shift to the northwest.

Common dodge: Where the agency has defined the APE narrowly, and you point out that it doesn't include, say, those areas where visual effects will occur, the agency may smoothly respond that it's really OK, because they consider such effects under NEPA and don't really need to do so under Section 106.

Response: What they do under NEPA is all well and good, but Section 106 is a separate statute with its own regulatory requirements. They can't logically say that they've complied with Law 1 by complying with Law 2 unless the laws themselves, or their regulations, allow them to do so.

Reviewing existing information

Having established what the APE is, the agency is supposed to find out what's already known about it. The regulations don't say why this is necessary, but it should be obvious. If I look out in a field and see a tumble-down old house, all I can tell from seeing it is that it's a tumble-down old house. If I've done background research, though, I may know that it's the house in which the town's first mayor launched his campaign for governor, which led to his election as president. Or imagine we're setting up a team to look at the area's historic properties. If we don't know that very ancient archaeological sites have been found in the area, or can be predicted to be there based on the geology and soils and what's known from other areas, we won't know that we ought to include a specialist in very ancient buried archaeological sites on our team, or schedule some deep testing with a backhoe.

It's not uncommon in some areas for CRM contractors, agencies, and SHPOs to reduce background research to just a "records check," to see what's already been recorded by archaeologists, and what's already on the National Register. There's nothing wrong with records checks, but they're not enough. If nobody has previously recorded the tumble-down house as the one the mayor lived in, just checking the records isn't going to help me appreciate its significance.

The agency or proponent ought to ask, "What do I need to know in order to predict what's in the APE?" And then go get the necessary information, or contract with someone to do so. If they haven't done this, that's a weakness that can be attacked. It's not reasonable to expect them to have done the equivalent of a doctoral dissertation on the area's history at the scoping stage, but they certainly need to have done enough research to have a handle on what's likely to be there and what they need to do to find it.

Seeking information from others

The regulations say that as part of scoping an agency must:

> Seek information, as appropriate, from consulting parties, and other individuals and organizations likely to have knowledge of, or concerns with, historic properties in the area, and identify issues relating to the undertaking's potential effects on historic properties. [36 CFR 800.4(a)]

The agency isn't supposed to just look at books and files. It's supposed to *talk with people*, see what people know about the area, think about it, predict is likely to be there, and what makes it important. Of course, the term "as appropriate" can cover a multitude of sins, but the intent of the regulatory language is clearly to have the agency access bodies of expertise outside its own personnel and files.

Note that the regulations say that the agency is not to ask only about an outside party's knowledge of the area, but also about his or her "concerns." The agency should be talking with people during scoping about what they think makes the area important, what's sensitive for them, whether and how the project plans create problems for them that have something to do with its historic or cultural significance.

Agencies that rely on some standard way of doing identification almost surely will *not* seek information from others—except that they'll always ask the SHPO to tell them what he or she has in the state's files. And they may not *want* to learn about people's concerns—because, of course, they don't want to pay attention to them. These are inadequacies that can be exploited.

The agency has special responsibilities toward Indian tribes, because federally recognized tribes are sovereign governments entitled under the Constitution, many treaties, and piles of case law to what's referred to as "government-to-government consultation." This is a semi-formal process—though as informal as the tribe and the agency agree to let it be—of notification and response, opportunities to comment, and negotiation to resolve problems. It dovetails, though not always very neatly, with Section 106 consultation. A lot of what the agencies call government-to-government consultation is pure window-dressing, however. Send the tribal government a letter so full of governmental gobbledygook that nobody can understand it, give them 30

Place-Saving Strategies — Getting Your Place Noticed

days to respond, and then go forward with the agency decision, patting the staff on the back for being so culturally sensitive.

And some agencies get so focused on tribal consultation that they forget to consult with anyone else—except the SHPO. They pretty much always talk to the SHPO if they talk to anyone at all. The regulations refer to local governments, property owners, and other "interested parties" as groups that ought to be consulted, but this doesn't always, or even often, happen. This, again, is an exploitable vulnerability.

Identifying issues

Based on its discussions with others, and whatever other sources of data it can access, the agency must, according to the regulations, identify "issues" that may have to be addressed as identification goes forward. What's an "issue?" Examples might be that detecting some kinds of historic property requires the use of special techniques, or that some information is very sensitive from the standpoint of a tribe, or that Rancher Rick wants any artifacts that archaeologists find on his property. Or that Rancher Ruth won't let people on her property at all, or that the site of the Seven Day Massacre may lie somewhere in the APE, so everyone will have to be especially careful to keep an eye out for bones. Or that there's unexploded ordnance in the area, or toxic wastes, or really voracious mosquitoes.

Special attention to tribes and Native Hawaiian groups

The regulations repeatedly return to the theme of giving special attention to the concerns of Indian tribes and Native Hawaiian groups. That's because there's language in the NHPA, added in 1992, requiring such special attention. Other ethnic groups sometimes get irritated that they're not included in the language, but they're not, and that's that. They have the same rights as any other group of American citizens, but agencies aren't formally required to give them "special" attention.

> **Common dodge:** You assert that the agency needs to consult a particular group of people—local horticulturalists, say, because there are lots of gardens in the APE. The agency people and the proponent's consultants look at you like you just landed from Mars and patiently explain that they're really required only consult with the SHPO and Indian tribes; everybody else gets to "comment" through the NEPA process.

Response: Look back at them with matching incomprehension and ask if they don't think the horticulturalists may have "concern with the undertaking's effects on historic properties." If they may have such concerns, then 36 CFR 800.2(c)(5) says that they may be entitled to be consulting parties. The agency can choose not to recognize them as such, but it's their choice, not a matter of law. Agencies tend not to like being reminded that they have free will, and the responsibility that goes with it.

The main tribal/Native Hawaiian concern that the regulations highlight is confidentiality, which we'll deal with a bit later. For the moment, suffice to say that if a tribe wants to keep information on its ancestral sites secret, the agency is supposed to try to oblige, to the extent it can within the constraints of law. This can get pretty complicated—which is why we'll deal with it later.

THE RESULTS OF SCOPING

The results of scoping ought to be—ta-da!—a scope of work for identification, tailored to the actual needs of the project, the area, the concerned parties, and the kinds of historic properties the area may contain. In a nutshell, the scope ought to predict what's likely to be out there in the APE, and spell out what has to be done to find out if the predictions are correct.

One of the important things the scope of work should do is establish what specialists ought to be involved on the identification team. Are there old buildings in the area? Better have an architectural historian. Lots of documents to go through? Sign on a historian. A need for consultation with a tribe or other group outside the American mainstream? Consider a cultural anthropologist or sociologist, or someone from the group itself. Does the whole landscape, or some part of it, seem to have special qualities of some kind? Bring in a landscape historian or cultural geographer. Are there likely to be archaeological sites? Then an archaeologist is needed—or maybe archaeologists of several types: historic archaeologists and prehistoric, specializing respectively in periods since the Europeans arrived and before; geoarchaeologists, who can find deeply buried sites and interpret landscape features; ethnoarchaeologists, who can relate archaeological data to the ways of life of contemporary people. Exactly what's needed in terms of expertise, and in terms of discovery methods, depends entirely on what's come out of scoping. The regulatory requirement is that the agency make *a reasonable and good faith effort* to identify historic properties. Scoping

Other common identification activities:

Architectural documentation

Aerial survey

Interviewing long-term local residents, local historians, and tribal elders, both at home . . .

. . . and in the field

Use of ground-penetrating radar and other detection technology

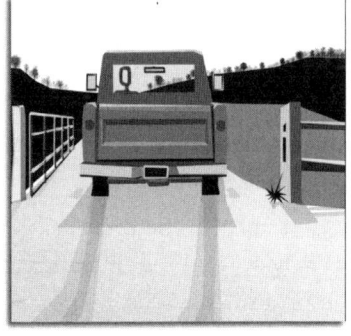

"Windshield survey" which means simply driving through an area and looking for buildings or sites that look old

defines what's reasonable to do, and the agency is then supposed to get it done honestly—that is, in "good faith."

What really happens

The above is what the regulations say the agency *has* to do. What really happens is something else again.

Typically, an agency won't really do scoping at all, or if they do something they call scoping, it will be a matter of holding a public meeting or two. They'll usually do that under NEPA, with no particular reference to the concerns of Section 106.

Much less commonly, people working on identification will try to understand the cultural and historical character of the whole landscape.

The form letter

They'll contact the SHPO, or require the project proponent to do so. What they ask the SHPO depends on how savvy they are. Here are some examples:

- ☐ "Please advise if this project will have adverse effects on historic properties."
- ☐ "Within 30 days, please tell us if you have any concerns."
- ☐ "Please inform us of any historic sites within 3 miles of the project site."

None of these queries—and there are innumerable variations on each theme—has anything to do with what the regulations require, and most ask the SHPO to do things that are not the SHPO's job to do—assuming they're even feasible. The SHPO is unlikely to know where all the historic properties are, within 3 miles of the project site or anyplace else, and it's not the SHPO's job to find out. It's the responsible agency's job to find out what damage the project may do, and that includes finding out what's out there to damage. The "tell us of any concerns within 30 days" business is a pure, unadulterated dodge; they're not interested in finding out the project's effects, they're interested in ticking off an item on a checklist: "No comment from the SHPO within 30 days, check." But the regulations don't say to ask the SHPO about concerns and give them 30 days to respond; they say to consult.

Place-Saving Strategies – Getting Your Place Noticed

Common dodge: The agency official will fold his hands piously and say that, sadly, his agency is just not expert in historic preservation matters and must therefore defer to the SHPO. You know, Congress gives us money to build (whatever)—not to do archaeology (or history, or whatever they think the discussion's about).

Response: Be very sympathetic, but point out that however stupid the agency may be about historic preservation, the law nevertheless makes the agency—not the SHPO or anybody else—responsible for assessing the impacts of its actions. It's really not kosher to say, "Well, I don't have the money or personnel to comply with this law, so I'll fob off the responsibility on somebody else."

They'll send out a similar form letter to Indian tribes, Tribal Historic Preservation Officers, maybe to local governments, maybe (though seldom) to others on a mailing list perhaps given them by the SHPO, perhaps left over from a case 10 years ago and still hanging around the office. It is likely to say about the same thing as the SHPO letter: tell us if you have any problems, or where all your sacred sites are, or where your ancestors are buried. Tribes respond to this sort of thing about as well as you'd expect them to.

The problem, though, is that if the SHPO or the tribe doesn't respond, the agency is very likely to say, "OK, they had their chance," and go ahead. What do they go ahead and do? We'll get to that in a moment.

Dumb responses and their outcomes

First, let me highlight another problem. Some SHPOs and/or tribes *do* respond to stupid contact letters, and actually try, or seem, to give the agency what it asks for. Some SHPOs feel obligated to go check their archaeological site files—which of course contain information on only those sites that are recognized as "archaeological" and that someone has recorded and filed—and advise the agency of the results. Sometimes this advice is very poorly set forth. Consider this example:

> We have checked our site files for your project area and there are no properties listed in or eligible for the National Register within its boundaries.

The SHPO probably means that their records show no listed or eligible properties, which is probably true. This is probably a reliable indicator that there really are no *listed* properties, because if they were listed they'd be recorded. But it doesn't mean that there are no *eligible* properties. There may be a 7,000-year-old Indian cemetery in the middle of the project area that nobody's noticed because it's covered with poison oak, or a surface parking lot. It's really just sloppy language use on the part of the SHPO, but it's probably resulted in the destruction of a lot of important places that just hadn't been listed in the National Register.

The "Class N survey"

Very commonly, though, an SHPO will be smart enough not to let the project off the hook without any attempt by the responsible agency to identify historic properties. Unfortunately, they're not always—or even often—smart enough to tell the agency or proponent to do the scoping that the regulations require. Instead they'll try to provide a helpful shortcut. They'll write back to the agency saying, "You have to carry out Section 106 review; to begin this, we recommend that you perform a Class I Survey as described in our survey guidelines." Or a Phase I survey, or a reconnaissance cultural resource investigation—it goes by a lot of names but basically what it means is this:

- Hire a "cultural resource" (read "archaeological") consulting firm.
- Have it line its people up along the edge of the project site and march across it at measured intervals, looking at the ground.
- At further specified intervals, dig holes, or rake the ground, or something to give you an idea of what's under the plow zone, leaf mold, or drifting sand. Maybe put the dirt through a sieve. Collect flakes of stone, sherds of pottery, and so on.
- Based on this, lay out the boundaries of all the archaeological sites.
- Write a report that the SHPO will approve.

Now, this may be OK—if a bit uncreative—with respect to archaeological sites within the top half-meter or so of the soil, within the boundaries of the project site, but it's not going to reveal:

- More deeply buried archaeological sites
- Sites in the area of potential effects but not within the physical project site (for instance, those that may be eroded away downstream or upstream)

Place-Saving Strategies – Getting Your Place Noticed

- Historic places that aren't archaeological sites—old buildings and structures, sites of historical events that didn't leave obvious traces, natural places and things associated with a group's traditional culture, locations where people do culturally important activities

Moreover, this sort of approach automatically means that the focus of attention is on the ground, and on small things in and on the ground. When you're looking at the ground, thinking about the little things in the ground, it's very hard to notice the big picture—what's on and in the land around you. This kind of survey can totally miss the existence of big landscape features, whole landscapes, whole historic neighborhoods, and those living people whose association with such places make them historic.

Sometimes the SHPO's standards, or common practice, or the moderately clear head of the consultant will result in adding further studies to identify non-archaeological properties. Maybe there'll be a "windshield survey" by architectural historians, driving the roads and looking at the older buildings, taking pictures, filling out record forms. Maybe there'll be a survey for "traditional cultural properties" (TCPs), places in the environment that living communities value for traditional reasons. Although every community has places important in its traditions, there's a tendency among agencies and contractors to think that only Indian tribes can have them, so TCP surveys tend to be studies of tribal attitudes toward specific locations in the APE, carried out by people with some kind of anthropological or sociological credentials. Very rarely there may be an effort by someone involved in the survey to stand back and look at the whole landscape to consider whether it, rather than or in addition to little pieces of it, may be eligible for the Register. These tend to be add-ons, though, often rather uncomfortably integrated with the overall survey if they're integrated at all (sometimes they're reported only in appendices). And they're rare; most surveys are all about archaeology.

So the proponent's consultant conducts the "Phase I" or "Class One" Survey and then writes a report, which the proponent submits to the SHPO. Here things can get especially squirrely.

SHPO clearance

When an SHPO doesn't respond to a letter request, or responds with a dumb statement like the example given earlier, or when an agency submits a "Class (whatever)" report to the SHPO and the SHPO approves or adopts or certifies or accepts it, this is often referred to (colloquially) as "SHPO clearance." The SHPO has, in essence, "cleared" the project; Section 106 is done, all is well, and it's full speed ahead. The same thing can happen where a Tribal Historic Preservation Officer is the one the agency coordinates with.

However, there is simply no such thing as SHPO clearance under the Section 106 regulations. It's not part of the process. It's really antithetical to the process, because the process is all about multi-party consultation, while "clearance" assumes that there's some authoritative figure who can say yea or nay, regardless of who has or has not been consulted and how. It also assumes that the SHPO is in the driver's seat, and that's not the way the system works. The agency is in the driver's seat, whether it wants to be there or not.

Common dodge: Many agencies have learned that SHPO clearance really isn't appropriate, so they call it something else—SHPO coordination, SHPO comment, or whatever. But they still treat it—and here's the problem with it—as the exclusive measure of a project's compliance with Section 106. If the SHPO says the project's good to go, it's good to go. If not, we gotta do more work.

Response: Try to get the agency to focus on what the regulations actually require them to do and to consider whether and how they've done it.

Agency belief in getting SHPO clearance makes SHPO review of reports a tremendous bottleneck. Agency review of such reports can be equally complicated and time-consuming, and things get really crazy when agency and SHPO staff start arguing—between themselves and with the proponent's consultants—about whether a report is adequate. All the parties involved are usually archaeologists, and the arguments become pretty esoteric. Was the spacing of surveyors over the landscape correct? Were shovel test pits excavated correctly, to the right depth, sifted properly? Were the boundaries of sites appropriately defined? Were the recovered artifacts properly identified? Are the consultant's conclusions about the age or character of each site correct? These arguments can go on at considerable length.

Ironically, your interests and the interests of the project proponent may converge at this point, though neither of you may recognize it (or want to do so). You want the agency, SHPO, and other consulting parties to focus on the serious issues, particularly about your special place. The proponent wants the agencies to just get on with it. The reviewers are happily debating technical minutiae that may be irrelevant to you both.

Eventually the proponent may get tired of it all and apply political pressure to the agency and SHPO, whereupon the professional staff members get told to resolve their differences and put the thing to bed. *This is a very dangerous time for you,* because they may put it to bed without ever considering your place or what's important about it.

So, although extended debate on the road to SHPO clearance may delay the process, and that may seem like a good thing, I don't think that's true if the debate is about things that are actually marginal, or technical. It's too easy to find these being "resolved" by executive fiat, in the process ignoring less marginal, less technical matters—like your special place. You need to try to keep everyone focused on the important things, as opposed to mere technicalities. It's in this way that your interests and those of the proponent may coincide.

What's Really Supposed to Come Out of Identification

If achieving SHPO clearance isn't the point of the identification effort, what is? The answer is simple in concept, but sometimes hard for people to get their arms around.

There's a guideline for identification that's cited in the Section 106 regulations—the *Secretary of the Interior's Standards and Guidelines for the Identification of Historic Properties,* issued back in 1983. Standard number 1 is that "identification of historic properties is undertaken to the degree required to make decisions." In other words, what ought to come out of the identification process under Section 106 is enough information to let the agency make reliable decisions. How much and what kind of information that is depends on a host of circumstances.

"Decision" at this point almost never means "decision as to whether to proceed with the project." It does mean "decision about the effects of the project on historic properties"—because that's the decision an agency makes under Section 106, in order to take those effects into account as the law requires. Based on that taking into account, and many others, the agency makes the decision about whether and how to proceed.

So what does the agency need to know in order to decide how historic places will be affected? As usual, there's no standard answer, and as usual there are all kinds of more or less arbitrary, entirely made-up standards the agencies and SHPOs try to impose. In many cases such standards are—or at least seem to be—necessary in order to give the review system order and predictability. But it's important to remember that they *are* made up, they're not inscribed in the regulations; they can be changed. And unfortunately, sometimes they work at cross-purposes with the actual regulatory requirements and can make your job harder.

> CONTACT: The Secretary of the Interior's Standards for Identification:
> http://www.cr.nps.gov/local-law/arch_stnds_2.htm

Realistically, the agency may need to know different things, and gather different amounts and kinds of data, about different properties. The rule of thumb is that they need to figure out what makes a place eligible for the National Register, and how that quality of the property may be changed if the project goes forward. In the next chapter we'll talk about what makes a place eligible for the National Register, and in the following chapter, what's involved in determining effects.

For your purposes, though, you want to make sure that your special place is identified, and recognized as significant. That means communicating with the people doing the identification work—probably contractors—and insisting on reviewing their reports. Make sure that your place is represented, and correctly represented.

The agency or proponent or contractor people you talk with very likely will tell you that they can't share the report with you, because they're obligated by law to keep it secret lest some terrible person misuse the information. The bogeyman that's usually conjured up is the vandal who's going to destroy the place. Sometimes there's something behind this, but often it's either just a knee-jerk reaction or a desire to keep you in the dark.

There *are* legal requirements regarding keeping records on historic properties confidential—Section 9 of the Archaeological Resources Protection Act, and Section 304 of the National Historic Preservation Act. ARPA applies only on federal and Indian tribal lands, only to "archaeological resources" over 100 years old, and only if there's concern on the part of the land managing agency that releasing information can lead to loss or destruction of a "resource." Section 304 applies more broadly to places identified in connection with all kinds of federal undertakings, regardless of landownership. It also provides for keeping information confidential for a wider range of reasons, such as to avoid invasion of privacy or impeding use of a religious site.

Place-Saving Strategies – Getting Your Place Noticed

But Section 304 can't be applied unilaterally; the agency must consult with the Keeper of the National Register in deciding whether to keep information secret, and the keeper gets to decide who gets access to it. So if worse comes to worst, you can petition the keeper to release the information and lobby the Advisory Council on Historic Preservation as well—because in 106-related Section 304 cases, the keeper has to consult with the council. Lobbying the council may help when an agency misuses Section 9 of ARPA too, provided it's in the context of a Section 106 review. If nothing else, you ought to be able to get the council to insist that the agency explain itself, and that often results in information being coughed up.

Of course, you may not want your special place *over*identified—maybe it's a place you think has some kind of spiritual character that will be disturbed if the wrong people know about it, or too many people visit it, or maybe you use it for private activities that you don't want disturbed, or maybe you just don't want too many people knocking on your door. If that's the case, then Section 304 may help you keep the information under wraps, but the trade-off may be that it makes it harder for everybody to consult about effects in an intelligent manner. The consulting parties literally won't know what they're talking about. There's a balance that has to be struck between protection of sensitive information and knowing enough to consult sensibly. Exactly where that balance should be struck varies from case to case.

Which is OK under the regulations. "Identify" doesn't necessarily mean "document extensively," though people will tell you it does. Some State Historic Preservation Officers want to see a National Register nomination form filled out on every place found during a Section 106 identification effort, and the National Register staff in NPS will tell you that's a good idea too. In fact, sometimes it is and sometimes it isn't; but in any event, it's not required by the regulations. What's required is a reasonable and good-faith effort to identify historic properties to the extent necessary to make decisions about their eligibility and about how they may be affected. Exactly what that means is negotiable among the consulting parties and should be negotiated.

It's also worth noting that there's no requirement in the regulations to identify *all* the historic properties in an APE, though again some people will tell you there is. Actually, identifying all historic properties is usually impossible; even the most qualified person, with the best team working in the most effective manner, can't be sure she's found everything. And it's not required. What is required is enough information to provide a basis for knowing what's out there, to the extent needed to understand and deal with effects. Often we can get by perfectly well with very incomplete information. There have even been cases where it was only necessary to know that *something* made an area sensitive, so the agency had to consult with people about how that sensitivity could be respected.

The bottom line is this: You need to work with whoever is doing the identification, and with the project proponent and agency staff, to make sure the work is done thoroughly and professionally, and to make sure your special place is identified to the extent and in the manner you want it identified. How exactly that's done is something you'll have to figure out.

Historic Property Identification and NEPA

The National Environmental Policy Act (NEPA), via the regulatory system described briefly in Chapter Four, requires consideration of project impacts on all aspects of the human environment, including historic places. So historic property identification ought to be done early enough in planning to get its results into the NEPA analysis and resulting documents—whether those documents support assigning the project to an excluded category (categorical exclusion), or are parts of an environmental assessment (EA) and finding of no significant impact (FONSI), or are in an environmental impact statement (EIS) and record of decision (ROD). And identification ought to involve paying relatively equal amounts of attention to all the alternatives under consideration.

This doesn't always happen, in part because of the notion that all historic properties have to be identified in great detail. This can ratchet up the price of historic property identification to the point at which it's completely disproportionate with what's being spent on assessing any other environmental variable—endangered species, water quality, even toxic wastes—and proponents understandably balk at that. That's one reason it's important to keep it in mind that the regulations require something much more reasonable—identifying things to the extent needed to make the decisions the agency has to make.

Generally speaking, it will serve your interests to promote good, early coordination between NEPA impact analyses and Section 106 identification work. Such coordination should get your special place identified—again, to the extent it needs to be—at a point in planning when multiple alternatives are open for consideration. That will make it easier for the proponent to opt for one of those alternatives and leave your place alone.

So keep track of what the agency is doing, or causing the non-federal proponent to do, with regard to NEPA and get after them to coordinate their Section 106 work. If they tell you, "Oh, we do that later, when we can carry out the SHPO's direction about identifying everything down to the last jot and tiddle," don't accept it. Point out that historic properties are part of the environment that NEPA requires be considered, that the 106 regulations don't require an unreasonable level of identification work, and that their NEPA documents will be deficient if they don't include a reasonable level of historic property identification. And work on the SHPO, who may actually be misadvising the agency; some SHPOs, unfortunately encouraged by the National Park Service (which holds the purse strings of their federal grants), actually promote identification practices that can't be carried out until an alternative has been selected and land acquired, thus almost guaranteeing last-minute conflicts and thwarting the purposes of both NEPA and Section 106. This often puts SHPOs in hot political water, but they never seem to learn.

How the BPS Did It

At Broad Run Bridge, the responsible agencies didn't really do scoping. The Virginia Department of Transportation (VDOT) corresponded with the SHPO, but that was about all. No one forced the issue. The village of Buckland, its associated manor house, and the battlefield were already included in the National Register, so arguably not much further identification was needed, and VDOT, rather automatically following its standard procedures, had archaeological surveys done of the bridge's immediate vicinity—which they took for granted constituted the project's area of potential effects (APE).

The Buckland Preservation Society (BPS) challenged the adequacy of VDOT's identification work. BPS argued that the bridge reconstruction was part of the long-term effort to widen the highway through the village, and that the cumulative effects of this entire action, including the way it would facilitate sprawl, had to be considered. BPS shared its views with the Federal Highway Administration (FHWA), the SHPO, the Advisory Council, the National Trust, and the NPS American Battlefield Protection Program. FHWA expectably sided with VDOT, wanting to focus solely on the direct physical impacts of the project on archaeology. The Trust and Battlefield Program either agreed with the BPS or added their own concerns (the Battlefield Program wanted further study of the battlefield, for example). The SHPO and Advisory Council said there was a need for more study. VDOT agreed to do more archaeology in the right-of-way, which of course did nothing for the cumulative effects issue.

Meanwhile on a parallel track, the BPS was working at the state level to promote the idea of a bypass around Buckland and the battlefield. This would eliminate any need for a high-speed, high-volume highway through the historic places to accommodate through traffic, and potentially allow the land acquired in the 1950s to be returned to the village. The BPS organized support in the state legislature, and funds were appropriated for a study of the bypass alternative. BPS also began working with the Battlefield Preservation Program, the National Trust, and a variety of historical organizations and institutions in and around the state to document Buckland's history and plan for its future—a future without a bisecting highway.

CONTACT: For regulatory language pertinent to this chapter go to http://www.achp.gov/regs-rev04.pdf and see 36 CFR 800.4

CHAPTER SEVEN

Evaluation

Is Your Place Eligible for the National Register?

FOR THOSE WHO JUST TUNED IN . . .

This may be the first chapter you turn to. You have a place you think is special. It's threatened by some change. You're wondering if Section 106 of the National Historic Preservation Act (NHPA) can help save it. You know, or have learned, or have been told, that your place may be protected if it's on or eligible for the National Register of Historic Places. So you want to find out what this Register is all about.

If that's what you've done, here are some things you need to know, all of which are discussed in the preceding chapters:

- Section 106 says that *federal agencies* must *consider the effects* of *undertakings* on places *included in or eligible for* the National Register. This doesn't mean they can't destroy them, just that they have to give them a fair shot at survival.

- "Undertakings" are projects that federal agencies undertake, or help others undertake (via a grant, for example), or permit others to undertake (as, for example, when the Corps of Engineers issues a permit to fill a wetland).

- *Federal agencies* are responsible for compliance with Section 106, but they can delegate most of the legwork to others.

- Agencies have to *consult* with State Historic Preservation Officers (SHPOs), Tribal Historic Preservation Officers (THPOs), Indian tribes and Native Hawaiian groups, and others as they go through the Section 106 process. If you want to protect something, it's important to get recognized as a *consulting party*.

Saving Places that Matter

- ▣ Section 106 doesn't apply to undertakings where the federal government isn't involved, no matter how significant the threatened places may be.

- ▣ "Affect" means change. Change can happen in many ways. It can be direct or indirect, or cumulative (part of a pattern of change by multiple factors). It can be physical (knock it down, dig it up); it can be visual or auditory or olfactory (put something in the visual environment, or generate inappropriate noise or smells). It can be change in the way a place is used (economic development that alters the character of a neighborhood, land-use policies that keep people from accessing a place).

With that as prelude, and with encouragement to dip into the preceding chapters for detail, let's talk about National Register eligibility.

REGISTER ELIGIBILITY IS *REALLY* IMPORTANT

If a place isn't eligible for the Register, it doesn't get considered under Section 106. Period—no ifs, ands, or buts about it. It may be considered under other federal, state, tribal, and local laws, but not under 106. If you want to use Section 106 to protect your place, you *have* to get it recognized as eligible for the Register.

This does not mean you have to nominate it to the Register, though sometimes that's the only way to get the job done. It doesn't even mean that you need to document it in any particular way, though different agencies, and different SHPOs, insist on various kinds of documentation. Sometimes nomination may be the best or only thing to do, but often it's not. Sometimes you'll need lots of supporting documentation; other times you can get away with less, and there are good reasons to do so. We'll talk more about this.

Evaluation – Is Your Place Eligible?

What the Register Is

The Register is a list maintained by the National Park Service (NPS). It's a list of "districts, sites, buildings, structures and objects" that have been found by the Register's professional staff to have significance in American history, archaeology, architecture, engineering, or culture. The places can be significant at the national level, the state level, or the local level; the fact that it's the *National* Register doesn't mean that everything on it has to be important to the whole nation.

On the other hand, the importance of a place *does* have to make sense to professional historic preservation people in the SHPO office and in the National Register Division of NPS. The National Register Division is headed by an official called the *Keeper of the National Register*, who has absolute power over what gets determined eligible. In the final analysis, after all the studies and documentation

and review, if the keeper says it's eligible, it's eligible; if the keeper says it's not, it's not. This may seem like a strangely centralized, authoritarian way for a democracy to decide what's valuable about its heritage, but that's the way it is.

The Register is continually expanded through nominations, which can be submitted by anyone. Private parties submit nominations through the SHPO, who has a "State Review Board" that pronounces on them.

But Section 106 gives consideration not only to places that are *on* the Register—that have been nominated and gone through formal review—but to those that are *eligible* for it. That is a critical fact, without which Section 106 wouldn't be worth much. An eligible property is a place that meets the Register's criteria—whether anyone has ever applied the criteria to it or not.

> ## The Importance of Being Eligible
>
> The existing Section 106 process is far from perfect, but it has afforded the Coalition an opportunity to be heard and have input into the design of Port Authority's proposed facility. The original World Trade Center was not listed on the National Register. None of the federal agencies involved, nor the Advisory Council on Historic Preservation, would accede to our request that a formal determination of eligibility be made by the Secretary of the Interior. Requests from members of Congress went unheeded. It was only the requirement that "eligible" properties be identified that caused the redevelopers of the World Trade Center site to consider our concerns. If only properties listed on the National Register had been considered during the Section 106 process, not only the Coalition, but every citizen who believes that September 11 was a transcendently significant event in our nation's history would have suffered irreparable harm.
>
> Anthony Gardner, Coalition of 9/11 Families, in a letter to Congressman Devin Nunes during consideration of amendments to the National Historic Preservation Act, April 18, 2005

WHAT AGENCIES ARE SUPPOSED TO DO

Agencies are supposed to conduct (or make someone else, like a non-federal project proponent, conduct) appropriate *identification efforts* in the *area of potential effects (APE)* of the undertaking under review (see Chapter Five). This typically means surveys of some kind, usually by consulting firms under contract. These studies are supposed to provide the consulting parties with enough information about places in the APE to allow the parties to decide whether they're eligible for the Register.

In order *to* decide, the agency is supposed to apply the *National Register Criteria* to the places its studies have identified. The criteria are set forth in regulations issued by NPS (36 CFR 60.4), which has also published exhaustive guidelines to assist in applying them.

Evaluation – Is Your Place Eligible?

Agencies apply the criteria in consultation with SHPOs—or with a THPO where that tribal official has assumed SHPO functions on tribal land. They *should* involve other consulting parties too, but the regulations are soft on this point, because what's appropriate in terms of involvement varies with the situation. If the property being evaluated is a tribal burial site, for instance, and one of the consulting parties collects  Indian artifacts for a hobby, the other consulting parties may want to be cautious about how they share information with him. But at a bare minimum the SHPO or THPO has to be consulted, and the other consulting parties should be kept in the loop so they know what's going on.

If the agency and the SHPO (or THPO) agree that a place is *eligible*, *does* meet the criteria, then they can treat it as eligible for the purposes of Section 106 review. If they agree that it's *not eligible*, *doesn't* meet the criteria, then it's treated as not eligible, and that's that—*unless* the Advisory Council on Historic Preservation (ACHP) or the Keeper of the Register requests that the agency seek a formal determination of eligibility from the keeper, in which case the agency must seek such a determination. If the agency and SHPO or THPO can't agree on whether a place is or isn't eligible, then the agency also seeks a formal determination from the keeper.

Pretty straightforward—deceptively so. There are, as we'll see, all kinds of ways to finesse application of the criteria and either short-circuit the determination process or ball it up.

Regarding as Eligible, Determining Eligibility, Listing

The consulting parties on a 106 case (meaning at least the agency and SHPO or THPO) can agree to regard a property as eligible for the Register, for purposes of the Section 106 review then in progress, without much ceremony. They simply say "OK, property X is eligible for purposes of this consultation," and get on to the next step in the process. This is the simplest way to deal with eligibility, for all concerned, and it's the most flexible. There are no particular documentation requirements. But some agencies, and some SHPOs or THPOs, get nervous about being so informal, and often there are reasons for more formality. Maybe someone is rightly or wrongly worried about litigation, or proving to his or her superiors, congresspeople, or a doubting public that the place really is important. In such cases the agency and SHPO or THPO can formally agree in writing that the place is eligible—usually with an exchange of letters or a concurring signature on a letter or report. This is usually called a *consensus determination of eligibility*. Once the signatures are in place, we move on with the process. Because it is more formal, and somewhat more heavily documented, a consensus determination tends to be a bit more permanent; agencies and SHPOs tend to regard a property that's been determined eligible to be eligible for all time. The Keeper of the National Register can also determine the property eligible; we'll see shortly how that happens.

The most formal way of documenting eligibility, of course, is by nominating the place and getting it accepted on the Register. This is very time-consuming, requires a lot of paper, and usually costs a lot. It involves numerous steps and lots of different levels of review. It really has nothing to do with Section 106—except that properties placed on the Register are unquestionably eligible and are treated as such.

In all these cases, in theory, the parties are simply recognizing that the property meets the National Register Criteria. They aren't *making* the place eligible; they're recognizing that it *is* eligible—and always has been, even before anybody found it or considered it with the criteria in mind.

And, of course, the consulting parties can agree to regard the property as *not* eligible, or it can be formally determined not eligible. We'll discuss a bit later what happens in that case, and what you can do if you disagree.

A property that's nominated to the Register and doesn't make it—gets washed out somewhere in the review process—may or may not wind up being treated

as not eligible; it depends on how it's been washed out. If the SHPO or keeper has said, "This place does not meet the criteria," then that's usually it. But if either has said, "We're not sure," or "we need more documentation," or "please demonstrate X, Y, or Z," then the eligibility of the place is undetermined, and the parties in a 106 consultation can still treat it as eligible or determine it so.

THE CRITERIA

Here are the National Register Criteria, as published at 36 CFR 60.4:

The quality of significance in American history, architecture, archeology, engineering, and culture is present in districts, sites, buildings, structures, and objects that possess integrity of location, design, setting, materials, workmanship, feeling, and association and (a) that are associated with events that have made a significant contribution to the broad patterns of our history; or (b) that are associated with the lives of persons significant in our past; or (c) that embody the distinctive characteristics of a type, period, or method of construction, or that represent the work of a master, or that possess high artistic values, or that represent a significant and distinguishable entity whose components may lack individual distinction; or (d) that have yielded, or may be likely to yield, information important in pre-history or history.

To be eligible, a place has to meet *one* of the criteria labeled (a) through (d), and it has to have *integrity* as outlined in the first sentence. The place also must *not* fall under any of seven *criteria considerations*, which we'll discuss a bit later.

WHAT THE CRITERIA MEAN

The National Register Criteria are subject to a lot of interpretation, and most of that interpretation is highly subjective. You need to know enough about them to promote their interpretation in ways that serve your interests, that illustrate the significance of your place.

Integrity

First, note the reference to "integrity of location, design, setting, materials, workmanship, feeling, and association." The place has to be more or less *in* place, at its original location. Its design—assuming it's a designed thing like a building—has to be somehow coherent, a reflection of its time and historical context. It can't be made of phony material, and the way it's built (assuming it's built) has to have some authenticity. Its original sur‑

roundings—to the extent they're relevant—can't be too messed up. If the place has some kind of aesthetic or other cultural feeling that people think is important—if it's regarded as beautiful, or spiritual, or expresses the community's identity—that quality can't be too badly compromised. If it's associated with some set of historical events or patterns or people, that association needs to be real, not manufactured—a Civil War battlefield, not a Civil War theme park.

If that threshold criterion—"integrity"—seems pretty loose, well, no argument. At base, it just means that the place has to be real and not terminally impaired. But there's room for a tremendous amount of interpretation, lots of opportunity for argument here, as we'll see.

Criterion (a) for Association

"Association" can be with very specific events—the Battle of Blueblood Bottom, the murder of Mayor Smith. Or it can be with bunches of less specific events that collectively contribute to some broad pattern of history—the settlement of Kansas, ancient urbanization in the Southeast, Chinese migration to the western gold fields. The event patterns can be national or international in scale—space exploration, World War II—or regional, or local, like Cochise's struggles for Apache freedom or the development of the chicken industry in Petaluma, California. They can be with a community's traditional history too—the travels of the Ojibwe ancestors from the Great Wigwam at the bottom of Lake Superior to the eastern salt sea and then back to the shores of the lake where the sacred wild rice was found, or the Matachines dance traditions of hispanic communities in New Mexico.

Criterion (a): Association with significant events. The Buckland Mills Battlefield. Photo by author.

Criterion (b) for Big People[1]

Criterion (b) is about association with historically significant people. These include the usual suspects such as George Washington and Davy Crockett, but also people whose significance is more local: the central California bandido Joaquin Murrieta; Harry Truman's Kansas City political mentor Tom Pendergast; early Nevada bordello operators. They can also be "people" whose precise character isn't historically documented—the *katsinas* of the Southwestern pueblos, or the volcano goddess Pele in Hawaii.

Criterion (b): Big People. Grave of Choctaw Chief Pushmataha. Actually this grave is not eligible because graves and monuments are ordinarily excluded, but really is eligible because it's in the Congressional Cemetery in Washington, DC, which is on the Register even though cemeteries usually aren't eligible (except when they are). Photo by the author.

Criterion (c) for Characteristics (or Cute Buildings)[2]

This one could also mean "catch-all," since it embraces so many possibilities: high artistic value, work of a master, and so on. Buildings, structures, and other kinds of built things like parks and parkways are commonly found eligible under criterion (c). This may be because they represent some particular style of architecture (such as Federal, Queen Anne, or Moderne), a period of construction (World War II, for example), or some particular method of building things (reinforced concrete, timber framing). Or they may be the "work of a master" like Frank Lloyd Wright or Eero Saarinen. Sometimes the "master" isn't actually known by name—he's the unidentified enslaved African who built really good cabins all over some chunk of the Southeast. Similarly, a place can exhibit high artistic value that reflects the work of a known artist or someone completely unknown—a really good street artist, a prehistoric rock-art inscriber.

Criterion (c): An example of a style or type. Truss bridge, Idaho. Photo by the author.

And then there are the places "that represent a significant and distinguishable entity whose components may lack individual distinction." A bit counterintuitive? Imagine a dockyard made up of warehouses, piers, docks, cranes, rail cars and engines, slips, bollards, barges, sail lofts. No single piece may be terribly "distinctive," but put them all together and they're quite distinguishable as a dockyard, which perhaps is significant as a good example of its type, or because of association with important events. Places like this are commonly referred to as "historic districts"; examples include mining landscapes, ports, railyards, warehouse complexes, industrial areas, commercial strips, farm and ranch landscapes, parks, villages, and urban or suburban residential neighborhoods.

Criterion (d) for Data (or Dig)

Criterion (d) is the one under which sites that archaeologists want to excavate are commonly found eligible for the Register. We don't have to *know* that the site contains important data; if it appears *likely* to contain useful information,

Criterion (d): Data. Nineteenth-century copper processing site in central New Mexico, which contains data on historic mining technology, economy, and social organization. Photo by the author.

that's sufficient. Or it may have yielded such information in the past, even though today it's been worked out, dug out of existence. In theory, other kinds of place can be eligible under criterion (d) too: a building for its architectural information, or historical documents sealed up in its walls, attic, or basement; or an urban neighborhood district for what it can tell us about the social life of its occupants. But it's rare to see this criterion applied to anything but archaeological sites, with reference to anything but archaeological kinds of data.

STRATEGICS

You obviously want your place to be recognized as meeting at least one of the four criteria, and as having integrity. The project proponent would probably prefer that the place not be seen as meeting any of the criteria. If it obviously *does* meet one or more of them, then the project proponent probably wants its integrity to be seen as compromised.

Generally speaking, fights over eligibility work in your favor. They can delay the 106 process, which in turn can delay the overall project planning process. This can become expensive for the project proponent and encourage him to seek a negotiated way out. The smart thing for a proponent to do, in most cases, is to concede eligibility and move forward with review. Eligibility is a topic about which the proponent is almost certainly not expert; he's going to have to rely on his consultants, or on the review agency's experts, or the SHPO. Once one gets beyond eligibility and starts arguing about how the project will affect something and what can be done about it—real-world stuff as opposed to academic fine points—the proponent is usually on much more solid ground. He can bring forth engineering arguments for the idea that the project won't have much serious effect. He can bring forth economic and public policy arguments for the idea that the effects are justified—it's too bad, but they just have to be accepted in the larger public interest. As long as he's stuck on eligibility, he's at the mercy of the archaeologists, the architectural historians, and all the other professionals who may get involved, who can engage in almost indefinite hair-splitting debate.

So it may benefit you to do what you can to keep the argument going. Keep feeding new data to the consulting parties, keep offering new arguments for eligibility, demand lots of documentation to support every decision or agreement. There are limits to the wisdom of this strategy, however. Someone finally may decide they've had enough and decide to bounce the question to the keeper for a final determination. This too may work in your favor; the keeper will take time to analyze the data and may well come down on your side. On the other hand, the keeper may not come down that way, or may produce a determination that is so obscure that everyone is left scratching their heads. Or someone may put political pressure on the keeper to fall into line with the proponent and the review agency. The keeper is not immune to such pressure. But when the keeper gets worried about the political implications of a decision, the most common reaction is to ask for more data. "We can't really tell whether this building meets criterion (c); we need more information on its period of construction. Please supply the information and we'll take another look." This of course works in your favor too, by further gumming up the works.

What To Do

You need to muster information on what makes your special place special, and translate it into terms that will resonate with people who spend their lives working with the Register. Then offer your arguments in favor of your place's eligibility in whatever way you can—at meetings, in writing, whatever. If the significance of your place isn't obvious, be prepared for arguments. Try to find similar places that have been included in the Register or found eligible for it; your SHPO should be able to help, as may the National Register staff in the National Park Service. See how the significance of such places has been presented, and model your own presentation accordingly.

Let's briefly consider a few hypothetical examples, featuring places that aren't obviously important buildings, structures, or archaeological sites.

Grandpa's homestead

If your special place is something like your (or someone else's) ancestral farm, ranch, cottage, or other kind of home place, you'll probably want to argue for eligibility under criterion (a). If it includes standing structures that seem interesting architecturally or in terms of engineering, landscape architecture, or something of the kind—if it's also grandpa's mill, for example—you may want criterion (c) as well. If Grandpa was a big guy in the community, you can throw in criterion (b). Try to couch the significance of the place in a way that relates to as large a number of people as possible—some social entity larger than just your family. If the place has been changed a good deal over the years, think about ways to show that these changes haven't seriously detracted from its historical or cultural significance—or even that they've *enhanced* its significance, by linking it to historical developments in the area. Yes, the fine stone barn that was an important feature of the place isn't there any more, but it was knocked down to build breastworks during the Civil War. Yes, there was a sort of ugly wing tacked onto the henhouse in 1948, but the reason it was built was to house returning Japanese-American internees.

A natural place

If your place is a natural one that shows little or no human modification—a spring, a grove of trees, a valley, a stretch of seacoast—you need to find some kind of historical or cultural connection to make it eligible. Look for particular events or important people who've been associated with the place. Walden Pond is a natural place, after all, and its association with Henry David Thoreau and his writings is sufficient to make it eligible for the Register under criteria (a) and (b). Or consider more general cultural associations. Does an Indian tribe or other indigenous group regard it as their place of origin or as having spiritual power of some kind? Or does the nearby town, or tribe, or civic group hold special events there? Or does everybody in the area fish there, or gather boysenberries? These kinds of things may constitute significant enough patterns of events to qualify it under criterion (a) as what's called a "traditional cultural property."[3]

A neighborhood

If you're trying to use Section 106 to save your neighborhood from being demolished to make way for a highway or courthouse or a federally subsidized fast-food fabrication facility (if such things don't exist now, they probably will before long), you're using it for very much what the authors of the National Historic Preservation Act (NHPA) intended, but sadly it's something that isn't much encouraged by the way the Register is usually viewed today. There's probably a good argument to be made for the significance of your neighborhood on cultural grounds. Maybe it's been the Ethiopian-American neighborhood since the 1960s; perhaps it's where immigrants from Appalachia came to find work after World War II; perhaps it's got the best collection of salsa clubs in town. These characteristics—very expressive of the kind of urban diversity that the authors of NHPA wrote and spoke about as justifications for the law—are often rather difficult for people in SHPO offices and at the National

Register itself to deal with. Register specialists tend to be a lot more comfortable with more straightforward historic or architectural districts—the main street around which the town developed, a neighborhood full of handsome Queen Anne houses or Moderne apartment blocks. If your neighborhood has these kinds of characteristics, you should certainly play them up. But if it doesn't—if it's significant to you simply because it's where you and your ancestors have lived for a few generations, or because it's the kinkiest 17 blocks in town—you still may be successful in arguing for Register eligibility, though you may get some blank looks along the way. You're going to need to research the role that the kinds of people who live in the neighborhood have had in building the community, or the roles they've played in the larger history of the state or region. You're going to have to emphasize the importance of those roles and discuss how they're reflected in the social life of the neighborhood, perhaps in the architecture of its buildings or the organization of its outdoor spaces, in its businesses, public facilities, or gathering places. You're going to need to base your argument on criterion (a)—that is, show that the people whose neighborhood it is have been a significant influence on the history and culture of the community, that this influence constitutes an important "broad pattern" of local, state, national, or other history. Based on this sort of argument, you may be able to show that your neighborhood is an eligible traditional cultural property, even if its architecture isn't any great shakes and no monumental historical events have taken place there.

A big place

What if your special place is really big? A whole river valley, a mountain, a group of farms or a desert? Whole landscapes can be eligible for the Register; they're usually found eligible as districts, typically under criterion (a) with a bit of (c) thrown in because their individual components—this grove of trees, that old barn—may not be particularly distinctive, but collectively they make up something special. But big places tend to make SHPO and Register staff nervous; they worry about the political implications of seeming to bestow official historical status on an area where many people's oxen may be standing around to be gored. You need to be sensitive to this nervousness, and do what you can to assuage it. Obviously the more local interests you can line up in favor of eligibility, the more you'll assure the reviewing authorities that they won't get in trouble for saying it's eligible. On the other hand, eligibility isn't a

Evaluation – Is Your Place Eligible?

popularity contest; the mere fact that 98% of the citizenry thinks the place is significant and ought to be saved doesn't make it significant in the eyes of the SHPO or the keeper. To demonstrate significance you have to do the same thing with a landscape that you do with any other kind of property: show that it somehow relates to broad patterns of history, or that it's associated with important people, or that it exhibits the attributes of some type of architecture, landscape architecture, agriculture, or just culture. Among the difficulties you'll probably encounter are that people will fret about what the boundaries of the landscape ought to be, and about what elements ought to be understood as contributing to it. If you're trying to fight off a project in one part of the valley, you'll almost certainly find the proponent—and maybe the SHPO—very resistant to considering the significance of something much larger than the area the project can be easily seen to affect. When this happens, it's important to remember, and remind the other consulting parties, that for Section 106 purposes you don't necessarily need to establish boundaries or precisely define the size, shape, and character of the property. The consulting parties can agree that, yes, this 100-mile-long valley is eligible for the Register for its association with Amish culture and agriculture, and whatever its precise shape and size and boundaries may be, taking out Jacob Vondervleet's barn will diminish its character. Having agreed on this, they can get on to discussing what, if anything, can be done to reduce, minimize, or mitigate that adverse effect.

A place worth studying

Maybe your place is the site of an ancient village, or a 19th-century fort, and you think it's worth keeping around so that people in the future can study it, learn from it, interpret it for the public. It probably won't be hard for you to make a case for its eligibility under criterion (d), for the information it contains—though depending on who you need to have buy your argument, you may have to go to some lengths to demonstrate what kinds of information the place probably contains, and what might be learned from it. But if you really want to keep the place, rather than just dig it up and write a learned paper about it, you'd better try to get it recognized as eligible under another criterion too. This is because, as we'll discuss in a moment, there's a widespread (though unsubstantiated) belief that if a place is eligible only under criterion (d), it's OK to document and destroy it. It shouldn't be too hard for you to make a criterion (a) case for a place that's eligible under criterion (d). After all, if it contains information important in history or prehistory, it's almost got to be associated with some important pattern of past events. There are people in the Register game who have trouble with this kind of thing, however—who feel that if it's eligible under criterion (d), that's the end of it, and it's a waste of time, or even something of an affront, to discuss its historical associations. This may be fine if everybody understands that a (d) place is just as worthy of preservation as an (a), (b), or (c) place, but often that's *not* a shared understanding, and the proponent may find it in his interests to view (d) places as expendable.

Common Proponent Dodges

Argument about eligibility can be fierce and can go on for a long time. Many of the archaeologists and architectural historians who do Section 106 work are frustrated academics who like nothing better than to fight over esoteric fine points of history, architecture, or prehistory. The smart project proponent will get past eligibility questions as quickly as possible—accept eligibility and move along.

But many proponents aren't smart enough to concede eligibility and move on, and neither are a lot of agency people. Very often one or the other, or both, will decide to fight over eligibility, to argue that your special place, maybe every place affected by the project, isn't eligible. When someone opts for this approach, there are several predictable arguments they're likely to advance. Let's look at each one and at what you can do to counter it.

Squeeze it out of the APE

The proponent may argue that the place really isn't in the area of potential effects—though someone must have thought it was or it wouldn't have been identified. Maybe the APE has changed as a result of a project redesign. Maybe the folks doing the survey didn't really understand the project plans, so they overestimated the project's effects. Or maybe we can flag and avoid the place, so it's not going to be affected, so it's no longer an issue.

Sometimes this argument is legitimate. If your special place is on the north side of the lake and they've redesigned the project to put the road on the south side, then maybe it's *not* in the APE any longer, and there's no use considering it further. You've won.

Evaluation – Is Your Place Eligible?

But don't pop the champaign cork until you've examined the fine print. Make sure they're really committed to the south shore route; it's down in black and white, in budget and planning documents, resolutions by planning bodies, and so on. And make sure it's not still going to have noxious visual or auditory effects, or stimulate development of the lakeshore. If it will arguably have such effects on your special place (or other possibly eligible places), then you want the process to go forward, which includes resolving questions of eligibility.

It doesn't have integrity

From the proponent's point of view, the next best thing to gerrymandering the APE is to assign no "integrity" to your place—without which, of course, it can't possibly be eligible.

The idea of integrity is a simple one. If the place has been so messed up that it doesn't retain whatever made it significant in the first place, it's no longer significant. But how messed up is sufficiently messed up? How do we decide? The National Register has given us a certain amount of guidance on this subject, which unfortunately can be used mischievously.

The most common "integrity test" that people apply based on Register guidance is the "recognition test." If somebody who lived in the time the place gained significance came back and looked at it today, would they recognize it? If they would, it's retained integrity; if they wouldn't, it hasn't.

So, would Grandpa recognize his homestead if he came back today? Well, let's say he wouldn't be likely to: the house burned down, the barn fell over in a windstorm, there's tract housing all around. But it's still Grandpa's homestead, and the whole extended family (thousands of people by now) and all the other people who recognize Grandpa's role in the community still honor the place, come there every year for the annual Grandpa Gabfest, give speeches, enjoy picnics. Does it really matter whether Grandpa would recognize the place? Isn't it a place that allows people to connect with history, and isn't that what the National Historic Preservation Act is about?

Or what if you're trying to save the burial place of your ancestors, the last of whom was interred 200 years ago, and there's a spacecraft fabrication plant on the site now. Would the ancestors recognize it? Hardly. Does that make it insignificant? Of course not.

Examples like this can be proliferated, but the bottom line is that one way or another, the project proponent may find a consultant, or an agency "expert," or somebody in the SHPO's office, who'll say, "Well, I'm terribly sorry, but the Register has spoken on this subject, and that's just the way it is." It may be important for you to get in the first shot: argue for the integrity of the place, and if it looks like somebody may play the "recognition" card, play it first: "It may be that Grandpa wouldn't recognize the place if he came back, but considering the nature of the property's significance, this does not indicate a lack of integrity, for the following reasons...."

Insufficient data

"Well," the proponent or agency may say, "you make an interesting point about the significance of your grandpa's homestead, but we simply don't have enough data to allow our experts to reach a conclusion."

The appropriate response to this is to ask politely what further information they need, and whether there's any way you can help them get it. Keep reminding them—politely, of course—that it's the agency's responsibility to comply with Section 106 and hence to decide whether affected properties are eligible. If the agency doesn't have the information it needs to do its job, then the agency is responsible for getting it. It's not the responsibility of the public to supply the needed data without cost to the agency—though of course, you'll be as helpful as you can, within reasonable fiscal limits.

You may also want to discuss whether the information they think they need is really needed. If you're arguing that your grandpa's homestead is eligible under criterion (a) because it's associated with early settlement of the valley, nobody may need to know exactly how many buildings were on the site, how many times the house and barn were renovated over the years, and whether the orchard grew pears or apples, but the proponent may very well assume that he has to pay for all that data. Why? Because he has a proposal from his consulting firm saying that in order to determine eligibility to the SHPO's satisfaction, they'll have to do a study to make all these things clear—at a cost of $200,000 and six months. The SHPO, or some standards issued by the SHPO, may really suggest that all this information must be gathered; after all, it's no skin off the SHPO's nose. On the other hand, the SHPO may have no idea what standards are being imposed in her name. If the parties can sit down and discuss what really needs to be known in order to evaluate the place, a reasonable conclusion may be reached that's satisfactory to everyone. They may actually need *no* further data, or just a little bit, of a particular type.

Evaluation — Is Your Place Eligible?

You may, of course, be tempted to insist that they fund every imaginable study, in hopes of bleeding the proponent dry, but the likelihood of actually accomplishing this is negligible, and it's wiser, I think, to demand only the information that's really needed.

But the bottom line is that the proponent can't legitimately say, "We don't know if Grandpa's homestead is eligible, so we'll assume it's not." That's not taking effects into account as Section 106 requires; it's quite the opposite. They *can* say, "We don't know if Grandpa's homestead is eligible, so we'll assume it *is*"—because that means the place will get further consideration as the review process proceeds.

"Why don't you nominate it?"

The proponent, or the review agency, or some other helpful party, may suggest that if you think the place is so important, you ought to nominate it to the Register yourself. If all else fails, you may indeed have to do this, but it's not your responsibility under the law, and it's a costly, time-consuming thing to do. Assuming this responsibility means taking onto your shoulders the burden of proving the place eligible, and that's not where the burden is supposed to be. Under the Section 106 regulations the agency is supposed to figure out whether the place is eligible, in consultation with the other parties. It's their burden to do this, not yours.

So the response to the suggestion to nominate is to remind the agency that determining eligibility is its responsibility, and to urge them to get on with it—offering, of course, your fullest assistance in doing so and advancing your arguments with as much supporting evidence as you can reasonably provide. If your special place is special because you regard it as sacred—some kind of highly sensitive spiritual location—there may not be much information you can bring forward without risk of spiritual harm to someone, but if it's grandpa's homestead you may have lots of documents and garrulous relatives to bring to the table.

If the agency is really recalcitrant—just won't accept its responsibility— or if you don't trust them to do the job honestly, then you may actually have to nominate the place. This may be particularly tempting when you think the agency or proponent and the SHPO are in cahoots—cutting a deal under which they'll find your place not eligible. Unfortunately, though, you nominate the property through the SHPO, so if she's inclined against your point of view, she's as likely to oppose your nomination as to cut a deal with the agency. However, nomination is a very public process, which may enable you to put more pressure on the SHPO than you could in the more private determination process. As usual, it all depends.

"It's only locally significant"

The word "National" in "National Register" can confuse people, or be used to confuse. "No doubt grandpa's homestead is important to *you*, Mrs. Smith, but it's not significant to the whole *nation*, so it's not eligible for the *National* Register."

The Register in fact is explicitly designed to include places of national, state, and local significance. The *Register* is national, but the places on it don't have to be. All Grandpa needs to have been is an important guy locally to make his homestead eligible. First homesteader in the valley, notable African-American banker, whatever. Or he may have been part of a pattern of local history—sodbusting, mining, stealing land from the Indians—that is itself important, and his homestead is important for its association with that pattern. Or the way he chinked his log cabin may reflect a characteristic kind of local vernacular architecture.

You are probably going to have to figure out some way that Grandpa or his homestead are important to some group of people more inclusive than your family, unless you're a Rockefeller or a Kennedy. But if Grandpa played some kind of role in local history, or exemplified some type or trend or pattern in history, or was part of some special social or ethnic group, his homestead is probably eligible, and being "nationally significant" has nothing to do with it.

It's not unique

"It's a nice old homestead site," the proponent's experts may say, "but, gee, there must be 700 such sites scattered over the state. There's nothing particularly special about this particular one, so it can't be eligible."

Of course, if there *is* something special about Grandpa's homestead, you ought to bring this information forward. But your first response to the "nothing special" argument should be to ask, "So what?"

There's nothing in the Register criteria that demands uniqueness; in fact, the word *unique* is never used. On the other hand, being *representative* of something—in other words, *not* unique—is an argument for eligibility under criterion (c). There's a limit to how far you can push this argument; every fence post is representative of the structural type "fence post," but that doesn't make every fence post eligible for the Register. On the other hand, though, it's certainly not the case that only the biggest, best, most unique fence post in the state—or more realistically, the best shotgun house or prehistoric shell midden—can be eligible for the Register. Uniqueness is simply not a National Register criterion.

It doesn't fit into a theme/context

In an effort to bring order to the process of nominating things to the National Register, the National Park Service sometimes encourages SHPOs to develop "interpretive themes" or "historic contexts." An example might be "The development of hydropower in Northwestern Texas." The idea is that once such a "theme" or "context" is in place, people will nominate places that somehow exemplify it, and it will be possible to decide whether this place or that exemplifies it better than some other place. It's kind of a variant on the notion of uniqueness—that somehow the Register ought to include only the best and brightest of each kind of thing. There might be some merit in this notion as it's applied to nominations; it surely makes sense to invest an SHPO's limited nomination dollars in the really neat stuff before investing it in stuff that's less interesting. But it makes no sense at all in a Section 106 context; the fact that my Grandpa's homestead isn't—by somebody's calculation—as good an example of 19th-century homesteads as your grandpa's doesn't mean that mine shouldn't be considered in planning the highway that will bulldoze it out of existence. But "themes" and "contexts" can provide very sophisticated-sounding dodges. "The SHPO has established 75 historic contexts for our state, and your grandpa's homestead doesn't relate to any of them, so sorry, Charlie, it can't be eligible."

There is, of course, nothing in the Register criteria that requires relevance to anybody's contexts or themes. And however much the Register may encourage people to develop such things, it is certainly not Register policy that places have to fit into such artificial constructions in order to be eligible. Don't let anybody tell you that your special place isn't part of American history because it doesn't fit into someone else's idea of how that history ought to be organized.

Your history's wrong

Suppose you've asserted that Grandpa's homestead is where the Treaty of Big Gray Oak was signed with local Indian tribes. That's been the tradition in your family, and it's inscribed in the family Bible in Grandpa's own hand. But the proponent's consultant, or the SHPO, or some other ostensible authority, says nope, it's just not true; the Treaty of Big Gray Oak was really signed on the other side of the river, where the Wal-mart parking lot is today.

They may be right, of course, and that will take a lot of wind out of your sails if you've based your arguments for the significance of Grandpa's homestead on its association with the treaty signing. But they may also be wrong, or there may be open questions about where the event actually took place. They may be citing a second- or third-hand account by somebody with fancy credentials—a professional historian or high government official, say—but your Grandpa-inscribed Bible is a first-hand account and may really be more authoritative. You shouldn't be afraid to argue the point.

There may also be an argument to be made about documentary records versus customary knowledge. If everybody in the area has believed, all these years, that the treaty was signed on Grandpa's homestead, and if remembering the treaty has been a big part of the annual Salute to Grandpa festival, does it really matter that perhaps the treaty was "really" signed somewhere else? Has Grandpa's homestead achieved some degree of historical, cultural, social significance from its long-assumed association with the treaty, regardless of its "real" association?

There's no question, though, that you're on shaky ground if it looks like you have your historical "facts" wrong. You should guard against this by being careful about what you claim for your place. Remember that you don't necessarily have to have some clear-cut association with a specific historic event in order to make an argument for eligibility. Association with events that are part of the broad pattern of history is sufficient. You can document with certainty that Grandpa lived at the homestead and that he played a certain role in the history of the community. You can document your family's ongoing association with the place. You can document community beliefs about the place, and the importance of those beliefs, without necessarily claiming that they reflect absolute historical facts. You need, in short, to be careful about how you characterize your special place's significance; avoid giving the proponent and his experts a way to nail you for shoddy research. They have everything to gain from doing so and nothing to lose.

Eligible under criterion (d)

The agency may find your place eligible, but only under National Register criterion (d): possession of some kind of significant information about the past.

Evaluation — Is Your Place Eligible?

Many archaeologists have a hard time thinking of any criterion *other* than (d), so finding your place eligible under only that criterion may not reflect malice—just narrow-mindedness. Unfortunately, the assignment to (d) status can have implications. Lots of agencies, lots of SHPOs, lots of consultants, even lots of Indian tribes think that if a property is eligible only under criterion (d) it's OK to destroy it, provided you first record the information in it. In terms of actual preservation, criterion (d) properties are second-class citizens; a (d) classification is probably a prelude to a proposal to document and destroy. This is particularly likely if the project you're dealing with is a transportation project. Under Federal Highway Administration rules implementing Section 4(f) of the Department of Transportation Act, a property that's significant for reasons other than research can't be used by a transportation project unless there's no feasible and prudent alternative to doing so, but a property that's significant only for research can be blown away without detailed consideration of alternatives, provided the information it contains is recovered. And among transportation agencies, criterion (d) is generally taken to indicate significance only for research.

There's nothing in either the National Register or Section 106 regulations that makes criterion (d) properties expendable, and it's really a stupid idea. It's kind of like saying that it's OK to set fire to a handwritten medieval manuscript after scanning it to your hard drive. Worse, actually, because a scanner and good character recognition software might actually capture all the content of a manuscript, but we can never be sure we've recovered all the information in an archaeological site or any other kind of property. In fact, it's a sure bet that however carefully we've studied the place, we've missed things. But be that as it may, it's become quite customary in some areas and some agencies to write off, document, and destroy criterion (d) properties.

So be on the lookout for criterion (d) assignments, and be sure to argue from the very beginning that your place is important for reasons other than its information content. Look at the other three criteria and figure out how to relate your place to one or more of them.

Playing the Criteria Considerations

As if the Register criteria weren't complicated enough, and sufficiently subject to abuse, the Register has confused things further by creating seven "criteria considerations." These describe circumstances under which a place that might otherwise seem to be eligible *isn't*. To add to the fun, most of the "considerations" allow for exceptions—situations where a place that might seem to be eligible but *isn't* because it falls under a consideration actually *is* eligible. I am not making this up.

There's a lot of mischief to be made with the criteria considerations, both by people who want to use them as loopholes, allowing them to blow away significant historic places, and by people who just want to gum up the 106 process. If you're going to play the Register game, unfortunately you need to know how to play the considerations.

Like the criteria themselves, the criteria considerations are set out in the Register's regulations, 36 CFR 60.4. Here they are:

> *Criteria considerations. Ordinarily cemeteries, birthplaces, or graves of historical figures, properties owned by religious institutions or used for religious purposes, structures that have been moved from their original locations, reconstructed historic buildings, properties primarily commemorative in nature, and properties that have achieved significance within the past 50 years shall not be considered eligible for the National Register. However, such properties will qualify if they are integral parts of districts that do meet the criteria or if they fall within the following categories: (a) A religious property deriving primary significance from architectural or artistic distinction or historical importance; or (b) A building or structure removed from its original location but which is significant primarily for architectural value, or which is the surviving structure most importantly associated with a historic person or event; or (c) A birthplace or grave of a historical figure of outstanding importance if there is no appropriate site or building directly associated with his productive life. (d) A cemetery which derives its primary significance from graves of persons of transcendent importance, from age, from distinctive design features, or from association with historic events; or (e) A reconstructed building when accurately executed in a suitable environment and presented in a dignified manner as part of a restoration master plan, and when no other building or structure with the same association has survived; or (f) A property primarily commemorative in intent if design, age, tradition, or symbolic value has invested it with its own exceptional significance; or (g) A property achieving significance within the past 50 years if it is of exceptional importance.*

EVALUATION – IS YOUR PLACE ELIGIBLE?

Let's imagine some situations in which your special place might run afoul of the considerations.

Religious property

Suppose you're the members of a religious sect that has a place on the slopes of a mountain where you go to meditate. You've done this for many years—maybe since your sect was established in America back in the early 20th century. Let's suppose further that the place is wholly natural; there are no buildings or other constructions that might be argued to have architectural or artistic distinction.

The "religious property" exclusion will make it a bit more difficult to demonstrate its eligibility for the Register than might otherwise be the case, but it doesn't make it impossible. You'll need to focus on the historic significance of the place. Think about the role that the place has played in the history and culture of your sect, and the role that your sect has played in the larger community. You've been in existence for almost a hundred years and been an important force in the community, encouraging peace, harmony with nature, and nonviolence. Figure out how to document that. And figure out how to document the role your place has played in maintaining the character of your group. Maybe it's the place where for generations sect members have sat in quiet contemplation before meeting to take a decision on some important issue. Maybe it's the place where your founder had a vision that told her to establish a religious community. Document that historic significance—the significance of your place to your group, and of your group to the larger community.

Whatever you do, do *not* say your place is eligible because it's a sacred place, or because it has spiritual power. That would suggest that you're trying to get the keeper to bless your particular religious beliefs, and that's a very serious no-no under the "establishment clause" of the First Amendment to the U.S. Constitution. The establishment clause says that Congress will make no law "respecting the establishment of religion," which means in essence that the government will do nothing that might tend to establish an official U.S. sect. For the keeper to decide that your place is eligible for the Register because it's sacred would very much smack of establishment. You can certainly say that it's the group's *belief* that the founder had a vision here, and describe the vision, but don't put the keeper or SHPO in the position of appearing to say that this vision was real. Historical and cultural significance aren't determined by whether the vision was real, but rather by the historical and cultural effects of belief in the vision.

Of course, if your place is a church, synagogue, mosque, temple, or other built facility, don't neglect to offer arguments based on its architectural character, the distinction of the architect, the quality of its artwork, and so on, along with its historic and cultural values.

Moved structure

Imagine two examples. First, suppose your place is an old railroad engine used in logging that's parked on a siding in the woods where it's been rusting away for years. You shouldn't have a problem with the "moved structure" consideration for two reasons. One, it's an inherently movable property; it would be ridiculous for the Register to accept the eligibility only of trains that didn't work—that is, that didn't move. Two, it's been sitting out there in the woods for quite a number of years; arguably it's in its "original" location. If it's recently been dragged out of the woods and put in the local railroad museum, you may have more trouble with eligibility, but the "inherent movability" argument still ought to hold. If it's been moved to the railroad museum, taken apart, and partly restored, you may have integrity issues, but that depends on how careful the restoration has been.

Or, imagine that your place is an old bordello that used to be located in town but was dragged out into the sticks when the town fathers and mothers began to complain about its influence on the community's upstanding youth. You're going to want to document when the thing was moved, because if it was over 50 years ago it will be easier to verify its significance than if it was more recent. And you're going to want to document historic events and associations that have been tied to the place *in its current location*. Who has frequented it? What political deals have been cut there, what gunfights have occurred? If its architecture is distinctive, as a bordello's architecture may very well be, you'll want to document that, and if it's the only or best old bordello left in the area, that will help too.

Birthplace or grave

Maybe rather than being Grandpa's homestead, your special place is where Grandpa was buried, up on Windy Hill. It's going to be hard to convince people that this grave isn't ineligible because of the birthplace/grave exclusion, unless Grandpa was a super-important guy and there's no place else left that's associated with him.

If the grave is close to the homestead, see if you can wrap them together; define the homestead to include the grave. Now you're not asking that the grave, as grave, be regarded as eligible; the homestead is the focus. Or look for other things that have happened on or around the grave, preferably associated with Grandpa but not necessarily. Was Windy Hill the place he used to like to sit and think, plan his activities? Was it where he and Grandma got married? Was it where he announced to the assembled multitude that he was running for governor? Or—quite apart from Grandpa—was it where the Treaty of Windy Hill was negotiated, or the site of the Windy Hill Massacre or the Windy Hill gold discovery? If nothing ever happened there but that Grandpa got planted, and it's not associated with anything else that's significant, you're probably out of luck.

Cemetery

Cemeteries are actually determined eligible for the National Register quite commonly, based on their historic, cultural, and archaeological significance, but if your place is a cemetery and somebody's trying to destroy it, they'll probably trot out the "cemetery consideration" as a basis for saying it's not eligible. To counter this, you'll need to stress the cemetery's association with events or, more likely, patterns of events significant in the history or culture of the area. Is it an ancient (or not so ancient) tribal (or other) cemetery where your ancestors have started their journey to the spirit world? Talk about the importance of this passage, and of the ancestors, in your cultural traditions. Is it the little rural cemetery where all your family members have been buried since they came into the area back in 1815? Talk about that history, and how it's reflected in the graves and "grave furniture"—headstones, footstones, and so on. Are you an archaeologist concerned about the research value of an ancient or historic cemetery? Talk about that. Is it a really ancient cemetery—maybe thousands of years old? Emphasize that. And, of course, if it has particularly handsome, complicated, old, or otherwise impressive grave furniture, don't fail to describe it.

There are a couple of ironies in the way cemeteries get evaluated under the "cemetery consideration." For one thing, ancient unmarked cemeteries tend to be more easily found eligible than marked ones with gravestones and crosses and such. This is probably because ancient cemeteries are often viewed (at least by those doing the evaluations) as archaeological sites, or parts of such sites, which contain information useful in understanding the otherwise obscure distant past. And they're often the cemeteries of Indian tribes or other minority groups, and both SHPOs and the keeper tend to be pretty sensitive to minority concerns. Another irony is that "graves of persons of transcendent importance" can help make a cemetery eligible, even though such graves by themselves are the subjects of their own criteria consideration and are usually *not* eligible. However inconsistent it may seem, if Grandpa's buried in the cemetery and was really important in the history of the area, you should emphasize that, and be sure to use the word *transcendent*.

Reconstructed building

It's rare, but occasionally the property at issue in a Section 106 case is really a modern building that's a reconstruction of something old. Say, for instance, that the town hall burned down in the 1980s and a faithful replica was built. The criteria consideration indicates that the town hall probably isn't eligible. But if you can show that it really *is* a faithful replica, very accurately replicating the original, and as the town hall it's a very important part of the town, you may have a chance of getting it determined eligible. If you can argue for it as part of a district that contains a lot of original buildings, that will improve your chances—say, for instance, that it's on one end of a line of elegant public buildings, or the town's main street with well-preserved commercial buildings on either side.

Besides the exceptions to the criteria consideration actually listed in the regulations, it's commonly accepted that when buildings or structures were meant to be rather transient, a more or less new building or structure built in accordance with traditional principles can be eligible for the Register. In the Pacific Islands, for example, most buildings were traditionally built of thatch, matting, and logs, materials that don't last long in the tropical environment. Relatively recent examples of such buildings have been determined eligible and sometimes placed on the Register, as have relatively modern sailing canoes built according to traditional principles. These buildings and structures remain eligible as they're maintained through time too, even though at some point all the original stuff they were made of gets replaced. Oddly, it's been difficult to prevail upon SHPOs and the keeper to apply the same principle on the mainland, with respect to tribal dance lodges and other structures. It certainly won't hurt to try, though, if this is the kind of place you're concerned about.

Commemorative property

The consideration doesn't quite mean simply that statues aren't eligible, but that they're not eligible for their association with the thing they commemorate. So a monument in the town square honoring those killed in the Civil War isn't eligible for its association with the Civil War, but it can be eligible because its designer was a famous architect or engineer, or because it was the target of major civil rights marches in the 1960s. If you want a commemorative property to be determined eligible, you're going to have to find something significant about the property itself, apart from the event it commemorates. Of course, if the commemorative property is at the place where the event that it commemorates happened, then the fact that there's something commemorative there doesn't disqualify the site, and the commemorative property may be found to contribute to the character of the eligible place. When people try to portray the site of the Trinity nuclear test explosion, where the world was introduced to nuclear power, there's not much for them to portray other than the commemorative monument that now stands there.

Place that got significant less than 50 years ago

If your place became significant within the last 50 years, you'll have to make the case that it's "exceptionally significant," and the project proponent, of course, will argue that it's not. Most of the exceptionally significant places that Register people talk about when they give examples of eligible recent properties are places that are clearly important to everyone: NASA's Mission Control in Houston; an ICBM silo; the site of the World Trade Center in New York, and the spot where United Flight 93 went into the ground on 9/11/01. But "exceptional significance" doesn't mean only "significance to the whole nation or world." A place can be exceptionally significant at the state, local, regional, or tribal level. Suppose, for example, that there's a terrible flood somewhere next year and a little town is threatened with imminent destruction. At the last possible moment a heroic bulldozer driver arrives at the levee that's about to break and plugs the hole, saving the town. The town might very well, if it wishes, argue that the site of this event is exceptionally significant in its history, and regard the place as eligible for the National Register or even nominate it. There's also a move afoot among Register aficionados, as I'm writing this in 2007, to do away with the "50-year rule," so this criteria consideration may not be a problem in the future.

Back to the Process

So in a nutshell, you need to get your place recognized by the consulting parties—or at least by the responsible federal agency and the SHPO—as eligible for the Register by virtue of:

1. having integrity;

2. meeting at least one of the Register criteria; and

3. not falling under one of the criteria considerations, or falling under one but qualifying as an exception.

There's tremendous room for argument about these things. As a result, it's in the process of eligibility determination that the whole Section 106 process most commonly gets bogged down. This can be good for you if your purpose is to delay the process and the project, but that said, I don't want to encourage you to string things out, offer tricky arguments, bring up new properties or new aspects of significance at the last minute. That probably won't work very well for you, because eventually it will tempt people to try to boot you out of the consultation process, or at least pay less attention to what you have to say.

The question of documentation

There's often a question about how much and what kinds of documentation the agency—or somebody—needs to develop as the basis for deciding to regard a property as eligible or ineligible, or to formally determine it one way or the other. Actually, questions about documentation may not be raised as often as they ought to be; often everybody just accepts that there are hard and fast "documentation requirements." Some SHPOs want everything written up as though it were being formally nominated to the National Register, and the Register staff itself certainly prefers this kind of documentation. Other SHPOs want particular state forms filled out, or reports to be developed following particular format standards. Some agencies have their own preferences or requirements, as do tribes, professional organizations, and even consulting firms.

Evaluation – Is Your Place Eligible?

In fact, the regulations—the Section 106 regulations, that is—prescribe no documentation standards whatever. Whatever the consulting parties agree is sufficient, is sufficient. This can be very handy when, for instance, it's necessary to keep information about a place confidential because you're afraid someone will break in, damage it, disturb someone's privacy, or otherwise make mischief. The bottom line, though, is that there needs to be enough documentation somewhere to show that the agency based whatever decision it makes on a reasonable body of data, a showing of facts. How much that is depends on how controversial matters are, whether anybody's likely to challenge the agency's decision, whether the case is likely to wind up in court.

It may be beneficial to you to promote a lot of documentation, because it takes time, slows things down, and creates more opportunities for disagreement and delay. I suggest being careful about how far you push this, however. As usual, there is a point beyond which you seem to be obstructing things for the sake of obstructing them, and that's going to hurt your credibility.

If the case goes to the keeper for a formal determination, there are some pretty specific documentation requirements, which the keeper will impose on the agency.

What happens if they say no?

So at the end of the day, when you've made your arguments and everything's been discussed, what if the agency and SHPO agree that your place isn't eligible—doesn't have integrity, doesn't meet any of the criteria, or is knocked out by one or more of the criteria considerations? There's at least one course of action you can take to get the decision reversed, and sometimes two, or more. I usually recommend taking all actions available to you.

First, if the agency has an administrative appeals process that applies to your situation, you may be able to invoke that. Maybe it's the forest supervisor in the Forest Service who's decided your place isn't eligible; you may be able to appeal that decision in a quite formal way to the regional forester. Many agencies have appeals processes, but they may or may not be open to you. The Corps of Engineers, for instance, has a process by which someone can appeal a decision *not* to issue them a permit, but no process for appealing decisions *to* issue one. But check with the agency; it can't hurt and it might give you an avenue worth pursuing.

Then there's the general process that's provided for in the Section 106 regulations. If the agency and SHPO don't agree about eligibility/ineligibility, *or if the Advisory Council or the Keeper of the Register request*, the agency has to go to the keeper for a determination. So what you need to do is persuade the keeper and/or the Advisory Council to so request.

By all means try the keeper, but I can't hold out much hope that the keeper will be much help. The National Register has its own (quite obsolete) regulations—36 CFR 63—that say something totally different about eligibility determinations, and besides that complication, the Register's people tend to be frightened of political shadows and unwilling to tell another agency to do anything. The Advisory Council can be pretty chicken at times too, but they tend to be more responsive than the keeper. So write them, email them, phone them; explain the situation and ask them to ask the agency to seek a keeper's determination.

If neither the council nor the keeper will help you, and you can't get action out of the agency, then you've no choice but either to give up or to move into the political or legal arena. Go up the agency's chain of command, write or call your congressperson, call in whatever chips you can, and try to force somebody to do something. Or get a lawyer and take them to court—but be warned; if they've dotted all the procedural *i*'s and crossed all the procedural *t*'s it's a very rare court that will tell them to rethink their decision.

If the council and/or the keeper so request, the agency must ask the keeper for a determination, sending the keeper a whole lot of information on which to make a decision. This takes time, during which the project should be dead in the water. You can file information and arguments with the keeper too; so can anyone else. Partly as a result of all this inflow of data, the keeper can take a fair amount of time to reach a decision, though the Register staff tries to be pretty prompt. It's not uncommon, though, for them to decide they need more data, and the agency has to supply it. This, of course, can take more time.

Eventually, though, the keeper will make a determination. Sometimes it can be a pretty strange one; the keeper's people are good at splitting esoteric pseudoacademic hairs. But the bottom line is, he or she will say—more or less—that your place either is or is not eligible for the Register. This determination is final; there's no appeal. So if the answer is no, you're dead. If it's yes—well, see below.

The difficulty of getting a keeper's determination, and the uncertainty surrounding what it will be, highlight the importance of influencing the agency and SHPO before *they* make a decision. Encourage them in any way you can, without making a total pest of yourself, to find your place eligible. If you know somebody the SHPO or agency official will listen to—a superior in the chain of command, a member of the legislature—it may be a good idea to ask that person to lend encouragement too, though this can be a double-edged sword. Agency decision-makers usually are pretty jealous of their prerogatives and hate to be pressured, and their superiors may be reluctant to pull power plays too. Too much political pressure can cause people to dig their heels in.

If the agency you're struggling with is the National Park Service (NPS)—perhaps they're trying to evict you from your historic cabin on an inholding in a national park—you're unlikely to get much help from the National Register. The Register is embedded within NPS, after all, and its people are painfully aware of who butters their bread. If you have to take an NPS case to the keeper, you'll need to make special efforts to apply your own political pressure. Try to enlist your congressman, activate any contacts you have within the administration of the Interior Department—within which NPS is lodged. Try to give the keeper some pragmatic, fear-based reason for making an honest and honorable determination despite what others in NPS may want.

I should mention again that another thing you can do if the agency and SHPO say your place isn't eligible is nominate it to the National Register. But nominations go through the SHPO, and if the SHPO has already decided your place doesn't cut the mustard, nomination is likely to be a futile enterprise—unless you know somebody on the State Review Board, which rules on nominations, or somebody else who can jerk the SHPO's chain. Even if you can get a hearing from the board, however, there's nothing that requires the agency to hold up its project waiting to hear whether your place gets accepted. So by the time you've filled out all the cumbersome paperwork, filed it with the state, and prevailed upon the State Review Board to review it, your special place may be history. Sometimes nomination is a good last resort, but usually it's not.

What if they say yes?

If the agency and SHPO agree that your place *is* eligible, or if the keeper says it is, then the agency, SHPO, and other consulting parties go on to determine what the project's effects on it will be. That piece of the process is the subject of the next chapter.

Don't Forget NEPA

As we move on with the 106 process, remember that the agency should be coordinating its Section 106 compliance with its responsibilities under the National Environmental Policy Act (NEPA). Historic properties are obviously one part of the "human environment" that NEPA says the government cares about, so theoretically, the agency should be figuring out what's eligible for the National Register while it's doing its NEPA studies, and folding the results together.

You probably want the agency to do a higher level of NEPA analysis than the agency wants to—an environmental assessment (EA) if the agency thinks the project is categorically excluded (CX); an environmental impact statement (EIS) if the agency wants to do an EA. If you've gotten your place determined eligible, you need to ask the agency how it's going to work this information into its NEPA analysis, and whether in its view the presence of your Register-eligible property means they have to do whatever level of analysis you want them to do. The NEPA regulations (at 40 CFR 1508.27(b)) list some factors the agency is supposed to consider in deciding whether to do an EIS. Included in the list are the presence of historic properties and public controversy on environmental grounds. You now have the former; you may have to generate the latter. But bear in mind: the agency doesn't *have* to do an EIS if there's a historic property and environmental controversy—unless its own regulations require it, as some do. Historic properties and environmental controversy are just some of the things the agency has to consider. So to get a high level of NEPA review, look for other kinds of impacts: endangered species, potential release of toxic materials, mucking up a wetland, whatever you can find. And involve yourself in the NEPA process, though as we discussed in Chapter Five, it's nowhere near as consultative or participatory a process as Section 106 review is—or at least is supposed to be.

How the BPS Did It

At Broad Run Bridge, eligibility wasn't really a question. Both the village of Buckland and the Buckland Mills Battlefield are already included in the National Register, nominated to it years ago. There were and are questions concerning their boundaries and characteristics, however. Several buildings that would have contributed to the significance of the village—a "district" in National Register terms—were demolished by the Virginia Department of Transportation (VDOT) in the 1950s when it acquired right-of-way through the village for the widened highway it claims to have no plans to build. The archaeological remains of these buildings and their 18th-century sur-

Evaluation – Is Your Place Eligible?

roundings might still exist within the right-of-way and be destroyed by the bridge project. Oddly, documentation about these buildings seemed to have gone missing. Arguments erupted between VDOT and the Buckland Preservation Society (BPS) about how close the buildings had stood to the bridge project's area of potential effects (APE) and whether their remains might still exist in the ground. VDOT sponsored additional archaeological testing, which BPS members watched like hawks and closely critiqued. The issue has never really been resolved, but as we'll see, the project plans have been changed in ways that greatly reduce its importance.

> CONTACT: For the National Register regulations, see
> http://www.cr.nps.gov/nr/regulations.htm
>
> CONTACT: For pertinent Section 106 regulation, go to
> http://www.achp.gov/regs-rev04.pdf and see 36 CFR 800.4(c)

– Notes –

1. Of course, "Big People" is not a term the National Register uses; the National Register is much too solemn.
2. With thanks to architectural historian/attorney Lea Keatinge, who as far as I know invented this memory aid.
3. If you're dealing with this kind of property, let me shill my textbook *Places That Count: Traditional Cultural Properties in Cultural Resource Management* (AltaMira Press, 2004).

CHAPTER EIGHT

Will There Be an Adverse Effect on Your Place?

SO YOUR PLACE IS ELIGIBLE

Now what? Well, your place isn't saved by being regarded as eligible, determined eligible, or even formally included in the National Register. It's not guaranteed a place in the sun. It simply becomes something the agency has to "take into account" in planning its action, in consultation with the SHPO and other consulting parties—including you, assuming you've been successful in getting to the table.

People are sometimes put off by learning that finding a place eligible for the Register, or even formally listing it, doesn't make it inviolable. In fact, though, the law couldn't work that way or one of two things would happen. The first possibility is that very, very few places would be determined eligible. Why? Because determining something eligible would then mean forgoing the opportunity to do anything other than preserving the place, and because we often need projects such as highways and housing and military maneuvers—projects that tend not to preserve the things in their path—it would mean we'd have to be very selective about what got viewed as historic. As a result, for the majority of special places there would *no* consideration under Section 106. The other alternative would be for all progress to stop, because we would have elevated historic preservation above all other public interests. As long as we like to have highways, sewers, energy, and national defense, the latter isn't going to happen, and I for one don't think that the former would be a good idea. I'd rather see my special places get *some* consideration, and have a fighting chance to talk everybody into saving them, than to have only a few super-special places—the Mount Vernons and Mesa Verdes of the country—given consideration in agency planning.

What Being Eligible Means

What happens if the consulting parties agree to regard your place as eligible, or the agency and SHPO or THPO determine it eligible, or the keeper determines it eligible, or it's formally listed on the Register, is that the agency consults further about what effect, if any, the project is going to have on your place. Effects under Section 106 come in two basic flavors: *adverse* and *not adverse*.

The kind of effect a project is going to have, as defined in the regulations, can be very, very important. In fact, it's at this stage in the review that you may have your best shot at stopping the project in its tracks. Either because of internal agency procedures or unreasoning fear, some agencies and quite a few applicants for assistance and licenses will do almost anything to avoid being seen as having adverse effects—even to the point of abandoning a project or selecting an alternative that they otherwise don't much like. So if you can box them in to a point at which they can't avoid determining that their project will have adverse effects, you just may find that the danger to your special place will suddenly go away.

But don't count on it. If the agency or proponents are experienced in Section 106 review, or well advised, or just intent on having their way, they can press the other consulting parties to accept the adverse effects with some kind of mitigation—as we'll see in the next chapter. They can also find various more or less sneaky ways to avoid an "adverse effect" determination.

"No Historic Properties Affected"

One possible angle is for the agency to make a determination that there are "no historic properties affected." This usually happens only when the agency decides, and the SHPO agrees, that nothing in the area of potential effects (APE) is eligible for the Register. But the same determination can be made if the agency finds that there *is* something there—like your special place—that's eligible but somehow the project won't affect it.

If your place is going to be affected, you obviously don't want the agency making a "no historic properties affected" determination. Such a determination brings the Section 106 process to a close, and the project can go forward.

So, if you find the agency making a determination of "no historic properties affected" and you don't agree with it, you want to scream bloody murder.

The SHPO or THPO has 30 days to concur or not concur in the determination, so you want to be in front of his or her desk—or at least in his or her email queue—just as quickly as possible. The Advisory Council isn't formally involved in this kind of determination unless the agency and SHPO can't reach a meeting of the minds, and probably doesn't know a thing about the case, but you can and should complain to them too. And make whatever other noise you can to let the agency and SHPO know that the determination is wrong. Call your congressperson, go to the media, whatever.

Most times, though, if your place—and/or any other properties in the area of potential effects—are regarded as or determined eligible, or if they're on the Register, of course—then the agency is going to recognize that there will be an effect. The question now becomes: is the effect adverse?

Determining Adverse/No Adverse Effect

Well, of course the effect is adverse, you may say; otherwise why would you be going through all this grief? True, true, but some adverse effects are a lot more obvious than others. To make sure they all get attended to, the regulations have a process that the agency is supposed to follow to determine objectively whether a given effect is adverse. If it is, there's more consultation to do; if it's not, then the process comes to a speedy end—usually.

As usual, it's the responsible federal agency that's supposed to call the shots—in this case, to determine whether the effect is adverse. As usual, the agency is supposed to do it in consultation at least with the SHPO and hopefully with other stakeholders like you. As usual, agencies often try to play fast and loose with the process, in this case determining that effects aren't adverse when they really are. And as usual, agencies often try to consult with as few people as possible.

As soon as your place is determined eligible for the Register, it's a good idea to start asking the agency about its schedule for effect determinations, and how you can participate. Put them on notice that you know what the process is and you want to be a part of it. Of course, communicate with the SHPO or THPO too, and with any other consulting parties.

Generally, the agency will write a letter to the SHPO, and copy other consulting parties, setting forth its determination of effect. Or determinations, since they may be dealing with multiple properties, though recommended practice is to make a single determination covering the whole project. Sometimes the agency will file a contractor's survey report with descriptions of all the properties found and simultaneously determine eligibility and effect: "We think property X isn't eligible for the following reasons. We think property Y is eligible, but it won't be adversely affected for the following reasons. We think property Z is eligible and will be adversely affected because we're going to bulldoze it off the cliff." Sometimes the agency will just send all the information to the SHPO and expect the SHPO to decide—often about both eligibility and effect. They're not supposed to do this; it's not the SHPO's job to make the determinations. But some SHPOs think it's fine, or at least tolerable, and some agencies do it this way because it relieves them of the need to think.

Anyway, documents go to the SHPO and *someone* applies what are referred to as the "criteria of adverse effect," laid out in the regulations at 36 CFR 800.5(a). If the "criteria" are met, there's an adverse effect; if they're not met, there's not.

The criterion of adverse effect

There really aren't any "criteria" of adverse effect—there's just one criterion, and a string of examples; it's the latter that most people mean when they refer to the "criteria." The core criterion says that an adverse effect is one that may alter characteristics that make the property eligible for the National Register, in a way that alters the place's integrity.

What does this mean? Suppose we're dealing with a big old commercial building—maybe a department store. Suppose that the building has a grand lobby with distinctive elevator doors. Suppose we want to modernize the building by ripping out the elevators and putting in escalators. To decide whether this is an adverse effect we have to decide whether the character of the lobby, and particularly the elevators, contribute to the building's eligibility. If they do, then taking them out will reduce the building's integrity. If they don't, then it won't.

Applying this criterion can be tricky, because it requires you to know a lot about the property—what makes it eligible, what will compromise its integrity. This complicates things when, for example, an Indian tribe wants to keep information about a place secret, or when we just want to regard a property as eligible without much documentation and move on with the process.

This is one reason that most people turn to the examples, which follow the criterion in the regulations. But one not-uncommon proponent dodge is to insist that whatever will be changed about the place does not contribute to its eligibility, or that what will be done to it won't reduce the property's integrity. This is something to watch for, so you can raise counter-arguments.

For example, suppose everyone has agreed to treat Grandpa's homestead as eligible for the Register under National Register criterion (b) (important people) because of its association with Grandpa. Suppose the proposal is to put up a power line that will cut through the fine view of the river from the front porch, or the view of the house from the road.

"Well," says the proponent (a power company that needs a permit from the Corps of Engineers to fill a wetland along the way), "our power line doesn't affect the homestead's relationship with Grandpa, so it's not going to diminish the integrity of anything that makes the place eligible."

How to respond? Well, you can talk about how much Grandpa used to like the view from the porch, or about how the community's attachment to the homestead, and hence to Grandpa's memory, will be diminished if there's an ugly power line in front of it. But this is pretty abstract stuff, and we can split hairs over it indefinitely. This is one reason that most people prefer to talk about the examples, which are more concrete.

The Criterion and Examples of Adverse Effect

(1) Criteria of adverse effect. An adverse effect is found when an undertaking may alter, directly or indirectly, any of the characteristics of a historic property that qualify the property for inclusion in the National Register in a manner that would diminish the integrity of the property's location, design, setting, materials, workmanship, feeling, or association. Consideration shall be given to all qualifying characteristics of a historic property, including those that may have been identified subsequent to the original evaluation of the property's eligibility for the National Register. Adverse effects may include reasonably foreseeable effects caused by the undertaking that may occur later in time, be farther removed in distance, or be cumulative.

(2) Examples of adverse effects. Adverse effects on historic properties include, but are not limited to:

(i) Physical destruction of or damage to all or part of the property;

(ii) Alteration of a property, including restoration, rehabilitation, repair, maintenance, stabilization, hazardous material remediation, and provision of handicapped access, that is not consistent with the Secretary's standards for the treatment of historic properties (36 CFR part 68) and applicable guidelines;

Will There Be An Adverse Effect on Your Place?

(iii) Removal of the property from its historic location;

(iv) Change of the character of the property's use or of physical features within the property's setting that contribute to its historic significance;

(v) Introduction of visual, atmospheric, or audible elements that diminish the integrity of the property's significant historic features;

(vi) Neglect of a property which causes its deterioration, except where such neglect and deterioration are recognized qualities of a property of religious and cultural significance to an Indian tribe or Native Hawaiian organization; and

(vii) Transfer, lease, or sale of property out of Federal ownership or control without adequate and legally enforceable restrictions or conditions to ensure long-term preservation of the property's historic significance.

The examples ("criteria") of adverse effect

The regulations give us seven examples of adverse effect. Let's look at each one and imagine how it might apply to a place, and what issues can arise in deciding whether it applies.

- **Physical destruction**. If the project will destroy the property—knock down the building, bulldoze the archaeological site or sacred boulder—that's an adverse effect. Pretty straightforward. The destruction doesn't have to be complete; destroying half, or a third of a place is good—or bad —enough. But people do start to quibble when it's a tenth or a fiftieth or just the bare little smidgin. When that happens it's useful to bring up one of the other examples, and one of them is almost always relevant.

Under a previous version of the regulations it was possible to destroy certain kinds of archaeological site and say it wasn't an adverse effect, provided a program of data recovery would be carried out, ostensibly removing all the important information from the site. Thanks to Indian tribes and Native Hawaiians who really didn't like the homes and graves of their ancestors treated like second-class sites, that provision was removed in 2000, but occasionally you'll find an agency, proponent, or consultant who thinks it still applies. It doesn't. Destroying a place is an adverse effect, period.

- **Alteration, except according to standards**. The *Secretary of the Interior's Standards for the Treatment of Historic Properties* prescribe what the Department of the Interior says are the right ways to maintain ("preserve"), restore, rehabilitate, or even replicate a historic building or structure. If a project will alter a place in a way that's consistent with the standards, then it's not an adverse effect; if it's *not* consistent with the standards, then it *is* adverse. Although the regulations make them sound like they're relevant to all kinds of property, the standards are really useful only with buildings, structures, and some kinds of landscape that are substantially constructed—parks, parkways, gardens, maybe some farmsteads. The standards are routinely used in federally funded rehabilitation of historic housing—through low-income housing programs funded by the Department of Housing and Urban Development, for example, and in private projects whose proponents are seeking federal income tax credits for rehabilitating historic buildings.

Damage or destruction; alteration of setting: Katamin, the center of the world in the beliefs of the Karuk tribe in California, has suffered heavy erosion since dams were constructed upstream, altering the flow of the Klamath River. Photo by the author.

Will There Be An Adverse Effect on Your Place?

Any other kind of alteration, in theory, is an adverse effect, which can get a bit tricky if it's an alteration that everybody thinks is a really good idea—for instance, stabilizing an eroding streambank in a historic landscape or through an archaeological site. There's a tendency on the part of many SHPOs to wink at this kind of alteration, which unfortunately causes some proponents to expect the same treatment for projects that *aren't* so benign. "Well, yes, we're going to take the north wing off the building, but it's the wing that was added in 1927 and nobody likes it much, so...."

- **Removal.** If the property's going to be picked up and moved, that's an adverse effect. Exceptions are usually made for things that are inherently movable—ships, for example, and airplanes. But if the project requires that Grandpa's barn be moved 20 feet to make way for the highway, or that the Old Truss Bridge be trundled off to the local park to be part of a walking path, that's an adverse effect.

In case you're getting worried about good-seeming actions like putting old bridges in parks being adverse effects, remember that there's nothing necessarily *wrong* with having adverse effects. There's nothing in the law or regulations that says historic places can't be adversely affected. Having an adverse effect simply means—as we'll see—that there has to be more consultation about it, usually leading to a memorandum of agreement (MOA) about what will be done. If everybody thinks that moving the bridge to the park is a dandy idea, the MOA should be quick to negotiate. But if the bridge is your special place, and you don't think moving it is a good idea at all, the regulations give you a basis for insisting that the project get more attention, that alternatives to moving the bridge be considered.

- **Change in use.** The example actually lumps "use" and "setting," but they're quite different things that can be affected in different ways, so I think it's clearer to talk about them separately. What do the regulations mean by "change of the character of the property's use?" They couldn't mean *any* change in use, or it would be an adverse effect every time an agency using a historic office building reassigned cubicles. In practice, change in use is something that most people don't deal with much under Section 106, unless the change will somehow also cause physical changes, visual effects, or something of the kind. But I have a hunch that change in use really is a serious issue in more cases than most Section 106 practitioners realize. It may be that it's the issue in your case.

Suppose, for example, that your special place is a canyon in a national forest where your family has run cattle under a special use permit or lease for the last three generations. Suppose that the Forest Service wants to terminate your lease or not renew your permit. Suppose that you've managed to get the Forest Service and SHPO to treat the canyon as eligible for the Register because of its association with the history of cattle ranching in the area. You can certainly argue that if you're kicked out, that will be a change of use that has an adverse effect, and in a just universe you ought to prevail. You're a lot less likely to prevail if the canyon's been determined eligible because of its archaeological sites, or because of the value it has to the nearby Indian tribe that regards it as a spiritual place, or because of the old railroad that runs through it. Yes, it's still a change in use, but the Forest Service is going to say that the use is irrelevant to the significance of the canyon, so the core Register criterion isn't met: the use change doesn't alter anything that qualifies the canyon for the National Register. This, of course, highlights the need to make sure—back when eligibility is being determined—not only that your special place gets determined eligible, but that it gets determined eligible for the right reasons. If you treasure running cattle in the canyon, don't be satisfied with a determination that it's eligible for its archaeological sites.

- **Change in setting.** In full, the regulations talk about changing "physical features within the property's setting that contribute to its historic significance." What does that mean? Something physical is going to be changed—not the smell of the place or its noises (but see the next example). That something is "within the property's setting"—the landscape or streetscape or riverscape within which it is set. And that setting contributes somehow to its historic significance. As usual, it's easier to imagine examples than to come up with an abstract definition. Imagine a water-powered sawmill, or the ruins of such a mill, in a forest, on the bank of a stream. The stream and the forest—or at least the stream within sight of the mill and the trees right around it—make up the mill's setting. Both contribute to its significance, because the stream made the mill work and the mill worked on the trees. The eight-lane elevated expressway that hangs overhead, spanning the valley, is part of the setting but does not contribute to the mill's significance. Simple.

But, of course, subject to a great deal of hair-splitting debate. Is the roughly paved road up to the mill part of its contributing setting, even though it replaced an earlier gravel road that was somewhat to the east? What about the stone wall along the county highway, over which passersby view the mill; it's in the foreground of almost every picture that's been taken of the place in the last 40 years and it's very picturesque, but—well, it was built in the 1960s by a youth employment program. But it replaced an earlier wall that was taken out by the highway, and. . . . If the state highway department wants to use federal funds to widen the road and take out the wall, they're almost certainly going to argue that the wall is not part of the contributing setting. If you want to keep the mill just as it is, you're going to argue the opposite.

What can really be maddening is that preservation professionals can argue about this sort of thing even if it makes no difference whatever. You and the highway department may be prepared to agree that the wall can come down provided it's reconstructed 20 feet closer to the mill, outside the highway right-of-way. But the highway department's cultural resource consultant and the SHPO's wall guy may still insist on duking it out over whether the wall is part of the contributing setting. And a stickler for the step-by-step structure of the Section 106 process may insist that you can't even talk about moving the wall until all questions about eligibility and effect have been resolved. The regulations aren't really that inflexible, but some practitioners are.

- **Introduction of elements.** This example deals with the setting too, but it's a bit easier to work with. The full text is: "Introduction of visual, atmospheric or audible elements that diminish the integrity of the property's significant historic features." A visual element might be a power line crossing between the mill and the road, or a wireless telecommunications tower across the stream. Atmospheric elements might be the smell of the new hog farm upwind, or the particulates from the power plant over the hill. Audible elements, of course, are things you can hear: aircraft overflights, traffic noise, screaming kids on a playground.

The trick to applying this "criterion of adverse effect" is linking the element to a significant feature of the property, and showing that the element will diminish the feature's integrity. You may say that one important feature of the mill is that it still looks like a mill, or that it's a picturesque ruin, that another is the water running down the millrace, whose gurgling and bubbling people like to listen to. A tower across the stream, or a playground whose denizens make so much noise that you can't hear the millrace, clearly diminishes the integrity of those features. The proponent of the wireless tower may say no,

Introduction of inconsistent elements: modern aircraft and ancient traditions often don't mix well, nor do power lines and culturally important landscapes. Illustrations by Greg White.

the fact that people like to look at the mill and take pictures of it has nothing to do with its historic character: if nobody ever takes another picture of it, it will still be historic. The proponent of the playground may say something similar: the mill was for cutting lumber, and that made a helluva lot of noise. Nobody could hear the millrace gurgling then; what makes it part of the mill's historic character now? Honorable people can disagree about this kind of thing, and dishonorable people can have a field day.

- **Neglect**. Suppose some wealthy family deeds a big chunk of desirable land to the National Park Service on the edge of Purplestone National Park. Suppose there's a handsome old mansion on the property. Suppose the mansion is eligible for the National Register. If NPS doesn't maintain the mansion, and it begins to deteriorate or even—heaven forbid!—falls down, that's an adverse effect. But, of course, the purpose of Purplestone National Park is to preserve the area's spectacular natural resources and to accommodate visitors who want to wait around in hopes that Old Faithless Geyser will spout. There's no money in the budget for maintaining a mansion that has nothing to do with the park's purpose, and Congress isn't likely to appropriate any. If you have fond memories of playing as a child in the mansion and want to see it kept standing, or if you really like its Remingtonian Rustic architecture (I made that up), you can probably get attention by using this example of adverse effects. By not maintaining the building NPS is certainly having an adverse effect on it. It's probably violating another section or two of the National Historic Preservation Act too—Section 110(a)(1), which charges agencies with "preserving" historic properties under their care (though "preserve" is defined very broadly in NHPA)—and maybe Section 111, which says that if an agency controls but doesn't need a historic property, it should reach out to others who may take care of it under leases or management agreements. Having NPS dead to rights isn't necessarily going to get Congress to allocate any maintenance money, but under Section 106 NPS is at least going to have to think and talk about ways to keep the building standing, and something may come of this that will make you happy.

There's an odd-reading exception to the "neglect" example. If letting the thing deteriorate is a "recognized quality of religious and cultural significance to an Indian tribe or Native Hawaiian organization," then it's OK to let it deteriorate. This is to take care of situations where a tribal burial site on federal land is eroding into a river, and the tribe views this as a natural part of the ancestors' passage to the spirit world. The agency that manages the land in this case can let the site erode, let the ancestors pass, and not call it an adverse effect. Or if a totem pole is rotting away in the woods, and that's what the tribe thinks should happen to it, then the agency that controls the woods doesn't have to run out and slather it with preservative.

Telecommunications towers are some of the most common intrusive elements today.

- **Transfer.** If a federal agency is going to get rid of a historic property through sale, lease, exchange, or other form of transfer, that's an adverse effect because the property will no longer have the protection of Section 106 and other federal laws. Here too there's an exception: if the agency imposes restrictions to protect the property, and these are enforceable, then they can say the transfer is not an adverse effect. Exactly what constitutes a good, enforceable restriction varies from state to state, because it depends on the state's real estate laws. Ironically but not surprisingly, transfer of non-federal property *into* federal ownership is not held to be an adverse effect. If you've been taking good care of a historic place that the feds now want to acquire, however, you can certainly argue under the core criterion that this transfer—given the vagaries of federal land management and budgeting—may diminish its integrity. The adversity of transfer between federal agencies similarly depends on how the core criterion applies. If the Forest Service wants to transfer land to the Army, which will run tanks all over it, that will clearly diminish the integrity of any historic properties that exist there, and ought to be called an adverse effect. But the Army may piously say that it, after all, has all the same responsibilities under Section 106 as does the Forest Service, so the transfer is a wash. This, of course, is nonsense; the Forest Service is sadly lacking in heavy weaponry.

The determination process

The responsible federal agency is supposed to apply the "criteria" of adverse effect, in consultation with the SHPO or THPO and other consulting parties. Typically the agency will send a letter to the SHPO with copies to everyone else saying, "We've determined, subject to your concurrence, that this undertaking will have no adverse effect on properties A, B, and C for the following reasons, and adverse effect on property D for the following reason." The SHPO and the other parties have 30 days to respond. Though the regulations don't say so, in practical terms the SHPO can respond by saying that she needs more time, or more data, or both, thus extending the review period. Others can say that too, of course, but the SHPO has more clout. In most cases the SHPO concurs in the determination—perhaps after a bit of negotiation—and others either don't know what's happening or don't take advantage of their opportunity to object, so the determination goes into effect. If the SHPO doesn't concur, or other consulting parties object (in writing), and the disagreement can't be worked out, the agency refers the matter to the Advisory Council. The council gives the agency an advisory opinion, and the agency makes the final call.

A determination of "no adverse effect" can be conditioned. That is, the agency may offer, or the SHPO or other parties may propose, that changes be made in the project plans, or controls imposed, to make sure that adverse effects won't occur. For example, say the project is a pipeline and the property is an archaeological site. A condition that might be imposed is that the pipeline will be routed in such a way as to avoid hitting the site. Conditions

Will There Be An Adverse Effect on Your Place?

are documented and agreed to by the parties, or at least by the agency and SHPO, and then must be carried out or the determination is no good.

I say "must be carried out," but of course, whether a condition *really* is carried out depends to some extent on the goodwill of the agency and to a considerable extent on the quality of the condition. A condition that just says "the pipeline will be routed to avoid the site" probably isn't going to work; there's too much room for misinterpretation, and there's no guarantee that the people who can make it work—the planners, engineers, and construction people—even know about it. A condition that says "the pipeline will be routed along Alternative Corridor 'C' as shown on the construction plans entitled X and dated Y," with further provision for a sign-off by the project supervisor, briefings for key personnel, and reporting at key intervals to the SHPO or others, will probably work fine.

Most agencies, and most non-agency project proponents, like to get through the 106 process with determinations of no adverse effect—if they can't get away with even less. It's relatively quick, not too formal, pretty flexible, and it doesn't carry the psychological and public-relations onus of having adverse effects. It's actually often in an agency's best interests to accept adverse effect and move forward—because there can be a lot of argument over a "no adverse effect" determination—but even agencies that know that it's really OK to have adverse effects often prefer not to be seen as having them. Part of the reason for this, in some agencies, is that an adverse effect under Section 106 triggers a higher level of internal review of the project, and perhaps a higher level of review under the National Environmental Policy Act (NEPA). It's also usually quicker to move a determination of no adverse effect through the system than it is to negotiate a memorandum of agreement about how to deal with adverse effects. And it can be a less public process, carried out largely between the agency and the SHPO. So there's a very strong likelihood that the proponent of the project that threatens your special place will try to get concurrence in a determination of no adverse effect. You need to look out for this, to be vigilant.

How? By reminding the responsible agency and the proponent and the SHPO that you're in the game, and that you expect to participate in the determination of effect. Write letters, send emails, make phone calls, ask for meetings. It may be a good idea to point out in writing why you think there will be an adverse effect, referring to the relevant chapter and verse of the regulations:

> *As we are sure you will agree, the tower you propose to build across the river from Grandpa's homestead will introduce a visual element that is*

not consistent with the characteristics that make the homestead eligible for the National Register, and hence is an adverse effect under 36 CFR 800.5(a)(2)(v).

This, of course, is when the proponent may come back and say "visual effects aren't relevant to what makes Grandpa's homestead significant," and you're going to have to argue about that. They may also say, "The other side of the river isn't part of Grandpa's homestead, so obviously we're not going to have any adverse effect." There's a school of thought that holds that things must happen on or in the property itself in order to be adverse effects—or effects at all. It's a ridiculous argument, of course; it's like saying that you can't affect me without physically hitting, shooting, or spitting on me. In fact, you can have all kinds of effects on me by shouting curses at me, by exposing yourself to me or my children, or by running off with my wife; in the same way, a project can have visual, auditory, and atmospheric effects on a property without doing a physical thing within the property's boundaries. People who want to split hairs about it can argue that a visual effect really doesn't act on a property itself, because the place can't see; the effect is on people using the property, or living there, or looking at it. Which is true enough, but effects on people are really what we're concerned about in any case, isn't it? Congress didn't enact the National Historic Preservation Act to protect the tender feelings of old buildings and archaeological sites. Congress was concerned about the perceptions of taxpayers and voters—that is, people. And that's what we have to be concerned about in Section 106 review too. How is this project going to affect this property from the standpoint of those who value it?

If this seems pretty esoteric, I couldn't agree more. But it's the kind of argument we do get into, and you might as well be prepared for it.

The fact that agencies and proponents dislike acknowledging adverse effects gives the SHPO and other consulting parties—including you—something of an advantage, *if* those parties are interested in making a deal. The proponent may be willing to do quite a bit, make quite a few changes in the project, in order to get everyone to agree that there will be no adverse effect. If changes to the project are sufficient to protect your place to the extent you think it needs to be protected, this may be the time when you can get those changes made.

What kinds of changes? Relocating the road to the other side of the hill, doing the logging with helicopters rather than clear-cutting, incorporating the building into the project plans and rehabilitating it. There are lots of possibilities.

But in order for a determination of no adverse effect to be appropriate, such changes have to really make the adverse effect go away. Moving the road to the other side of the hill probably does this; moving it 3 feet may not, because the place may still be disturbed or there may be visual or auditory effects. Putting the road through the place after doing archaeological data recovery or architectural recordation certainly doesn't. Moving the property certainly doesn't, unless perhaps the property is a train or an airplane or some other kind of inherently movable thing to which its current location is irrelevant. And so on. Keep the examples of adverse effect in mind, and make sure the agency and the proponent do so too.

THE UPSHOT

The result of the adverse effect determination process is one of three things: agreement that there's no adverse effect, agreement that there *will* be adverse effect, or unresolved disagreement. The agreement or disagreement is between the agency and the SHPO or THPO; though other consulting parties can object and trigger Advisory Council review, in the vast majority of cases it's the agency and SHPO who decide on the adversity of effect.

If it looks like the SHPO is going to concur and you don't think she should, as a consulting party you can and should object strongly in writing, to the agency, to the SHPO, and to the Advisory Council. If you can get the SHPO or council to object, and the agency doesn't want to negotiate, then it has to refer the case to the council. What the council does in such a case is up to the council. The regulations say that it will render an "advisory opinion" about whether the criteria of adverse effect have been correctly applied, but it may try to broker a deal—which may or may not be good from your standpoint

If the council renders that advisory opinion, the agency can do what it pleases with it. It can, for instance, find that there's no adverse effect even though the council has said there is. But—here's an interesting twist—the council's opinion doesn't have to go only to the guy in the field, the local agency person responsible for the project. If the council chooses to, it can send the opinion to the head of the agency—the Secretary of Defense, Secretary of Housing and Urban Development, Administrator of the Federal Highway Administration, whoever the big boss is. Federal officials low in an agency food chain hate it when another federal agency tells the big boss that they've screwed up, so the council's advice does carry some weight, and it's something that agencies try to avoid. So if you can persuade the council of the worthiness of your cause, you may have a fighting chance, even if the SHPO has ducked the issue.

Bringing in the Advisory Council isn't a cure-all, of course. They may agree with the agency; they may come under political pressure to do so, or they may just be inclined to; they may honestly disagree with you. Often the council recommends a compromise that makes nobody happy. And no matter what the council says, the agency has the final say. But generally speaking, if you have a good case, it's worth trying to bring the council into the discussion. They provide a new, presumably authoritative voice, they're probably less vulnerable to political pressure than the SHPO, and they have that nice authority to get the head of the agency involved.

One way or another there's a decision—yes it's an adverse effect, or no it's not. If the answer is no adverse effect, the agency documents that fact, together with the SHPO's concurrence, and that's it; the Section 106 process is done and the agency can move forward with the project, provided it carries out whatever conditions have been attached to the determination.

If the answer is that there *will* be adverse effect, then the next and usually last act in the Section 106 melodrama opens. That, we'll discuss in the next chapter.

Don't Forget NEPA

Let's end with another reminder that the responsible agency should be doing its National Environmental Policy Act (NEPA) review concurrently with its Section 106 review, and the effects that it's now found (willingly or not) on historic properties should be factored into that review. It's rare for impacts on historic properties all by themselves to kick a NEPA analysis up from an exercise in categorical exclusion (CX) screening to an environmental assessment (EA), or from an EA to an environmental impact statement (EIS), but it can happen—particularly if there are other kinds of impacts too, and the agency is teetering on the edge of opting for the higher level of review. So you ought to keep track of how the results of 106 review are being factored into the NEPA analysis, and if it looks like you've a chance of success, push for that analysis to be ratcheted up a notch. The more analysis is done, the more likely it is that something will emerge that's a project killer, or that the proponent will just get tired and look for another option.

The agency may tell you—or you may know—that they've already finished their NEPA work. A lot of agencies don't coordinate NEPA and Section 106 very well, and it's not uncommon to see NEPA analysis and documentation done first—often as a sort of pro-forma exercise—while Section 106 review is put off until later in the planning process. In such cases the NEPA document (typically an EA, or some sort of annotated checklist for a screened CX) will include a "cultural resource" section made up of boilerplate about local history and prehistory, followed by an assurance that surveys will be completed and Section 106 review will be done, implicitly making all significant impacts go away.

If the agency in your case has "finished" its NEPA work that way and now has found (or been forced to acknowledge) adverse effects on historic properties, its NEPA analysis may be vulnerable to attack. After all, the NEPA analysis is supposed to reveal significant impacts; if impacts on historic properties are significant and the NEPA document didn't report that, there's a problem. How *big* a problem it is depends on how serious the adverse effects are on historic properties, what other effects have been identified, how the agency's NEPA procedures work, how much trouble the agency's already in over the project, and other project-specific variables. And don't forget that NEPA analysis of impacts on "cultural resources" shouldn't be limited to dealing with historic properties. If there are going to be effects on, say, the social composition of a neighborhood, this needs to be addressed, even if the neighborhood isn't eligible for the National Register.

How the BPS Did It

Acting for the Federal Highway Administration (FHWA), the Virginia Department of Transportation (VDOT) determined that the Broad Run Bridge reconstruction would have no adverse effect on Buckland or the battlefield—because their archaeological testing program hadn't revealed anything within the area to be physically disturbed by construction. The Buckland Preservation Society (BPS) objected, pointing out that the transportation agencies had considered only direct physical impact. The really important effects, BPS said, were indirect and cumulative. The widened bridge would facilitate widening the highway through Buckland, which would bring more development.

VDOT and FHWA said, nonsense; they were just fixing up an old bridge, and this had nothing to do with widening the highway, which in turn had nothing to do with stimulating development. BPS said *that's* nonsense; if you don't want to widen the highway, why are you widening the bridge? The agencies said they needed the extra width to accommodate construction work; BPS said this was laughable, but they weren't laughing. Instead they were lobbying the State Historic Preservation Officer (SHPO), Advisory Council on Historic Preservation (ACHP), and National Trust for Historic Preservation to join in their objection.

The big issue, BPS said, was cumulative effect, defined in the NEPA regulations as the effect of the present project when added to those of all other past, present, and reasonably foreseeable future projects. BPS spelled it out. VDOT's past acquisition of right-of-way through the village and its demolition of buildings were past effects, as was the sprawl that had been facilitated by highway improvements north of Broad Run. That ongoing sprawl was an obvious pattern of present adverse effects. The most obvious future effect was implementation of the "Northern Virginia 2020 Plan"—widening the highway to six lanes. The bridge project contributed to this pattern of cumulative effect, because it didn't do anything to stifle sprawl but instead facilitated it. The National Trust expressed its agreement with BPS, and the Battlefield Preservation Program said it was concerned about cumulative effects on the battlefield. The SHPO objected to VDOT's determination, but mainly on the grounds of uncertainty about archaeological impacts.

The ACHP really held the trump card here; under the regulations its recommendations about adverse effects, though only advisory, have to be given great weight. After a good deal of argument, the ACHP said—at the end of a vituperative conference call among the parties—that it thought the BPS's concern about cumulative effects was a legitimate basis—along with the questions about archaeological impacts—for objecting to the determination of no adverse effect. This strengthened the SHPO's hand, leaving FHWA with no reasonable option but to assume adverse effect and continue consultation.

CONTACT: For pertinent Section 106 regulation go to http://www.achp.gov/regs-rev04.pdf and see 36 CFR 800.4(d) and 36 CFR 800.5

Chapter Nine

"Resolving" Adverse Effects on Your Place

STRATEGICS

If there's going to be an adverse effect (see Chapter Eight) on a place or places included in or eligible for the National Register (see Chapter Seven), then the Section 106 regulations call for more consultation about "resolving" that effect. Generally this means finding a way for the project to go forward with as little damage to historic places as the parties seeking their protection can negotiate.

If what you're trying to do is stop a project cold, or deflect its proponent into an alternative that completely protects your special place, this kind of "resolution" may mean that you've lost the battle. If you were going to make the project go away, you probably would have succeeded by this time: the proponent would have run from the presence of eligible properties, or adverse effects, in combination with whatever other problems (endangered species, wetlands, economic effects) the project may have run into. If the proponents have come this far, they're probably pretty determined to have their way, or something close to it.

But there are still opportunities to turn things around—either getting the project killed or forcing major changes to it. And if your intent hasn't been to kill the project altogether, if what you want are adjustments to reduce or mitigate impacts on your place, then your chances may still be pretty good.

Recall that Section 106 does not prohibit having adverse effects; *it is perfectly legal to destroy a historic property.* But federal agencies, and hence applicants for federal assistance or licenses, have to consider alternatives to avoid, reduce, minimize, or mitigate the adverse effect. And they do that in consultation with the SHPO or THPO and other consulting parties, like—we hope—you. It's in this context that you have a chance of saving your special place, even now on what may be the brink of its destruction.

Importantly, "considering" ways to resolve adverse effect under Section 106 doesn't—or at least shouldn't, if the regulations are followed—mean just thinking nicely about them before going ahead with one's project. The regulations are designed to get all concerned talking about what to do, with the goal of reaching a formal, written agreement. The agreement, if reached, is set forth in a *memorandum of agreement,* or MOA.

I wish I could say that consultation about resolving adverse effect is an orderly, fair process that always, or at least often, produces "win-win" solutions. I can't. The whole Section 106 process can be pretty rough-and-tumble, and when we get to consultation about resolving adverse effects, it can be truly nasty. This is when (if not before, of course) political power is wielded, veiled and not-so-veiled threats are put on the table, and slimy deals are cut, particularly between powerful proponents and frightened SHPOs. What you can do to counter this depends on what sort of power *you* bring to the table, or can wield elsewhere.

What the Agency Has To Do

The regulations require an agency to do specific things when there will be an adverse effect. You should try to make sure that the agency does them, because they can all help you.

Notify the Advisory Council

The agency has to notify the Advisory Council of the adverse effect, providing a prescribed body of documentation. This is an important requirement because it gives the council the opportunity to enter the consultation. I do not want to make the council seem like the white knight; sometimes the council can be tough, but often it's wimpy, and quite often just obscure. But even at its wimpiest or most opaque, it's another player—usually a new player since it probably hasn't been involved before now—and a new player can stir things up. It's also a player from Washington, DC, with all the aura of power that (however unjustifiably) creates. More importantly, it's a player who, as we'll see, can go far over the heads of the people you're dealing with in the responsible agency.

Then there's that body of documentation the agency has to send in. The agency puts the documentation together, but you and other consulting parties can suggest content and send in your own contributions. It's an opportunity to get the record of the case on the table, and demonstrate where the holes are, what's been done and not done, and how. It may be the first time the agency has been confronted with all the ramifications of the case, the first time they've seen it whole. That can be enlightening. And the submittal typically goes to the council from somebody in authority—the district engineer, the state director. And he or she is likely to have the general counsel or solicitor—the agency's legal people—look at it. They may have never heard of the case, and their prime interest is in keeping the agency out of court. It's possible—not necessarily very likely, but possible—for someone in this review chain to ask embarrassing questions: Why are we taking this position? Isn't that inconsistent with what we did in that other case last year or last month? Don't we need to do an environmental impact statement? Isn't this just like the case that our sister agency got busted for big time a couple of years ago?

So you ought to remind the agency—and the other consulting parties—that the agency needs to notify the council, and you can offer to help pull together the documentation. If the agency says, "Nah, that's all right, we can do it ourselves," be a bit more insistent, and ask at least to look at it before it goes in. The agency isn't required to let you look, but if it doesn't, that's something you can complain about to the council, while supplying the information or arguments you think the agency left out.

Consider bringing in more consulting parties

The regulations remind the parties that the agency and SHPO can agree to invite more parties to take part in the consultation. Of course, they can do this at any time in the process, but it's at the "resolving" stage that the Advisory Council felt compelled to encourage it. If there are people you think can help your cause by taking part in consultation, and they're not currently at the table, this is the time to suggest to the agency that they be brought in, and to suggest to them that they ought to beat on the agency's door. They should send in written requests, and tedious as it is, it's a good idea here, as at other points, to cite chapter and verse of the regulations: "Pursuant to 36 CFR 800.6(a)(2), we request the opportunity to participate as consulting parties...." Agencies can get incredibly picky and petty about this sort of thing, and it's usually best to give them no excuse—however silly and trivial—to deny consulting party status.

Consult

So with the preliminaries done, the parties consult. The regulations go on at some length about consulting with and without the council, but really it's all done the same way—or should be. Everybody talks, exchanges notes, debates, considers, argues, negotiates.[1] If the council's taking part, their staff representative is part of the discussion; if it's not, the other parties consult by themselves, and if they come up with a memorandum of agreement, it goes to the council to be filed.

CONSULTATION: AVOIDING AND CLIMBING OUT OF PITFALLS

You most likely want a full, detailed discussion, considering a wide range of alternatives in an evenhanded manner, looking seriously for ways to avoid, reduce, and mitigate impacts. The project proponent probably wants to consult for as short a time as possible, with the smallest possible number of people, consider the smallest range of alternatives, and ram the project through. The federal agency that's responsible for 106 compliance may be in the proponent's pocket, or they may try to maintain some level of objectivity and evenhandedness. Occasionally the agency may even be biased in your favor, particularly if the proponent's been difficult or annoying during earlier stages in the process.

There are federal agencies that are very conscientious about doing their job on behalf of the public, but often the agency simply wants to get out from under the case as quickly and simply as possible, while covering its legal tail. Unfortunately for you, this puts them in bed with the proponent even if they aren't especially attracted to each other. Both parties want the consultation to be quick, simple, and as quiet as possible. This brings them both to the SHPO.

The SHPO is a pivotal person in the consultation on resolution, because he or she is the only entity with which the agency *must* consult (unless the Advisory Council is involved too). A lot of agencies try to consult *only* with the SHPO, and in some states the 106 process has evolved into one of virtually getting the SHPO's approval, or "clearance," with little or no participation by others.

There are practical reasons why this kind of evolution has occurred. A whole lot of the projects that come through the agencies every year, every month, really don't require anything else. They're small scale, non-controversial, and don't involve anything terribly important. Technically, the properties are eligible for the Register; technically, the effect is adverse, but frankly, nobody really gives much of a damn. So the agency and SHPO stamp out a quickie MOA and everybody's happy. Unfortunately, people get used to this sort of thing and start to think it's the way it always ought to be.

And then there's the fact that agencies often don't have much expertise, and everyone's overworked. It's sometimes easier for an agency to just leave everything to the SHPO than to develop expertise, but the SHPO staff is so stressed that they can't do anything much more elaborate than quickie MOAs.

Bilateral consultation

Whatever the reason, trying to consult only with the SHPO is a common agency ploy, which you obviously need to block if you can. You'll know you have a problem if the agency and SHPO start exchanging letters without sending you copies, or having meetings without inviting you, or perhaps without even telling you. There's no requirement that all consulting parties be at, or even be invited to, all meetings, or copied on all letters, but there's nothing wrong with your insisting on it. What good is being a consulting party if you're not consulted?

"Let's write an MOA"

Whether the agency tries to consult only bilaterally or not, they're likely to try to move as quickly as possible toward an MOA. They may even conceive of the consultation process as starting with a draft MOA: "We will draft the MOA and send it to the consulting parties for 30-day comment." This may be a perfectly reasonable way to handle a simple, routine case, but of course you don't want your case regarded as simple and routine. So you need to point out to the agency, and quite likely to the SHPO, that the whole idea of consultation is to consult, that an MOA is supposed to be a negotiated document, and that in your eyes no one is close to being able to put an MOA on the table that everyone's going to sign. Of course, the problem is, everyone doesn't *have* to sign, as we'll see.

You may be presented with a draft MOA, more or less out of a clear blue sky. If it doesn't say what you want it to say (and it probably doesn't), you should scream bloody murder. Complain to the agency, to the SHPO, and particularly to the Advisory Council. Ask them to enter the consultation to protect you, the public, from having an ill-thought-out, premature MOA rammed down your throat.

Fixation on recordation/data recovery

We'll discuss MOAs more later, but suffice it to say that most quickie MOAs provide for the property in question to be sacrificed after some form of recordation. If it's a building or structure, "HABS/HAER" documentation will be proposed. That's "Historic American Buildings Survey/Historic American Engineering Record," a National Park Service program that documents historic buildings and engineering works and has published standards for doing so.[2] So the agency proposes to record the building or structure per HABS/HAER standards and then destroy it. If it's an archaeological site, or something definable as an archaeological site (even if it's your ancestral cemetery), what will be proposed is "data recovery," which means having archaeologists dig the place up and recover the artifacts and other material from which information can be gleaned—after which the place can be destroyed.

Unless what you've been angling for all along is a good record of your place, you ought to object strongly to the jump toward recordation or data recovery. These are measures of last resort, done if the parties can't agree to anything else, or done in concert with other things—selection of a different alternative, redesign, and so

"Flag and avoid" is a common strategy thought to make adverse effects go away; unfortunately, only direct physical effects are avoided, and even this doesn't always happen.

Salvage or rescue archaeology, euphemistically referred to as "data recovery," is often a proponent's preferred way of dealing with in-the-way archaeological sites.

"Resolving" Adverse Effects on Your Place

Documenting a building or engineering work to the standards of the Historic American Buildings Survey (HABS)/Historic American Engineering Record (HAER) before its destruction is the architectural or engineering equivalent of archaeological salvage.

on. We'll all agree to move Grandpa's house and outbuildings a quarter mile away farther from the highway, after they're recorded to HABS standards, and then do data recovery on the original house site. We'll move the project to Alternative Site 5 to avoid impacts to Grandpa's homestead, and do data recovery on the much less important old mule corral that once stood on the new project site. Certainly the parties can agree to do nothing but recordation/data recovery, but you ought to promote considering a wider range of alternatives and mitigation measures. Think up alternatives; put them on the table; insist that they be considered. Why can't you put the track in a tunnel under the town? Why not do helicopter logging? Why not rehabilitate the old building for new uses, rather than knocking it down and putting up a new one?

Don't Shoot Yourself in the Foot

It's regrettable, but almost no one involved in Section 106 consultation gets training in negotiation methods. There are some very predictable mistakes that people make in the course of consultation. You should try to avoid them yourself, help anyone at the table who's supporting you avoid them, and watch for ways to exploit them if the other side falls into them. Here are the errors I'm most familiar with:

Knowing that you're right

You believe that you're right, of course—that your place is important and ought to be preserved. Being right and $3.50 will buy you a tall latte. The consultation may honestly be about achieving a balance among conflicting interests; it may be about a contest of wills; it may be a chess match. What it is *not* about is doing the right thing as it's conceived in your ethical universe. Don't be wimpy about your beliefs, but don't think that they're going to be shared, or carry any weight at the consultation table. Being right is no substitute for being a good negotiator.

Thinking you have power

You don't—unless, of course, you do, based on some legal authority other than Section 106 or on sheer political or economic muscle. I've seen Indian tribal elders fall into this trap many times. "We've told you that you can't build on this site; why don't you listen?" The fact is that the project proponents *are* listening, they just don't intend to do what you're telling them to do, and in the end, you don't have the legal authority to force them. What you need is the skill to persuade or dupe them into doing what you want, and you won't develop that skill if you think you have some kind of power that makes it unnecessary.

Expounding

Try to be succinct, to the point. Don't ramble. Try to avoid long speeches. Recognize that your consulting partners have conflicting demands on their time; don't waste it. Make your points, ask your questions, carry the discussion forward, but try to do it succinctly, efficiently.

Failing to listen

Pay attention to what people are saying! It's a very common human failing to be so intent on what we're saying or getting ready to say that we don't notice what the other guy is saying. What he's saying may surprise you; it may be less hard-nosed than you expect. It may present openings for negotiation. For example, the proponent probably doesn't want to build her road through your special place just because she hates such places; she probably has a rational purpose, and what she says about that purpose may open up ways to discuss alternatives. If she says she needs the road because the town is growing and traffic is getting terrible, don't waste time thinking up zingers about how the residents should constrain their procreation or buy smaller cars; seize the opportunity to ask about or propose alternative ways to fix that problem.

Not asking questions or pursuing answers

Try to remember—even if the agency people don't seem to—that federal agency employees work ultimately for us, the voters and taxpayers. Don't be intimidated by them; don't be afraid to ask them to explain themselves. And don't be afraid of their (or anyone else's) experts. A lot of people who do environmental impact assessment in and around government agencies quite honestly believe that their business ends with making expert scientific analyses, and that they need to make themselves understood only by their fellow experts. That's nonsense. NHPA and the other laws were enacted for the benefit of the American public, and that's you. If the experts can't make their arguments and assumptions understandable to the citizenry, they'd better get themselves a translator. Ask questions, insist on answers, and don't be shy about formulating answers of your own, talking with other experts.

Being impolite

Treat those with whom you're negotiating with respect. That doesn't mean you ought to be wimpy, ingratiating, nicey-nice; you simply ought to follow the Golden Rule: treat them as you'd like to be treated. Insulting them, being nasty or overly aggressive, not letting them have their say will not only turn them off, it may alienate others you want to keep on your side—the SHPO, for example, or the Advisory Council.

Being polite

On the other hand, don't get carried away with being polite. There are times to interrupt, to confront, to shock into attentiveness. There are even (rarely) times to insult, to allude to past errors and evils. There are often times to call bluffs, to cut through the rhetoric with which an agency or project proponent may be filling the air, to challenge an assumption or assertion. Try to be tough without being nasty.

Letting them control the agenda

They'll try. They'll literally compose agendas for meetings, and circulate them in advance. They'll try to keep the negotiation "on track" as they define it—which means, of course, getting it wrapped up as quickly as possible, with a minimum of muss and fuss. Try not to let them get away with this. Challenge agendas that you think are incomplete or directed toward the wrong things; insist on inclusion of your issues, your concerns, your alternatives. You may not succeed, but agencies don't like to create administrative records indicating that they froze people out, failed to give full consideration to all reasonable public interests.

Getting sidetracked

Keep your eye on the prize. Try to avoid getting waltzed off into lengthy discussions of side issues. Of course, what's a side issue to you may be central to someone else, and everybody in the consultation deserves to have their issues given full consideration, but try not to waste time and intellectual capital on minor or peripheral matters. It may not really matter very much that they've mischaracterized the significance of a particular place, or the importance of a projected effect, if they've gotten to the point of treating the place with respect and addressing the effect in an appropriate way. It's probably not useful, or productive from your standpoint, to get into a detailed discussion of architectural recordation or archaeological data recovery, if you're trying not to let your special place get destroyed at all. Try not to let the consultation get embroiled in minutiae and marginal issues.

Accepting false statements

Your negotiating partners aren't above lying, and they're even less above small twists and tweaks of the truth to make their conclusions and assumptions seem correct. Don't accept things you think are wrong. If they say their blasting for the road won't shake the adjacent buildings, make sure they can back that statement up with hard data and respectable analyses.

"Resolving" Adverse Effects on Your Place

Focusing narrowly on "historic preservation" or "cultural resource management" issues

People sometimes believe—honestly or because it serves their interests, or both—that under Section 106 we can "resolve" adverse effects only by doing something that they understand to be of a "historic preservation" or "cultural resource management" nature—which they usually take to mean actions like rehabilitation of old buildings, archaeological data recovery, and architectural recordation. In fact, the consulting parties under Section 106 can agree to any means of resolving adverse effect that's legal. Is it important to the cultural character of the river to keep the salmon migrating up it? Then managing salmon migrations, construction of fish ladders, and demolition of dams are entirely open to discussion under Section 106. Can you tolerate the loss of Grandpa's homestead if the proponent puts half a million bucks into cultural programming on the local public television channel? There's nothing wrong with that as something the consulting parties might agree to—though it's certainly likely to raise some eyebrows and make some people mumble about extortion. Of course, the less related your concern or proposed solution is to something that may make a place eligible for the National Register, the less likely you are to get it considered—which is one reason it's important to take part in the determination of your place's eligibility. If everybody understands the river to be eligible only for the role it's played in steamboat navigation, it's going to be hard to argue for the cultural importance of the fish.

Assuming

Don't assume. Anything. Take nothing for granted. Make sure every point is covered, every issue is addressed. Don't assume that anybody is going to do the right thing, that they'll be responsible or honorable. Or that everybody shares an understanding of what's being discussed, proposed, written down on paper. For instance, it's very common for Section 106 consulting parties to agree that a given site or building will be "avoided" during construction of a project. All very well, but what does everybody mean by "avoid?" Physically avoid the place, or avoid all impacts on it, including indirect impacts, visual impacts, auditory impacts? Will it be avoided by 300 feet, 30 feet, or 3 feet? How will we make sure it's really avoided? What happens if it turns out that for some reason it can't be avoided?

The Memorandum of Agreement

If agreement is reached, the consulting parties draft and execute a memorandum of agreement, which then must be complied with if and when the project goes forward. Agreement doesn't have to be reached among all the consulting parties; notably, if the agency and SHPO agree on what will be done and you object to it, they can still execute the MOA and the project can proceed. The agency has performed its Section 106 responsibilities; it has taken effects into account and given the Advisory Council an opportunity to comment. You don't have a veto.

You can, however, move heaven and earth to keep the core consulting parties—agency, SHPO or THPO, and sometimes the Advisory Council—from signing. Some SHPOs are more responsive to citizen concerns than others, and the voice of sweet reason may not be enough to prevent them from signing what the agency puts in front of them. You may have to muster not only your best arguments but your political muscle as well. This may be another time when you'll need your congressperson, your governor, your lawyer, the National Trust for Historic Preservation, or the Sierra Club.

The fine points of writing an MOA are another topic altogether, which could be the subject of another whole book.[3] MOA writing is probably not very relevant to you; you're unlikely to draft one, and you probably don't want one to be signed at all. So we won't belabor MOA writing here. Just remember that:

There doesn't have to be an MOA

If no MOA is reached, then the agency reports this to the Advisory Council, which "renders a comment" to the head of the agency. The agency head responds, makes a decision about what to do, and that, like an MOA, concludes the Section 106 process. The agency has considered its effects, given the council an opportunity to comment, and taken those comments into account; it's complied with Section 106. We'll discuss council comment in the next chapter.

If There Is an MOA . . .

If you wind up with an MOA that doesn't say what you'd like it to say—that lets the proponent bulldoze or demolish your special place after doing some oral history or architectural recordation, for example—then you're pretty much stuck, as far as Section 106 is concerned. You may be able to do something under some other legal authority, whether federal, state, tribal, or local, but Section 106 review is over. It's almost unheard of for an MOA to be overturned by a court of law, and people *have* tried to do that. I don't recommend it. You'll probably be wasting your time and money.

To Sign or Not to Sign

If there ends up being an MOA that you *can* live with—say, one that requires the project to be built following Alternative X, which places it well away from your place—then you need to decide whether to sign it. Of course, first you have to be asked to sign, and there's no guarantee that this will happen. The agency can elect to ask a consulting party to sign, or not; only the SHPO or THPO is guaranteed signature authority. But most likely, if you've been a consulting party, the agency will ask you (however reluctantly) to sign.[4]

If you think the MOA is acceptable, you ought to sign it. Doing so keeps you in the game; it gives you more ability to monitor what goes on than would be the case if you didn't sign. At least one court has found that only signatories to an MOA have the authority to seek enforcement of its terms in court. And having signed, a signatory can seek amendment or termination of an MOA; if you don't sign, you can call for such things, but no one need pay any attention to you.

Monitoring compliance

Particularly if you become a party to the MOA, but even if you don't, if you like what an MOA calls for you'd better keep track of how it's implemented. The MOA will probably contain some kind of provision for periodic monitoring by the parties to make sure it's working. You should be prepared to participate in that activity and make sure others who support you do too. And keep track of how the project proceeds, how plans are transformed into reality. It's very common for things to come up during the project that cause changes to be made in the design and even the location of the work. Sometimes agencies and non-governmental proponents don't think about their MOA when they make those changes. Oh dear, there's solid rock where we want to dig that basement; let's move it 100 feet to the north. It's just a minor change, but of course 100 feet north is in the viewshed of Grandpa's homestead, while the original site was not.

So keep track, and if something happens that's not consistent with the MOA, scream. Scream to the proponent, the overseeing agency if there is one, the SHPO, the ACHP, the press, your congressperson. Actually, you ought to start out politely reminding the proponents that they can't make that change without amending the MOA, and show them what it says. If they ignore you, then scream. And if necessary, take it to court. In an MOA an agency promises to do things in a certain way. If it then fails to do them that way, a judge should see it as an open-and-shut case.

The fact that an MOA can, in theory, be enforced is one reason it's important to take part in its development, and to watch carefully what's written. A sloppy MOA has holes in it that a wily project proponent can drive dump trucks and front-end loaders through. If you wind up with an MOA, and you want to see it enforced, it's got to be as airtight as you and the other consulting parties can make it.

What can be in an MOA

The project proponent, or maybe the SHPO, may well tell you that only very highly specified, formalized provisions can be in an MOA: it can only provide for rehabilitation of a building, perhaps, or only for archaeological data recovery, and can't provide for taking care of artifacts from a dig, or putting design controls on the highway. In fact, an MOA can provide for anything that's legal and that the consulting parties agree to, provided it has some relationship to the historic properties and preservation issues involved. I've done MOAs that have provided for major project redesign, construction of a boat harbor to replace traditional fishing facilities, and the management of culturally sensitive animal habitat. If someone tells you that what you want in the MOA can't be included, insist that they explain why it can't, in real-world terms. Don't accept "we don't do it that way," or "that's not consistent with the regulations"—unless, of course, they can show you where the regulations prohibit it.

NEPA COORDINATION

Assuming the agency is preparing an environmental assessment (EA), and assuming it hasn't found some other kind of egregious impact—on an endangered species, a wetland, or whatever—its representatives will probably use a signed MOA to help justify a finding of no significant impact (FONSI). They may (and certainly should) include the terms of the MOA in the FONSI as measures they're adopting to keep the impacts from being significant; significant impacts would mean they have to do an environmental impact statement (EIS). If they're doing an EIS, they'll report the results of the Section 106 consultation in it, and may (and again should) adopt the measures laid out in the MOA among the mitigation measures outlined in their record of decision (ROD).

How the BPS Did It

The Advisory Council's finding that questions remained unresolved about the effects of the Broad Run Bridge project helped the State Historic Preservation Officer (SHPO) rebut the Virginia Department of Transportation's (VDOT) and Federal Highway Administration's (FHWA) insistence that widening the bridge would have no adverse effect. So did the strong support given the Buckland Preservation Society (BPS) by the National Trust for Historic Preservation and the insistence of the National Park Service (NPS) American Battlefield Preservation program that more attention be given to effects on the battlefield. The SHPO advised the FHWA and VDOT to find that the project would have an adverse effect. FHWA and VDOT never quite did that, but they did acknowledge that everyone *else* thought there was such an effect, and as a result bit the bullet and started consulting about how to resolve it.

The main issue was the width of the proposed new bridge deck—some 25 feet wider than the existing one. This required relatively wide approach lanes that could muck up the archaeological remains of Buckland village within their boundaries, and more importantly it seemed to be a step toward widening the highway through Buckland. FHWA and VDOT insisted that it was not such a step, that they weren't even thinking about widening the highway. The BPS politely said they were full of hooey. Why had they acquired the land for a wider highway back in the 1950s if they didn't plan to build it? Why did the Northern Virginia 2020 plan call for a wider highway if it wasn't planned?

Hey, said FHWA and VDOT, the 2020 plan isn't ours; we're not bound by it. Irrelevant, said the BPS; the plan obviously reflects a reasonably foreseeable future action in which FHWA and VDOT will undoubtedly participate, so it has to be part of a cumulative effects analysis.

No, said FHWA and VDOT, we simply will not discuss cumulative effects; this project has no cumulative effects as far as we're concerned. But by the way, we've come up with a new design that adds only 6 feet to the width of the bridge, instead of 25.

Now the BPS had to steer a very careful course. For all practical purposes they'd won, but they had to keep the pressure on in order to get an agreeable solution nailed down. And in the long run they still needed to get the highway agencies to acknowledge their contribution to sprawl and commit to doing something about it. So they thanked VDOT for knocking 19 feet off the bridge and pushed for further design changes to reduce the width still further. They also drafted a memorandum of agreement that stipulated the reduced width and also included a section on cumulative effects. This section would commit FHWA and VDOT to adopt the bypass alternative if the study of it then beginning showed that it was feasible and prudent, and thereupon to return the extra right-of-way through Buckland to the village.

One of the hardest things for BPS members to get their arms around at this point was that they had won; they had gotten the bridge reduced to a scale at which it could not by itself contribute to sprawl. It was time to nail down the deal, but to some, drafting the MOA seemed like climbing in bed with the enemy. At the same time, there was some feeling that insisting on too much more might cause FHWA and VDOT to get up and leave the table. As we'll see in the next chapter, they could have done that, but the best guess was that they wouldn't, so the BPS pushed on with its argument for further reduction of the bridge width and a section on cumulative impacts.

After a good deal of grumbling, VDOT tasked its very talented project engineer with looking into a further reduced bridge deck. He managed to design one that was only 3 feet wider than the existing one. But the agencies were adamant about not admitting in any way that they were participants in the cumulative effects of sprawl, and they wouldn't commit to be bound by the results of the bypass study.

"Resolving" Adverse Effects on Your Place

It became apparent that the Advisory Council and SHPO felt that they'd pushed the agencies as far as they could be pushed; the bridge width issue had effectively been resolved, and with it the cumulative effects issue—for this project—seemed to dissolve. Though the BPS wanted VDOT to take real steps toward getting over its romance with sprawl development, it appeared that this case was not the one on which to push the point.

In the end—because it had little or no faith in VDOT to do what it promised to do—the BPS pushed for strong language in the MOA stipulating exactly what bridge design would be followed, and providing for ongoing monitoring by all the parties. With many expressions of regret and dismay, BPS agreed to removal of the cumulative effects stipulations. But it held out long enough that VDOT agreed to throw it another bone: an admittedly vague stipulation committing the highway agencies to participate in a BPS-coordinated effort to develop and implement an overall plan for the preservation and best use of Buckland and the battlefield. Since cumulative effects would have to be addressed in this plan, this stipulation kept the issue alive.

The MOA was signed by all the parties, and its terms are being carried out as this is written. Appendix A is the signed MOA.

CONTACT: For pertinent Section 106 regulation go to http://www.achp.gov/regs-rev04.pdf and see 36 CFR 800.6

– Notes –

1. See Nicholas Dorochoff's *Negotiation Basics for Cultural Resource Managers* (Left Coast Press, 2007) for negotiation guidelines.
2. HABS/HAER has recently acquired a sibling—HALS for Historic American Landscapes Survey—which documents historic designed landscapes (parks, parkways, etc.)
3. It *is* the subject of a couple of chapters in my 2001 book, *Federal Planning and Historic Places: The Section 106 Process*, which are also available on the World-Wide Web at *http://www.npi.org/Stipulations.htm* if you need to refer to them.
4. The regulations distinguish between "signatories" to an MOA and "concurring parties"; you may be asked to be either. It's largely a distinction without a difference, but in theory, being a signatory gives you a little more power than being a concurring party, so it may be worth arguing for the former status.

Chapter Ten

Endgame— and Further Complications

How You Got To This Point

You've fought your way through Section 106 review of the project that threatens your special place. You got recognized as a consulting party, and influenced how the responsible federal agency initiated review, scoped its identification work, and conducted that work. You got the agency and State Historic Preservation Officer (SHPO) to recognize your place as eligible for the National Register. You got the agency to acknowledge that the project would have adverse effects on it. You've participated in consultation about how to resolve those effects. You've brought in other consulting parties, developed alliances, impressed the SHPO with the importance of your place and the seriousness of the project's effects, and gotten the Advisory Council on Historic Preservation (ACHP) involved. You've also worked the National Environmental Policy Act (NEPA) process, and whatever state and local environmental or historic preservation review systems apply.

But the bastards haven't given up. They're still determined to put their highway or reservoir or bombing range or national park in a place where it will do grave damage to your special place, or to its use and enjoyment by people like you. And they've been smart enough not to tumble into any of the pitfalls that have lain along their path through the process. They've made the determinations, conducted the studies, taken part in consultation, played by the rules.

What do you do now?

STOP THE MOA

As we discussed in the last chapter, unless you're satisfied with the compromise that a negotiated memorandum of agreement (MOA) probably represents—

Endgame and Further Complications

and you may be; it may entirely or mostly meet your needs—then you want to keep an MOA from being executed. That's likely to be hard to do; the SHPO and ACHP see executing an MOA as a good thing, and try to achieve it in almost all cases. But it *can* be stopped, if you can get the SHPO and ACHP to see your place as important enough, and the project's impacts on it as serious enough.

Convincing the SHPO is important, but not enough, because the regulations allow the responsible agency and the ACHP to execute an MOA over the SHPO's head. In the event you're on tribal land and working with a tribal historic preservation officer (THPO), it's a bit different; the ACHP *cannot* execute an MOA over the THPO's head, because the THPO represents a sovereign government. But in most cases it's the ACHP you have to convince that an MOA is a bad idea.

Very likely you've asked the ACHP to enter the consultation earlier in the process; if they've agreed to do so, you'll have a point of contact on the ACHP staff with whom to work. He or she may be sympathetic to your point of view. But the staff person doesn't have the last word; he or she has at least a level or two of supervisors, and then there's the council itself. The council, remember, is a 20-member body made up of the secretaries of Interior and Agriculture, various presidential appointees, and so on. The staff can influence the council, but they can't buck it. And for the most part the council members are political animals.

So work with your ACHP staff person, muster your allies and get them to do the same, and look for ways to influence the council members. One member is the president of the National Trust for Historic Preservation; see if that person will help. There are "citizen" and "expert" members who aren't necessarily highly political; see if you can get to one or more of them. And if you have political drag yourself, or know someone who does, use it.

Section 106 is all about consultation, and at the end of the process the negotiations can become very intense.

Generally what's impressive to the ACHP—and for that matter, to the SHPO and others—are factors like these:

- *The charisma of the place.* Do lots of people feel very strongly about it? Does it have some kind of special status under local laws or policies, or in state law, or is it a National Historic Landmark? Are there eloquent people who'll speak for it, or write about it?
- *The character of the threat.* Is the place going to be utterly destroyed, or just changed a bit? Does the threat come from a nasty source (a toxic waste dump, a surface mine), or from one that's more benign (low-income housing, a green energy program, a much-needed irrigation project)?
- *Threats to other things.* Is the project also going to knock out charismatic animals (bears, bighorn sheep), endangered species, really nice scenery, a living ethnic or low-income community or neighborhood?
- *Public interests.* Is the project one that's perceived locally to be badly needed? Or are there public interests besides you who are speaking out against it? Do they have good arguments? Are there Indian tribes, Native Hawaiian groups, other ethnic groups, low-income groups who'll be hurt by the project, particularly if they ascribe value to your place?
- *Alternatives.* Are there other ways to achieve the project's purposes at reasonable cost without harming your special place and doing whatever other damage the project will do if carried forward as planned?
- *Political risk and opportunity.* Does the project have heavy-duty political support? Or is it related to an industry or activity that has a lot of support? Telecommunications, for example, or national defense? Conversely, is there political support for stopping the project, or finding an alternative? What kind of political support? Remember that the ACHP chairman and many of the members are appointed by the president.

You need to convince the ACHP—through letters, phone conversations, emails, on-site discussions, visits to Washington—that taking the above kinds of factors into account, the project is not one that the ACHP should "bless" by signing or accepting an MOA. Their tendency will probably be to sign it, or avert their eyes when the agency files it with them, but if you've gotten the staff involved early enough, and if you have a good case, you may be able to get the ACHP to terminate consultation. Or, of course, the SHPO may do so, or the agency may get so irritated with the situation that it will terminate. Then, of course, there's no MOA.

And Then?

Then the ACHP "renders a comment."

Remember the words of Section 106? The responsible federal agency has to take the effects of its action into account and "afford the Advisory Council a reasonable opportunity to comment." Most of the 106 process is about how effects are to be taken into account, and the ACHP takes its "reasonable opportunity to comment" by supervising how the process is carried out. But in the final extremity, if the process doesn't result in something that at least the SHPO and/or ACHP staff can live with, then the ACHP actually has to comment in the formal sense. It has to announce its opinion.

Whereupon, it's important to understand, the responsible agency can do whatever it likes. It doesn't have to do what the ACHP says. So it might seem plausible that an agency intent on doing a project, or helping or letting someone else do a project, would just steam through the process, terminate consultation as quickly as possible, absorb the ACHP's comment, and do its thing. But there are reasons that most agencies don't do that.

For one thing, it's a pain to get the ACHP's comments. The agency has to pull together a lot of documentation and send it in. This paperwork typically moves some distance up the chain of command above the agency office that's actually in charge of the project, resulting in unwelcome scrutiny of that office's work and decisions. Once the ACHP has the documentation, its chairman may just write a letter providing the comment, but if the case has any legs—if it's complicated, controversial, political—then the council will probably have some sort of meeting. They may designate a panel to review the matter; they may set up a fact-finding group. They may review the case at one of their regular quarterly meetings, or they may have a special meeting, perhaps at or near the site of the project. The meetings are public and usually follow something akin to a classic public hearing model. There's often media coverage, sometimes a lot of it, and if people are fired up about the case, the meeting can be long and contentious.

And then, after whatever deliberation it does, the council writes out its comment and sends it to the very top of the agency. If it's a Corps of Engineers project, the comment will go to the Chief of Engineers or the Secretary of the Army, maybe even the Secretary of Defense. If it's a project of the Department of

Housing and Urban Development (HUD), it will go to the Secretary of HUD. And under Section 110(l) of the National Historic Preservation Act (NHPA), the recipient has to respond and can't delegate that responsibility. This doesn't mean that the Secretary of Defense or HUD has to tap out his or her own message in response to the ACHP, but it does mean that he or she is going to have to give the matter personal attention. And nobody, *nobody* in a federal agency wants the ultimate boss asking questions about how they do their jobs.

The public must be involved in Section 106 consultation, but some agencies like to reduce public involvement to just holding hearings.

For this reason—and because the ACHP staff and the SHPOs see it as their duties to negotiate MOAs if at all possible—very few cases go to council comment. But let's suppose yours has. What should you do to prepare?

Convincing the Council

What you want, of course, is for the council to support preservation of your place. It's by no means certain that they will. It's the Advisory Council *on* Historic Preservation, not *for* Historic Preservation. The council doesn't necessarily come down on the side of preservation every time. It seeks what it thinks is the public interest. It can say "knock the thing down," or "bulldoze it away."

Exactly what opportunities you'll have to influence the council depends on how the comment is rendered. If the council members or some group of members and staff come to the site of the project, you'll almost certainly have the opportunity to go with them. As, of course, will the other side, and the SHPO, and all the other consulting parties. You can try to make sure they see the right things and aren't misled. And then there will be some kind of public meeting, where you'll have an opportunity to speak and submit written testimony, and you can line up others to do so as well. Do this carefully. Don't overwhelm the

ACHP with people all saying the same things, or with masses of redundant documentation. Organize your presentations so different people, representing different groups, say different but complementary things. Give the council documents that help make your point, and explain how they do so. Think of what you're doing as a sales pitch. You have to sell the council on your place, and on what a loss it would be for the American public or some good-sized and sympathetic portion of it if your place were destroyed. And of course you have to undercut the credibility of the opposition's arguments. You have to do this in a polite way, but forcefully. Be dignified, be adult, but don't be a patsy.

This is—as far as Section 106 goes—your last chance to save your place. Don't blow it.

But...

But we can hope you'll never have to face this last chance. We can hope that reason will prevail, or the proponent will tire or run out of money or get drawn up short by higher authority, or run afoul of some other hazard of the development process, long before you get to the point of laying your case before the assembled ACHP. The vast majority of Section 106 cases are worked out in ways that satisfy most, if not all, the consulting parties. If you're smart, diligent, determined, and clever, you should be able to be one of the satisfied parties.

Playing By Other Rules

There's one other, somewhat discouraging, thing to touch on. Not everyone plays the Section 106 game according to the rules we've been discussing. The regulations provide several optional ways to achieve compliance with Section 106, and some agencies make up their own ways of doing business—which the ACHP tends not to like, and courts tend not to accept, but they do it anyway.

Programmatic agreements and other alternative processes

Under the regulations, an agency can adopt its own alternative process via regulations developed in consultation with the council, SHPOs and THPOs, tribes, and other interested parties. This process may exclude some kinds of project from review, on the theory that they have little potential for doing damage. Or it can adjust the standard review process somehow, or replace it with another procedure that better fits the agency's needs.

The ACHP can also issue program comments—comments on a whole agency program, rather than on individual projects. These comments are the council's overall recommendations about how the program can take proper care of historic properties, and they're more powerful than project-specific comments because if the agency doesn't follow them, the council can withdraw them, driving the agency back to project-by-project review.

The most common alternative way of doing Section 106 is under a *programmatic agreement* (PA). Such an agreement is negotiated among an agency, the ACHP, some SHPO or group of SHPOs, or the National Council of SHPOs if the agreement will apply nationwide, and (in theory) other interested parties—just as though it were a memorandum of agreement. Once it's in place, the agency can follow its terms in lieu of standard Section 106 review for projects under the program.

All these systems exist for a practical reason. The Section 106 process simply doesn't work well for every federal program. It may be unduly bulky and burdensome for the kind of action an agency undertakes. It may not guarantee proper attention to the kinds of project the agency gets involved in, or the kinds of effects such projects typically have. It's a "one-size-fits-all" process, and as a result doesn't necessarily fit anyone very well. Programmatic agreements and other such alternative systems are designed to adjust the fit.

But there are two downsides to such alternatives. The biggie for the purposes of this book is that they give agencies a way to flummox the public. "Oh, but we *are* complying with Section 106; we're just complying with it in this different way." You have to learn the alternative process to know whether they're telling the truth.

The other problem is that many alternatives are very, very poorly crafted. Most programmatic agreements I've reviewed have holes in them large enough to drive at least a modest-sized fleet of humvees through. Some are so poorly written that they're almost indecipherable.

If your concern is with a telecommunications tower—a "cell phone tower" in common parlance—you're likely to run into the "FCC NPA." This is a "nationwide" (or "national") programmatic agreement that the Federal Communications Commission "negotiated" with the Advisory Council, the National Conference of State Historic Preservation Officers, and others in 2005. I put "negotiated" in quotes, because in fact FCC—that is, the telecommunications industry, with typically unthinking congressional support and with FCC barking happily in its lap—rammed the travesty down the throats of its supposed consulting parties. In a nutshell, the PA lets FCC authorize construction of a tower provided there's been an archaeological survey of the project site, some rather formulistic consultation with tribes, and review of visual impacts on properties within a standard distance of the tower—*provided* those properties have been placed on or somehow formally determined eligible for the National Register. Never mind the explicit statutory direction to address effects on places included in or *eligible* for the Register; all the communicants need to worry about are places that the Register or an SHPO has somehow magically *determined eligible*. So if you live in a fine old house or a culturally significant neighborhood that nobody's nominated to the Register, FCC has no obligation to consider the visual impacts of letting Eavesdropp Telecommunications, Inc. build a 200-foot tower next door to you. Until, that is, some aggrieved party with sufficient money takes FCC to court and demonstrates how contrary the PA is to the plain language of the law. Whereupon the telecom industry, rather than sitting down in good faith and trying to negotiate something sensible, will doubtless send its lobbyists to Congress to get the law changed. It's a sad state of affairs, but not an entirely unusual one. The Bureau of Land Management has a programmatic agreement that effectively gives it a free rein with activities on public lands, subject to some control by SHPOs—who sometimes exercise this control pretty dictatorially but almost never do much to promote participation by affected parties other than themselves. The Army has similar carte blanche on its bases.

Unilateral inventions

Besides alternative ways of doing business that the Advisory Council blesses, like programmatic agreements, some agencies just decide for themselves how they're going to do Section 106 review, and if the council doesn't like it, tough. The Corps of Engineers is one of the worst offenders here. The Corps decided decades ago that the way to simplify its life when considering issuing dredge-and-fill permits under Section 404 of the Clean Water Act was to issue "Nationwide Permits" and "General Permits" for abstract classes of action involving only small-scale discharges of fill. Then they'd let anyone whose project fell into a category of action covered by such a permit go ahead with his or her project with very little fol-de-rol, subject to certain standard conditions. Not an unreasonable thing to do, in principle but then they created a set of processes-within-processes for managing Nationwide and General Permits, creating such a complicated situation that it's hard to know whether a given project is or is not under such a permit. Some literally shift back and forth in the course of planning. And while the Corps sort of complied programmatically with NEPA when it issued the Nationwide and General Permits, it dealt with Section 106 by including a kick-out clause saying that if a project could affect a historic property, it couldn't be handled under such a permit. It's left to the beleaguered Corps staff, or the SHPO, or the applicant, to decide whether such a property might be affected, and the record of their doing so is very, very spotty. The Corps also attached an appendix to its permit regulations about how applicants are to deal with Section 106 when they actually have to do so, and it is only marginally similar to the Advisory Council's regulatory process. Although the council has complained repeatedly about all this, it hasn't yet (in some 30 years of trying) brought the Corps to attention.[1]

The bottom line—and I realize it's a bit depressing, particularly coming along at the end of the book—is that you can master the Section 106 process backward and forward only to find out that the agency whose action is likely to mess up your special place follows a different set of rules.

However, most federal undertakings, most of the time, are reviewed under Section 106 more or less in accordance with the standard process. And indeed, most alternative procedures merely tweak the standard process a bit—though often making it more complex than it is otherwise and reducing opportunities for public and consulting party involvement. If you know the standard process, you should be able to figure out how an agency's adjusted process may work, how it differs from the standard ways of doing business, and what (if anything) can be done about it.

Emergencies and discoveries

There are also special procedures laid out in the regulations for handling emergency situations and unanticipated discoveries. The emergency section of the regulations uses lots of words to say, in essence, that in an emergency all bets are off—the agency is just supposed to do whatever it thinks it can do to address impacts on historic properties. Similar provisions apply when something is unexpectedly discovered after Section 106 review has been completed on a project: the agency basically informs the SHPO and other interested parties, and does what it decides to do.

Endgame and Further Complications

An Example: The Trail of Dreams

Let me wrap up with an example of a case—not yet quite concluded as this is written—that illustrates how Section 106 can be used—in concert with other laws—to influence project planning even to the extent of stopping a project cold in its tracks.

In the far southeastern part of the California there's a large patch of desert across which runs a complex of ancient trails, pounded into the desert surface by thousands of years of running or walking feet. Some of the trails are crossed by lines of rocks, and around and among them are circles scratched into the surface, petroglyphs inscribed on boulders, and rocks with fragments of quartz scattered around them. This is the "Trail of Dreams" landscape. Across this landscape, in the beliefs of the Quechan tribe, tribal members travel in dreams to access worlds of spiritual wisdom. Most of the land making up this landscape is federal government land, administered by the Bureau of Land Management (BLM).

In the 1990s Glamis Imperial Gold, a Canadian minerals company, sought a permit from BLM to put in a surface gold mine in the midst of the Trail of Dreams landscape. Glamis already had leased the minerals underlying the site; BLM takes the strange position that it can enter into such leases without compliance with Section 106 because the lease action per se doesn't authorize ground disturbance. This, of course, creates awful last-minute conflicts when a lessee does propose ground disturbance and BLM finally undertakes to comply with the law.[2]

So Glamis applied for a permit to mine, and BLM initiated Section 106 review, directing Glamis to perform identification of historic properties. Actually, what BLM directed Glamis to do was an archaeological survey, this being all BLM usually can imagine as a means of identifying such properties. The archaeologists surveyed and surveyed and recorded and recorded. Meanwhile other studies were also done, and BLM did an environmental assessment (EA) and sent it around for public review.

Whereupon the Quechan came to realize that their special place was about to be trashed. They demanded attention to the landscape in the NEPA process, and insisted on being consulting parties in BLM's Section 106 review.

There followed a long period of studies and restudies, consultations and negotiations. Finally BLM—which was between a rock and a hard place because a long-outdated law, the 1872 Mining Act, more or less gave Glamis a right to mine—determined that the landscape was eligible for the National

Register and that the mine would have an adverse effect on it. Glamis then proposed to design the mine to avoid direct impacts to the "archaeological sites"—put the pit over here, the tipple heap on the other side of the trail, and so on. BLM, with a good deal of foot-shuffling and averted eyes, proposed this as the basis for a memorandum of agreement.

The tribe rejected the proposal out of hand, pointing out that archaeology was not what the Trail of Dreams was about, and commenting on the difficulty of traveling in dreams through an industrial landscape. They persuaded the SHPO and ACHP to back them—which wasn't too hard, given how ridiculous the proposed "resolution" of adverse effects was. So BLM had to ask the ACHP to comment.

After a fact-finding visit and public meetings, the ACHP commented directly to the Secretary of the Interior, who oversees BLM. The comment was a strong one, and was delivered to the Secretary personally by the Chairman of the Council: Find a way not to issue the permit, because the mine would have devastating effects on the cultural practices and beliefs of the Quechan tribe.

The Secretary at the time—Bruce Babbitt in Bill Clinton's administration—probably didn't much want to issue the permit anyway, and he had a very sharp lawyer as his solicitor. The solicitor, John Leshy, found a way around the 1872 Mining Act, and BLM denied the permit.

At this point, George W. Bush became president, and Babbitt, Leshy, and the chairman of the ACHP were all out of jobs. The new Secretary of the Interior, Gale Norton, had Leshy's opinion rescinded, and reopened NEPA review of the case. Since the ACHP had commented, the Section 106 process didn't need to be restarted.

Things didn't look good for the Quechan at the federal level, but now the California legislature (encouraged by the tribe and its friends in the environmental community) stepped in. The legislature enacted bills containing the seemingly unremarkable requirement that surface mines be backfilled when done, particularly in the vicinity of tribal sacred sites. This in essence made it uneconomical for Glamis to put in the mine, even if they did get a permit from BLM.

So Glamis, being Canadian, took the matter to an international tribunal set up under the North American Free Trade Agreement (NAFTA), asserting that California was in effect expropriating its property and failing to treat it fairly, in contravention of the NAFTA treaty. Glamis sought compensation for California's action from the U.S. government.

This suddenly placed the tribe, the state, and the U.S. government on the same side of the struggle against the Canadian miners. That's where things stand as of this writing; if you're interested in an update, I'm sure Google will accommodate you. But my point in recounting the story of the Trail of Dreams is not to elaborate on this particular case. My point is this: the Quechan tribe used Section 106, together with NEPA, to get its foot in the door of BLM's permitting process. They slowed things down, made better impact studies happen, created a forum for consultation and used it. Section 106 took them only so far, though it was quite a way—all the way to consideration by the Secretary of the Interior and denial of the permit. But nothing is exempt from politics, and the presidential election of 2000 wiped out the Quechan's gains. But the federal government isn't the only game in town, and the Quechan's concerns overlapped with those of environmentalists pushing the California legislature to do something about surface mines. The Quechan were able to ally themselves with these interests and benefit from the new state legislation. Then the matter went international with Glamis's NAFTA ploy, which shuffled alliances and—well, you get the point. Section 106 was one arrow in the Quechans' quiver. Only one, but a very important one, that made the charging Glamis bison[3] hesitate long enough for other bows to be drawn and arrows put to flight.

How the BPS Did It

What about Buckland and the Broad Run Bridge? It's worth noting that the Federal Highway Administration (FHWA) didn't have to sign the memorandum of agreement on the Broad Run Bridge. They could have terminated consultation and sought the Advisory Council's comments. However, the Buckland Preservation Society (BPS) judged that this was pretty unlikely. It would have taken the agencies a lot more time, and they were anxious to move the project forward for the perfectly good reasons that the bridge was seen as dangerous and the money to fix it had been budgeted. It was also likely that if the council had commented, its comment would have been at least somewhat sympathetic to the BPS—particularly given the support of the State Historic Preservation Officer and the National

Trust. FHWA wouldn't have had to follow the council's advice, but the comment would have gone at least to the FHWA Administrator, and possibly to the Secretary of Transportation, neither of whom would likely take kindly to getting involved in some diddly-squat bridge project in northern Virginia. So, as outlined in Chapter Nine, the BPS could feel reasonably comfortable about pushing—up to a point—for an MOA that it felt was adequate.

The Broad Run Bridge case was only one tip of a very large iceberg with which the BPS had—and has—to deal. As this is written, the BPS is trying to prevail upon the Corps of Engineers to do a full and adequate job of Section 106 review on a major housing development, Bishops Run, on Route 29 southwest of Buckland. The project requires a Corps Clean Water Act permit, so it has to go through Section 106 review, but the Corps is not very excited about considering even such direct effects as visual impacts on the battlefield—let alone the cumulative effects of induced sprawl. And the Virginia Department of Transportation (VDOT) is back again, with a proposed widening of Highway 215, a north–south artery that runs right through the battlefield. Seemingly slow learners, VDOT has thus far failed to initiate consultation with the BPS, though it is funding the usual archaeological surveys and a landscape study whose scope of work they haven't shared. This thick-headedness seems to result from the fact that a different administrative VDOT district is responsible for the 215 project; apparently they don't communicate well with their fellows who had to deal with the Broad Run Bridge.

This is not an uncommon problem; agencies are slow to learn, and often their administrative structures discourage the free flow of information. The passage of time is often also a problem; one set of administrators may learn how to do Section 106 intelligently and with responsibility, but they move on, and the next bunch is likely to revert to old ways. Or invent new ones that are just as dumb.

In any event the BPS has a long campaign before it as it fights sprawl and works to restore something of Buckland's traditional character. Section 106 is only one tool they're using; they're also seeking and administering grants to study the area, develop literature, prepare plans, and set up partnerships with government agencies and academic institutions. They're using state and local law, and working to win state and local political leaders to their cause. But where the federal government is involved, Section 106 can be an important tool if it's used skillfully. From its experience with the Broad Run Bridge, the BPS now knows how to use it that way.

CONTACT: For pertinent Section 106 regulation go to
http://www.achp.gov/regs-rev04.pdf
and see 36 CFR 800.7 (ACHP comment) and 36 CFR 800.14 (programmatic agreements and other alternatives)

– NOTES –

1. As this is written, the Corps is embarked on an initiative to revise its procedures for doing 106 on regulatory actions, and from what I've been told it seems that they're pointed in a reasonable direction, but only time will tell.
2. Late in 2006, in *Pit River Tribe, et al. v. United States Forest Service, et al.* (469 F.3d 768 [9th Cir. 2006]), the Ninth Circuit Court of Appeals found that implementing this policy in at least one case violated NEPA, Section 106, and the government's trust responsibility toward Indian tribes. See *http://www.ca9.uscourts.gov/ca9/newopinions.nsf/67281897AF199DD98825721E005B6AE5/$file/0415746.pdf?openelement*.
3. Living as they do along the lower Colorado River, the Quechan in reality don't hunt a lot of bison, but a rabbit just doesn't make as colorful a metaphor.

AFTERWORD

Now That We Understand the System

Let's Fix It

If there's one thing that writing this book has taught me, it's that the Section 106 process is far more esoteric, complicated, and insensitive to the public than it ought to be. Living with it on a day to day basis, year in and year out as I do, I've become used to it, and it's only when I try to explain it to real people, like you, that I realize how crazy it really is. Why in the world should a citizen have to go through a lot of bureaucratic process to prove that the environment he or she cares about meets standards developed by a bunch of archaeologists and architectural historians in a federal agency? Why should such a citizen have to enlist the aid of another bunch of such federal employees, plus a similar group at the state level, to force other federal agencies to pay attention to his or her concerns? This is democracy?

The situation with NEPA is no better. NEPA practice—except in cases where thoughtful but beleaguered practitioners make it so—doesn't even pretend to be responsive to public interests; it's all about expert analysis. This may be all right where hard-science things like parts per million of pollutants in the water are concerned, or the carrying capacity of a given piece of forest, or even archaeological research, but it makes no sense at all when we're talking about the cultural, social, truly human aspects of the environment.

And then there's the problem that experts doing both NEPA and Section 106 review are almost all hired either by federal agencies or by non-federal change agents. Their—our—objectivity and openness to the public are automatically compromised. However much they—we—may try to make this not be so. They—we—are hired guns, however much we may like to think we're working in the public interest.

So, while the purpose of this book is to help you and other real people use Section 106 as it is, let me offer a modest suggestion to any reader who has influential access to the political process. Let's change the law.

- Let's uncouple Section 106 consultation from the National Register and the State Historic Preservation Officers. Let's require agencies simply to find and consult with concerned members of the public—including "experts," of course, but not limited to them—about the impacts of agency actions on whatever aspects of the environment people are concerned about.

- Let's replace the Advisory Council on Historic Preservation, and the Council on Environmental Quality, with an oversight and rulemaking agency that promotes, insists on, and facilitates true consultation, negotiation, and resolution of disputes about environmental impacts and their mitigation.

- Let's require that analyses of environmental (including, of course, cultural) impacts be done under the direction of objective organizations, rather than by the hirelings of those who want, and perhaps legitimately need, to change the environment. Let's set up systems to make such objective analyses happen, feeding their results in to fair, consultative systems of decision making.

If we did all this, I think we'd have a means of defining and dealing with impacts on the environment—including everyone's special places—in a much more sensible, balanced, efficient and responsible way than we have today. And it would be a simple enough system that books like this one would be unnecessary.

I don't for a moment expect such changes to take place, however, and since they won't, I hope this book will be helpful to anyone who has a special place that's under threat by the forces of change and development.

GOOD LUCK!

Appendix

Section 106 Memorandum of Agreement for the Broad Run Bridge

1.

**MEMORANDUM OF AGREEMENT
AMONG THE FEDERAL HIGHWAY ADMINISTRATION, THE VIRGINIA
DEPARTMENT OF TRANSPORTATION
THE VIRGINIA STATE HISTORIC PRESERVATION OFFICER
AND THE
ADVISORY COUNCIL ON HISTORIC PRESERVATION
REGARDING THE ROUTE 15/29 SOUTH BOUND LANE BRIDGE DECK
REPLACEMENT OVER BROAD RUN, PRINCE WILLIAM COUNTY, VIRGINIA**

WHEREAS, the Virginia Department of Transportation (VDOT) proposes to replace the Route 15/29 south bound lane bridge deck over Broad Run Prince William County, Virginia (VDOT Project No. 0015-076-1115, PE101; PPMS 55581; VDHR File No. 2004-0634), hereinafter referred to as the Project; and

WHEREAS, the VDOT anticipates receiving Federal financial assistance for the Project from the Federal Highway Administration (FHWA); and

WHEREAS FHWA determined that the Project would not adversely affect the Buckland Historic District (076-0113) and the Buckland Mills Battlefield (Battlefield. 030-5152), properties listed in or determined eligible for listing in the National Register of Historic Places (Attachments A and B), and requested that the Advisory Council on Historic Preservation (ACHP) review the finding in accordance with 36 CFR 800.5(c)(2)(i), by letter dated September 16, 2005; and

WHEREAS the ACHP responded by letter dated October 18, 2005, in accordance with 36 CFR 800.5(c)(3)(i), stating that the Project may adversely affect historic properties and result in cumulative impacts to historic properties; and

WHEREAS VDOT and FHWA have considered alternative concepts for the undertaking and have developed an alternative that reduces the effects of the undertaking on historic properties; and

WHEREAS FHWA has continued to consult with the Virginia Department of Transportation, the Virginia State Historic Preservation Officer (SHPO), the Buckland Preservation Society (Society), the American Battlefield Protection Program of the National Park Service (ABPP), the National Trust for Historic Preservation, the Piedmont Environmental Council , the Civil War Preservation Trust, the Manassas National Battlefield Park, the County of Prince William, and the ACHP to resolve concerns regarding the effect of the Project on historic properties; and

WHEREAS the Society is developing a master plan for the preservation of the Buckland Historic District and Buckland Mills Battlefield; and

APPENDIX

Memorandum of Agreement
Route 15/29 South Bound Lane Bridge Deck Replacement

2.

WHEREAS FHWA has invited all the above parties to sign or concur in this Memorandum of Agreement (MOA); and

NOW, THEREFORE, the parties to this MOA agree that upon FHWA's decision to proceed with the Project, FHWA shall ensure that the following stipulations are implemented in order to take into account the effects of the Project on historic properties, and that these stipulations shall govern the Project and all of its parts until this MOA expires or is terminated.

Stipulations

FHWA shall ensure that the following stipulations are implemented:

I. Design and Construction

  a. VDOT shall design and construct the Project in accordance with plans and specifications that are strictly in accordance with "Alternative D" as defined conceptually in the document entitled "Route 15/29 SBL Bridge Deck Replacement" distributed at the meeting of consulting parties held May 16, 2006 at Manassas National Battlefield, and attached hereto as Attachment C, employing the Kansas 32-inch Corral Rail as described in Attachment C.
  b. VDOT shall afford the SHPO and Society an opportunity to review and comment on the plans and specifications at the Field Inspection, Constructability Review, and Final Submission stages of project development. If no comments are received from the SHPO and Society within 30 days of confirmed receipt, VDOT can assume concurrence. Should any party have questions about or comments on such plans and specifications, VDOT shall consult with that party, or if necessary with several or all consulting parties, to address such questions or comments.
  c. VDOT shall not disturb the ground outside the northern edge of the existing northern shoulder, nor permit such disturbance by its contractor(s), and shall limit construction activities beyond the edge of shoulder to that necessary for surface erosion and sediment control (e.g., silt fencing or straw bales) to comply with environmental standards. VDOT shall delineate this boundary in a manner that does not compromise the safe operation of Route 15/29.
  d. VDOT shall specify in the contract documents that contractor parking, storage, and staging areas between the Prince William/Fauquier County line and the intersection with Route 15 north in Prince William County are limited to the highway median and existing shoulder, and shall monitor contractor performance to ensure compliance.

e. Notwithstanding Stipulations 1.c and 1.d, above, VDOT may utilize areas outside of the defined limits for contractor parking, storage, and staging with the consent of the Society.
f. VDOT shall ensure that its contractor and project engineer are fully aware of and attentive to the terms of this agreement, and of the sensitivity of the area in which the project is implemented.
g. VDOT shall arrange for its contractor and project engineer to meet with representatives of the Society before construction begins to ensure a full mutual understanding of issues and concerns, and to facilitate the routine communication of project information and status as construction proceeds.

II. Archaeology

a. To avoid any inadvertent effects to archaeological sites presently covered by highway fill, VDOT shall limit excavation to no more than two feet below existing grade within 250 feet of the existing bridge. Within 50 feet of the existing bridge, VDOT may excavate to the bottom of the existing footing, approximately 15 feet below existing grade.
b. VDOT shall provide the Society with copies of any documentary information in its possession concerning the locations and character of buildings, structures, and landscape features demolished or otherwise destroyed when VDOT acquired right-of-way through Buckland in 1953.
c. In the event that a previously unidentified archaeological site is discovered once construction of the project has begun, VDOT, in accordance with Section 107.14(d) of the VDOT's *Road and Bridge Specifications,* shall require the construction contractor to halt all construction work involving subsurface disturbance in the area of the resource and in surrounding areas where additional subsurface remains can reasonably be expected to occur. Work in all other areas of the project may continue. The FHWA, in cooperation with VDOT, shall then address the discovery in accordance with the process described at 36 CFR 800.13(b)(3).

III. Planning

The Society shall invite VDOT's Northern Virginia and Culpeper District Administrators, and the Northern Virginia and Culpeper members of the Commonwealth Transportation Board to participate in the Society's master planning efforts. VDOT's Northern Virginia and Culpeper District administrators, or their designee(s), will participate in the Society's master planning efforts to the extent practicable.

APPENDIX

Memorandum of Agreement
Route 15/29 South Bound Lane Bridge Deck Replacement

IV. Dispute Resolution

   a. Should any signatory or concurring party to this MOA object in writing to the VDOT or the FHWA regarding any plans or products prepared pursuant to this MOA, within 30 days of confirmed receipt, or should any signatory or concurring party to this MOA object in writing to the VDOT or the FHWA regarding the manner in which measures stipulated in this MOA are being implemented, the VDOT or the FHWA, whichever is responsible for the plan, product, or measure, shall consult with the objecting party to resolve the objection. If the FHWA determines that the objection cannot be resolved through such consultation, the FHWA or the VDOT, as appropriate, shall consult with the signatories to this MOA to resolve the objection. If the FHWA then determines that the objection cannot be resolved through consultation, the FHWA shall forward all documentation relevant to the objection to the ACHP, including the FHWA's proposed response to the objection.
   b. Within thirty (30) days after receipt of all pertinent documentation, the ACHP shall exercise one of the following options:
      i. Advise the FHWA that the ACHP concurs in the FHWA's proposed response to the objection, whereupon the FHWA shall respond to the objection accordingly; or
      ii. Provide the FHWA with recommendations, which the FHWA shall take into account in reaching a final decision regarding its response to the objection; or
      iii. Notify the FHWA that the objection shall be referred for comment pursuant to 36 CFR 800.7(a)(4), and proceed to refer the objection and comment. The FHWA shall take the resulting comment into account in accordance with 36 CFR 800.7(c)(4).
   c. Should the ACHP not exercise one of the above options within thirty (30) days after receipt of all pertinent documentation, the FHWA may assume the ACHP's concurrence in its proposed response to the objection. The FHWA shall take into account any ACHP recommendation or comment provided in accordance with this stipulation with reference only to the subject of the objection; the FHWA's responsibility to carry out all actions under this MOA that are not the subjects of the objection shall remain unchanged.

V. Changes

VDOT shall not alter the geometrics or appearance of the bridge, or cause ground disturbance beyond that specified in the final plans, without first affording the SHPO and Society the opportunity to review the proposed change and determine whether it will require that revisions be made in this MOA. If revisions are needed, the parties to

Memorandum of Agreement
Route 15/29 South Bound Lane Bridge Deck Replacement

5.

this MOA may amend this MOA. Such amendment shall go into effect upon the written agreement of the signatories.

VI. Duration

Unless amended in writing by its signatories to prescribe a different date, this MOA shall continue in full force and effect until its stipulations have been carried out , or until December 31, 2011, whichever is earlier. If the terms of this agreement have not been carried out by December 31, 2011, VDOT shall consult the parties to this agreement to determine the appropriate course of action..

Execution of this MOA by the FHWA, the VDOT, the SHPO, and the ACHP, and implementation of its terms, evidence that FHWA has taken into account the ACHP's opinion in accordance with 36 CFR 800.5(c)(3)(ii)(A) and that FHWA has taken into account the effects of the Project on historic properties.

FEDERAL HIGHWAY ADMINISTRATION

By: _____ Date: 11/13/2006

fa: Roberto Fonseca-Martinez, Virginia Division Administrator

VIRGINIA STATE HISTORIC PRESERVATION OFFICER

By: _____ Date: 11/13/06

Kathleen S. Kilpatrick

VIRGINIA DEPARTMENT OF TRANSPORTATION

By: _____ Date: 11-13-06

Earl T. Robb, Environmental Division Administrator

APPENDIX

Memorandum of Agreement
Route 15/29 South Bound Lane Bridge Deck Replacement

6.

ADVISORY COUNCIL ON HISTORIC PRESERVATION

By: *John W. Fowler*   Date: 12/16/06

John W. Fowler, Executive Director

Concur:

BUCKLAND PRESERVATION SOCIETY

By: *Linda L. Wright*   Date: 11/19, 2006

Linda L. Wright

Resources

Here are some things to do and things to get, in preparation for using Section 106 to help save a special place.

Read the regulations. They're pretty dry (though some people actually find a certain quirky pleasure in parsing them), but you ought to know what they say, and think about it. The 106 regulations—36 CFR 800—are at *http://www.achp.gov/regs-rev04.pdf*, the NEPA regulations are at *http://www.nepa.gov/nepa/regs/ceq/toc_ceq.htm*, and you can find others using any good search engine. The National Park Service's cultural resources website—*www.cr.nps.gov*—has a pretty comprehensive set of links. Some of my books, more technical than this one, discuss many of the pertinent regulations in detail (see *www.lcoastpress.com* and *www.altamirapress.com*).

Find out about, and meet, your State Historic Preservation Officer (SHPO). Go through the SHPO's website if there is one (usually there is). If you can't find it any other way, try searching for "SHPO" and your state's name. The Advisory Council's website lists the SHPOs (*http://www.ncshpo.org/stateinfolist/fulllist.htm*), including email addresses, but usually not website URLs. See if you have mutual friends or interests. Call him up or drop her an email. Understand that the SHPO is a political creature; accept that and work with it.

Take a look at the Advisory Council on Historic Preservation's website, *www.achp.gov*, which contains examples of Section 106 cases (*http://www.achp.gov/casedigest.htm*), discussions of case law (*http://www.achp.gov/pubs-caselaw.html*), and a "citizen's guide" to Section 106 review (*http://www.achp.gov/citizensguide.html*). Find out what staff member deals with the agency or agencies you're concerned about. Start with the staff directory at *http://www.achp.gov/staff.htm*; call them up or drop them an email explaining (as briefly and clearly as you can) what you're concerned about, and see if they can help.

Resources

Contact the Federal Preservation Officer for the agency you're concerned about. Some FPOs are very dedicated and helpful; others are—well, not. But it's worth a try. They're listed, most with email addresses and phone numbers, at *http://www.achp.gov/fpo.html*.

Consider who your allies might be, and try to mobilize them. Don't neglect people with interests that may be different from but dovetail with yours. Maybe you're a serious property rights advocate with little use for tree-hugging conservationists—or vice-versa—but those people on the dark side may have their own reasons for keeping your special place safe, and remember: the enemy of your enemy is your friend. Among others, think about:

- Indian tribes and other indigenous groups, especially if your special place may be special to them too (assuming, of course, that you're not a tribe yourself, in which case, think about *other* tribes and groups other than tribes). Some tribes have Tribal Historic Preservation Officers; a list with contact information can be found at *http://www.achp.gov/thpo.html*. Other tribes have cultural offices, cultural committees, museums, NAGPRA coordinators, and other entities that may be interested and willing to help. Many tribes have websites; *http://www.nativeculturelinks.com/nations.html* provides what appears to be a good, up-to-date set of links.
- Neighborhood organizations, church groups, civic and fraternal groups.
- Local historical, architectural, or archaeological societies.
- The National Trust for Historic Preservation (*http://www.nationaltrust.org*).
- Local and statewide historic preservation organizations. See *http://www.preservenet.cornell.edu/links.html#statewidenonprofits* and *http://www.preservenet.cornell.edu/links.html#citywide*. The National Trust's regional office for your region may be able to help you network. See *http://www.nationaltrust.org/regional_offices/index.html*.
- National, state, and local environmental groups. Try *http://www.environmentaldirectory.net*.
- Property owners.

- Property rights advocates. A good place to start is *http://www.landrights.org/*.
- Civil rights organizations, particularly if you're an ethnic minority or a low-income person, and think your environment is being screwed up unjustly.
- Children, elderly people, others with time on their hands and the ability to command a sympathetic hearing.

Learn about the environment within which your special place lies, and about its history, prehistory, and culture. There may be a bigger entity—an ethnic neighborhood, a valley, a mountain range—that includes your special place but has characteristics that make it easier to argue for its preservation, or easier to attract allies. And the more you know about your place and its surroundings, the better the case you're going to be able to make for it, and the more circles you can talk around the opposition.

Learn the language. Pages 222–234 of this book provide a glossary of some of the weird terms we use in Section 106 practice. The more familiar you can get with what they mean—and what they don't mean, and what they don't mean but people think they mean—the better. There are also likely to be special terms that 106 and "CRM" practitioners use in your particular area; it's wise to try to get a handle on them, too.

Build a website, create a blog, scan the Web for lists and chat groups whose participants may be interested.

Look into state and local law, which may turn out to be more helpful to you than Section 106. See *http://www.ncsl.org/programs/arts/statehist.htm* for a starting point.

Talk with a lawyer, but don't assume that he or she is an expert unless you have good reason for thinking so. Most are specialists, and all are human, whether they think so or not. Understand that most lawyers, when they hear the words "historic preservation," think of state and local laws dealing with formally designated local historic landmark buildings, building codes, tax credits, and the like. See *http://www.legalmatch.com/law-library/article/historic-preservation-lawyers.html* for a discouraging example of this bias. If you're trying to use Section 106, you'll have to make this very clear to any lawyer you talk with, and probably give them the code citation (16 U.S.C. 470f, and 36 CFR 800 for the regulations).

Resources

Get in touch with me. I do as much pro bono work as I can, but understand that I'm just one guy, and have to work for a living. I'll advise you if I can. My email is *tfking106@aol.com*. Or take one of my classes, given through SWCA Environmental Consultants; see *http://www.swca.com/training/descriptions*.

Glossary

Not all these terms are actually used in this book, and some that are, are used only in passing. If you get involved in Section 106 review, however, you're sure to run into a lot of them.

36 CFR 60. Title 36, Part 60 of the Code of Federal Regulations; National Park Service regulations governing the National Register of Historic Places.

36 CFR 63. Title 36, Part 63 of the Code of Federal Regulations. Another National Park Service regulation, about determining eligibility for the National Register. Out of date and substantially inconsistent with 36 CFR 800, but still (unfortunately) on the books due to inattention, laziness, and fear of the public on the part of the Park Service.

36 CFR 800. Title 36, Part 800 of the Code of Federal Regulations. The regulations of the Advisory Council on Historic Preservation for implementing Section 106 of the National Historic Preservation Act (NHPA).

40 CFR 1500-1508. Title 40, Parts 1500 through 1508. The regulations of the Council on Environmental Quality governing compliance with the procedural requirements of the National Environmental Policy Act (NEPA).

Abandoned Shipwrecks Act. A federal law (43 U.S.C. 2101–2106) establishing federal ownership of abandoned shipwrecks and transferring management authority over them to the states.

Advisory Council on Historic Preservation (ACHP, Advisory Council, Council). The independent federal agency that oversees and issues regulations for Section 106 review.

Administrative Procedures Act. A federal law (5 U.S.C. 511–599) that governs how federal agencies must administer their programs and activities; it governs how agencies issue regulations, how they share information with the public, conduct meetings, and so on.

Admiralty law. Law governing ships and shipping.

Glossary

Anthropology. The academic discipline that studies human culture, human society, and human biology, past and present. One of the disciplines from which many people who do historic preservation and cultural resource management are drawn.

Architectural history. The academic discipline that studies the history of architecture and building design, including vernacular architecture. One of the disciplines from which many people who do historic preservation and cultural resource management are drawn.

Archaeological site. From an archaeological standpoint, any place of past human activity where archaeological research may be done. A place an archaeologist digs, or might like to dig.

Archaeology. The academic discipline that studies the human past. One of the disciplines from which many people who do historic preservation and cultural resource management are drawn.

Architecture. The art and science of constructing buildings and other structures. One of the disciplines from which many people who do historic preservation and cultural resource management are drawn.

Area of potential effects (APE). According to the Section 106 regulations, the geographic area or areas where a project may have effects on historic properties, if any turn out to be there.

Building. According to the National Register of Historic Places, "a structure created to shelter any form of human activity, such as a house, barn, church, hotel, or similar structure" (36 CFR 60.3(a)).

CA, Comprehensive Agreement under the Native American Graves Protection and Repatriation Act (NAGPRA). An agreement about how an agency or other party and an Indian tribe or Native Hawaiian group will interact in dealing with ancestral human remains and Native American cultural items.

Case law. The corpus of decisions in court cases that provides a basis for interpreting a statute.

Categorical exclusion. A type of project that an agency determines has so little potential for a significant effect on the quality of the human environment that little or nothing needs to be done to analyze its impacts under NEPA. Variously called "CX," "CE," "CatEx," and other things by different agencies.

Class *n* or Phase *n* survey. May mean a variety of things. State Historic Preservation Officers (SHPOs) and others often adopt standard approaches to historic property identification which feature different levels of land inspection that are assigned "class" or "phase" designations. These standards are typically developed by archaeologists, and reflect archaeological thinking.

Consultation. According to the Section 106 regulations (36 CFR 800.16(f)), "the process of seeking, discussing, and considering the views of other participants, and, where feasible, seeking agreement with them regarding matters arising in the section 106 process."

Consulting parties. Those who consult about a project and its effects under Section 106, generally including at least the responsible federal agency and the SHPO, and often involving others, including concerned citizens.

Council on Environmental Quality. The oversight/rulemaking body for NEPA, lodged in the Executive Office of the President.

Criteria of Adverse Effect. In the Section 106 regulations, a single criterion and a list of examples. A project has an adverse effect when it may damage the integrity of those aspects of a property that make it eligible for the National Register. Examples of adverse effect include destroying the property, introducing things into its environment that aren't consistent with it, and transferring it out of federal ownership.

Cultural resource. A term that means many different things to different people, but that tends to be used very authoritatively by many people who work with NHPA. Archaeologists often use "cultural resource" to mean "archaeological site." People with a somewhat more interdisciplinary point of view may use it as a synonym for "historic property." Others recognize that other laws require attention to other aspects of the environment, and use it to embrace culturally important plants, animals, even the night sky. Others use it to mean artifacts, and others refer to libraries and light opera companies as "cultural resources."

Cultural resource management. Another ill-defined term. Generally, the practice of doing things with, to, or about "cultural resources," whatever that term means to the person using it. Often used as a sort of synonym for "historic preservation," particularly by archaeologists.

Culture. Generally understood in the historic preservation community to mean "the traditions, beliefs, practices, lifeways, arts, crafts, and social institutions of any

Glossary

community, be it an Indian tribe, a local ethnic group, or the people of the nation as a whole" (National Register Bulletin 38), though there are many more complex definitions.

District. According to the National Register, "a geographically definable area, urban or rural, possessing a significant concentration, linkage, or continuity of sites, buildings, structures, or objects united by past events or aesthetically by plan or physical development" (36 CFR 60.3(d))—for example, a neighborhood made up of many houses, streets, the corner store, and so on, or a landscape containing multiple sites or other locations having cultural significance.

EA, environmental assessment. Under NEPA, done to determine whether a given action may significantly affect the quality of the human environment and hence requires an environmental impact statement.

Effect. *See* Impact.

EIS, environmental impact statement. Under NEPA, the "detailed statement" of the environmental impacts of a major federal action significantly affecting the quality of the human environment.

Eligible, eligibility. As used in Section 106 review, eligibility for inclusion in the National Register. To be eligible, a place must meet standards generally called "the National Register criteria," which are published at 36 CFR 60.4.

Engineering. The design, manufacture, and operation of machines, structures, systems, and processes, usually applying scientific and mathematical principles.

Ethnography. Anthropological study of a living society.

Executive order. An order issued by a chief executive (in the U.S. government, the president) to executive branch agencies about how they are to do something—usually carry out some legally mandated function.

FACA, Federal Advisory Committee Act. Public Law 92-463, 5 U.S.C., App, a federal law governing how agencies involve non-governmental parties in their decision-making. Regulations at 41 CFR Parts 101–6 and 102–3

Facade. The face(s) or front(s) of a building, usually the most (or only) decorated part(s).

Federal agency. An agency of the United States government, such as the Department of Housing and Urban Development or the Federal Deposit Insurance Corporation.

Federal Register. Daily federal government publication containing notices of pending and accomplished agency actions such as projects initiated, regulations issued in draft or final form, and environmental impact statements undertaken.

Fenestration. The design or character of windows and sometimes other openings in a building.

Flag and avoid. Marking the boundaries of a historic property (or anything else) and trying to develop one's project around it.

FONSI, finding of no significant impact. Under NEPA, the end result of an environmental assessment where it is found that the project won't significantly affect the quality of the human environment.

Footprint. The location where a project will actually be built or otherwise placed.

Freedom of Information Act (FOIA). A law, 5 U.S.C. 552 (codified together with the Administrative Procedures Act), requiring that agencies provide information upon request about their activities, including documents received or created in the course of reaching a decision, with various exceptions and subject to a variety of rules.

Government agency. As used in this book, a department, bureau, or other administrative subdivision of any kind of government—federal, tribal, state, local.

Guideline or guidance. Generally non-binding direction from an agency (or other authoritative body) about how something ought to be done. Not regulatory, but may support a regulation.

HABS, HAER, HALS, or Historic American Buildings Survey, Historic American Engineering Record, Historic American Landscape Survey. NPS programs that document different kinds of historic properties.

Historic. Having something to do with history, or "prehistory," the period before written records were kept in an area.

Historic or historical architecture. Buildings and other structures, and their components, that have some kind of historical value that relates to their architectural characteristics. Also the practice of architecture working with historic structures, as in their restoration and rehabilitation.

Historic preservation. Depending on context, this term can mean actually physically preserving something historic like a building or site, or a much broader set of

Glossary

activities that includes finding historic places, documenting them, fixing them up ("rehabilitating" them), restoring them, managing them, even just recording them somehow before they're destroyed. In Section 106 practice, the broad meaning is usually the one used.

Historic property. According to the National Historic Preservation Act, "district, site, building, structure, or object included in or eligible for the National Register."

Historic resource. As used in NHPA, has the same meaning as "historic property."

History. The past, sometimes limited to the human past since the advent of writing in an area. One of the disciplines from which many people who do historic preservation and cultural resource management are drawn.

Identification effort. Under the Section 106 regulations, the effort an agency makes to identify historic properties subject to effect by its undertaking. The agency is required to make a "reasonable and good faith effort" to identify such properties.

Impact. Under NHPA and NEPA, generally means whatever bad things a project will do to something. "Impact" and "effect" are interchangeable terms. Impacts include:

Direct impacts: Things that happen at or close to the project site, more or less at the same time as the project.

Indirect impacts: Things that happen at a distance from the project in time and/or space.

Cumulative impacts: The impacts of the project when added to the impacts of everything else affecting the general area—past actions, present actions, reasonably foreseeable future actions, regardless of who's doing the acting. Patterns of change in an area, to which the project under review makes some kind of contribution.

There are many specific types of impact, such as:

Auditory impact: Making noise.

Economic impact: Causing a change in the economy of a town, neighborhood, or other area.

Land use impact: Causing a change in the way land is used.

Olfactory impact: Causing a smell.

Physical impact: Knocking something down, bulldozing it, blowing it up.

Social impact: Changing something in the society within which something like a historic property exists or has value.

Traffic impact: Altering the volume or pattern of traffic flow through an area.

Visual impact: Causing some kind of change that can be seen from a historic property, or that alters the view of a historic property.

Indian tribe. Variously defined, but under NHPA, an "Indian tribe (sic), band, nation, or other organized group or community, including a Native village, Regional Corporation or Village Corporation . . . , which is recognized as eligible for the special programs and services provided by the United States to Indians because of their status as Indians" (16 U.S.C. 470w(4)). Often used less formally to refer to groups that are ethnically Native American but not formally recognized as such by the government.

Indian treaty. A written agreement between an Indian tribe and the U.S. government (or in some cases, a predecessor government such as the British Crown), usually ceding tribal land in return for peace, a reservation, and various more or less specified (though not always delivered) benefits.

Injunction. In legal parlance, a court order telling someone not to do something—for example, telling a project proponent not to start a project until Section 106 has been complied with.

Keeper. The Keeper of the National Register, a National Park Service official who oversees the National Register of Historic Places.

Landscape. Landscapes can be historic properties, and generally are broken down into three categories:

Designed landscape: A landscape intentionally designed as such, usually by a landscape architect. Parks, parkways, and botanical gardens are examples.

Rural historic landscape: A landscape that has developed over time to reflect rural ways of life—for example, an Amish farm landscape.

Cultural landscape: Sometimes used as a broad term embracing a range of landscape types, other times to refer to a landscape that has some kind of special cultural value, such as a battlefield or a landscape associated with the traditions of an Indian tribe or other community.

Glossary

Landscape architecture. The design of designed landscapes. One of the disciplines from which many people who do historic preservation and cultural resource management are drawn.

Landscape history. The study of the development of a landscape or landscapes, or of the process of landscape design. One of the disciplines from which many people who do historic preservation and cultural resource management are drawn.

License. As used in Section 106 and NEPA practice, allowing another party to do something, whether the allowance is technically referred to as a license, a permit, an easement, a right-of-way, or something else. Government and non-government actions "licensed" by federal agencies are subject to review under Section 106 and NEPA.

Lithic. Having to do with stone. Archaeologists refer to things like spear points as "lithic artifacts."

Memorandum of agreement (MOA). The document executed by consulting parties under Section 106 that stipulates how the effects of a project will be "resolved."

Midden. In archaeological parlance, the debris making up much of many archaeological sites. Essentially, the garbage.

NAGPRA, Native American Graves Protection and Repatriation Act. Federal law (25 U.S.C. Chap. 32) requiring that ancestral Native American human remains and cultural items be repatriated to tribes and Native Hawaiian groups.

National Conference of State Historic Preservation Officers. A membership organization open only to SHPOs, which works to advance SHPO interests and generally supports historic preservation initiatives at the federal level.

National Historic Landmark (NHL). A place designated by the Department of the Interior (National Park Service) under the Historic Sites Act of 1935 (16 U.S.C. 461–467), a predecessor to NHPA that directed NPS to identify and promote the preservation of places significant in the interpretation and commemoration of the nation's history. NHLs are automatically included in the National Register.

National Register of Historic Places. A list of known places in the U.S. and a few other jurisdictions that have been judged by the National Park Service to be significant in American history, archaeology, architecture, engineering, and/or culture. The

Register is maintained by the National Park Service, which has a National Register Division (whose actual name changes from time to time) that takes care of it.

National Register Criteria. The formal criteria used to judge whether a place is eligible for the National Register, published in regulation at 36 CFR 60.4 and the subject of extensive NPS guidance.

Native Hawaiian. According to NHPA, "any individual who is a descendant of the aboriginal people who, prior to 1778, occupied and exercised sovereignty in the area that now constitutes the State of Hawaii" (16 U.S.C. 470w(17)).

NEPA. National Environmental Policy Act (42 U.S.C. 4321–4347).

NHPA. National Historic Preservation Act (16 U.S.C. 470).

Nomination. In NHPA parlance, usually refers to nominating something to the National Register.

NPS. National Park Service, an agency of the Department of the Interior. Besides managing national parks, NPS administers several "out-house" programs, including the National Register and a variety of other historic preservation programs.

Object. In National Register terms, "a material thing of functional, aesthetic, cultural, historical or scientific value that may be, by nature or design, movable yet related to a specific setting or environment" (36 CFR 60.3(j)). There's a more or less unstated rule that the object can't be too big; if you can walk away with it, it's probably not eligible for the Register.

PA, programmatic agreement. Under the Section 106 regulations, an agreement negotiated by an agency with the Advisory Council, SHPOs, and others that sets up a system for doing Section 106 review that is different from the standard system set forth in the regulations.

Petroglyph. A carving or other drawing cut, pecked, or scratched into a rock surface, usually by ancient people.

Phase *n* or Class *n* survey. *See* Class *n* or Phase *n* survey

Pictograph. A painting on a rock surface, usually by ancient people.

Place. As used in this book, any piece of real estate (or sometimes non-real estate, like a ship) that someone thinks ought to be considered in planning, whether or not it's eligible for the National Register as a "historic property."

Glossary

POA, plan of action. Under NAGPRA, a plan developed in consultation with a tribe to govern how to handle the discovery of human remains or Native American cultural items.

Pro bono. For free. Many, if not most, lawyers do a certain amount of pro bono work for causes they or their firms think are righteous, and some consultants do it too; I do more than is good for me.

Project. As used in this book, anything that somebody sets out to do—build a dam, replace a building, put in a rail line. Where a federal agency is involved, the project becomes a federal undertaking (*see* "undertaking").

Public comment. Comments on a project and its effects by members of the public, often in response to an agency's request. Some agencies routinely ignore such comments once they have received them, or give only lip service to their consideration. Some think that soliciting public comment is all they need to do to involve the public, and under NEPA they are not completely wrong.

Public hearing. A particularly formal public meeting, with an agenda that is usually very hierarchically organized. An old tradition in American politics, which today largely serves as a substitute for real public involvement.

Public involvement. Involving the public in some interactive way in project planning, through consultations, meetings, workshops, and the like—but many agencies confuse it with public notice or a public meeting.

Public meeting. A meeting with the public, often (unfortunately) designed to do nothing but satisfy some agency-perceived legal requirement. Public meetings can be important parts of public involvement, though, especially when they are interactive and consultative.

Public notice. Notifying the public of a proposed action, usually by publishing a notice in the local newspaper or in the Federal Register. Often a substitute for actually involving the public.

Public participation. Synonymous with "public involvement."

Reconnaissance. A more or less quick but systematic look at a project's area of potential effects to get an idea of what kinds of historic properties may be there. Usually (if well done) coupled with background research and consultation.

Record of decision (ROD). A document describing and rationalizing a decision made by an agency on a project after an environmental impact statement has been completed.

Regulation. Direction issued by an agency authorized by law to do so, that tells others how to carry out some action required or provided for by law. Codified in the Code of Federal Regulations (CFR).

Scope of work (SOW). Description of the work to be done on some aspect of a project, such as a survey to identify historic properties. Usually bid on by prospective contractors, or negotiated once the contract is awarded.

Secretary. The head of an executive department, a member of the president's cabinet. In regulations and other literature surrounding Section 106 review, almost invariably means the Secretary of the Interior.

Section 106. 16 USC 470f. The section of NHPA requiring federal agencies to "take into account" the effects of their actions on historic properties, and give the Advisory Council on Historic Preservation a "reasonable opportunity to comment" on such actions. The major statutory basis for the Section 106 process.

Section 106 process. The process of federal project review set out in the regulations for implementing Section 106 (36 CFR 800).

Section 110. 16 U.S.C. 470j. A section of NHPA that sets forth a wide range of federal agency responsibilities with regard to historic places, including their identification, management, adaptive use, and documentation.

Shard, sherd, potsherd. In archaeological parlance, a fragment of something like a pot, though "shard" is more often used with reference to glass and glassy material. Potsherds are often the major surface signs of an archaeological site.

SHPO. *See* State Historic Preservation Officer.

Site. In National Register terms, "the location of a significant event, a prehistoric or historic occupation or activity, or a building or structure, whether standing, ruined, or vanished, where the location itself maintains historical or archeological value regardless of the value of any existing structure" (36 CFR 60.3(l))—for example, an archaeological site, the site of a famous murder, or a site held by a tribe to have special religio-cultural value.

Standards. A particularly directive form of agency guideline, and sometimes embedded in regulation. A standard typically has to be met in order for something to be

Glossary

recognized as adequate. For instance, an archaeologist who doesn't meet the Secretary of the Interior's personnel qualification standards for archaeology isn't usually qualified to receive a federal grant or permit to do archaeology.

State Historic Preservation Officer (SHPO). The state official, designated by the governor, who administers many programs under the National Historic Preservation Act in his or her state. A very important player in the Section 106 process, who must be consulted at each step in the process.

Structure. According to the National Register, "a work made up of interdependent and interrelated parts in a definite pattern of organization. Constructed by man, it is often an engineering project large in scale" (36 CFR 60.3(p)). In practice, Register people tend to distinguish between buildings—designed to shelter human activities—and structures that aren't designed for such purposes. Bridges, sewer lines, dockyard cranes, and ships are examples of structures that are not regarded as buildings. Obviously, some structures (such as ships) that are not buildings do shelter human activities, so the distinction between "building" and "structure" is not always clear-cut.

Summary judgment. Quick disposal of a court case where the court determines that there are no genuine issues of fact to be decided.

Survey. In Section 106 practice, fieldwork and background research to identify historic properties. May include a broad range of activities: background research, consultation with knowledgeable people, inspection of the ground by archaeologists, of buildings and structures by architectural historians, oral historical studies, ethnographic studies, landscape studies, and so on. Often used simply to refer to sending archaeologists out to look closely at the ground.

Take into account. In Section 106 practice, consider the effects of an action and see what can be done to avoid, reduce, or mitigate them. Section 106 requires federal agencies to take into account the effects of their actions.

TCP, traditional cultural property. A place that is important to a community for the role it plays in the group's culture or identity. A TCP may be eligible for the National Register if it meets one or more of the Register's criteria and has integrity in the eyes of those who value it.

Undertaking. In Section 106 jargon, something a federal agency undertakes. An agency may undertake to build a road, license a power plant, manage a park, provide financial assistance to a low-income housing provider, and so on.

UNESCO. United Nations Educational, Scientific, and Cultural Organization.

Vernacular architecture. Construction of buildings and other structures by people not formally trained in architecture, usually of local materials, usually of a functional style, with the designer usually unknown. Examples include many barns, sheds, cabins.

Windshield survey. Driving through an area to find and look at buildings or other structures. Often done by architectural historians as part of a Section 106 identification effort.

Index

16 USC 470, 23
16 USC 470f, 24, 222
36 CFR 60, 33, 97, 126, 129, 148, 218
36 CFR 63, 156
36 CFR 68, 174
36 CFR 800, 25, 33, 47, 56, 82–84, 87, 89, 101, 102, 110, 163, 174, 181, 218, 222
40 CFR 1500–1508, 33, 60, 158, 218

A

Abandoned Shipwrecks Act, 35
Administrative Procedures Act (APA), 92
Admiralty Law, 35
Advisory Council on Historic Preservation (ACHP) 9, 25, 26, 33, 36, 47–49, 59, 77, 93–94, 102, 119, 121, 122, 126, 127, 156, 162, 172, 175, 176, 178, 180–183, 187, 190, 192, 194, 196–202, 206, 211, 218,
  described, 47–48
  comment by, 199–201
  what impresses, 198–201
Agriculture, U.S. Department of. *See* U.S. Department of Agriculture
Air Force, U.S. *See* U.S. Air Force
Alternatives, 38, 51, 66, 67, 106, 120, 147, 167, 178, 182, 185, 187, 188, 198, 202
American Battlefield Preservation Program, 94, 121–122, 178, 194
American Land Rights Association, 55
American Mining Association, 53
Archaeological Data Preservation Act, 69
Archaeological Resources Protection Act (ARPA), 118
Archaeological survey, 97, 99, 100, 105–107, 114–115, 121
Archaeology, archaeological, 20, 30, 52, 54, 56, 58, 62, 65, 66, 67, 68, 69, 113, 115, 122, 135–136, 147, 151, 152, 158–159, 165, 167–168, 172, 174–175, 177–178, 184, 185, 188, 189, 192, 193, 210
Architect/Engineering/Planning firms, 50–51, 63, 69
Architecture, architectural, 52, 97, 110–111, 115, 150, 153, 125, 129, 133, 136, 138–139, 140, 144, 150, 170, 185, 188–190, 210
Area of potential effects (APE), 57, 98, 102–107, 109, 110, 115, 119, 121, 126, 140–141, 159, 161
Army, U.S. *See* U.S. Army
Audubon Society, 78
Automated teller machine (ATM), 44

B

Babbitt, Bruce, 206
Bias, 63–65

Bishops Run, 208
Block Grant, Community, 75
Bonaparte, Napoleon, 71
Bonnichsen v. United States, 92–93
Bridge, Broad Run, 71–72, 93, 121, 158, 177–178, 193–195, 212–217
Bridge, truss, 133, 167
Buckland, 20, 31, 71–72, 93–94, 121–122, 158, 177–178, 193–195, 212–217
Buckland Mills, Battle of, Battlefield, 20, 71, 131, 158, 177–178, 194–195, 208, 212–216
Buckland Preservation Society (BPS), 72, 93–94, 121–122, 158–159, 177–178, 194–195, 207–209, 212–216
Bureau of Land Management (BLM) 15, 26, 40, 44, 55, 203, 205–206
Bush, George W., 206

C

Cabin, Dog-Trot, 20
Cabrillo College, 30
California, 15, 21, 30, 32, 34, 36, 58, 131, 166, 205–207
Canada, 205, 207
Capital, architect of, 48
Case law, 34, 92–93, 108, 209
Categorical exclusion (CX, Catex), 60, 85, 120, 176–177
Chattanooga, Tennessee, 27
Choctaw tribe, 132
Civil Rights Act, 33, 220
Clean Air Act, 45
Clean Water Act, Section 404 of, 28, 31, 44, 203–204, 208
Clearance by SHPO, 115–117, 182–183
Clinton, President Bill, 33, 206
Coalition of 9/11 Families, 17, 126
Code of Federal Regulations (CFR) 25, 33, 47, 55
Congressional Cemetery, 132
Consultation in Section 106 review, 19, 45, 49, 58, 67, 83–92, 95, 98, 123, 127, 129, 143, 154, 160, 162, 167, 172, 178–183, 185–186, 188, 193, 196–201, 203, 207–208
Consultation, common errors in, 185–189
Consultation, government-to-government, 108
Consulting parties, 57–68, 84–85, 88–93, 95, 108, 110, 116, 119, 123, 126, 127, 128, 135, 137, 142, 154, 155, 157, 160–162, 167, 172, 174, 175, 181, 183, 191, 196, 200, 201, 203, 205
Coastal Zone Management Act, 45
Coast Guard. *See* U.S. Coast Guard
Constitution, U.S. *See* U.S. Constitution

Conventions, UNESCO, 36–37
Corps of Engineers, U.S. Army. *See* U.S. Army Corps of Engineers
Council on Environmental Quality (CEQ), 33, 48, 60, 69, 211
Court, federal, district of Oregon, 92–93
Court, going to, 75–76, 102, 103, 191, 192, 208
Court, military, 34
Court of Appeals, Ninth Circuit, 34, 209
Court of Appeals, Tenth Circuit, 34
Court, District of New Mexico, 34
Court, Northern District of California, 34
Court, state, 34
Court, tribal, 34
Court, Supreme, of U.S., 34
Crozet, Claudius, 71
Cultural resource management (CRM), 9, 52, 57, 60, 64, 65, 69, 71, 169, 177, 189
   CRM consultants/firms: characteristics of, 52, 76–77, 105, 107, 169, 177, 210
Cultural survival, 55
Cumulative effect, 104, 121–122, 124, 164, 177–178, 194–195, 208
Custer, George Armstrong, 71

D
Defense, Department of. *See* U.S. Department of Defense
Delay, power of, 18–19, 24, 81, 98, 117, 135, 154–155
Dixon, Harold, 91
Document and destroy, 65–66, 139, 147
Dorochoff, Nicholas, 88, 195
Drake, Francis, 20
Dripping Springs Ranch, 88
Dumb responses, 113–114

E
Earthjustice, 55
East Fork Ranch 20
Effect determination, 58, 139, 124,
Endangered Species Act, 49, 51
Energy, Department of. *See* U.S. Department of Energy
Environmental assessment (EA), 60, 120, 158, 176–177, 192, 205,
Environmental Defense, 54
Environmental impact assessment firms, 51–52, 63, 69, 76, 187
Environmental impact statement (EIS), 60, 69, 120, 158, 176, 193
Environmental justice, 33, 92
Environmental Protection Agency (EPA), 41, 44, 45, 48–49
Executive Office of the President, 60
Executive Orders, 32–33, 92
   Executive Order 12898, 33, 92
   Executive Order 13352, 92

F
Farm Service Agency (FSA), 28
Federal agencies
   abuse of responsibilities by, 61–70, 81–92, 99–101, 107–110, 112–117, 121, 140–154, 182–185

agreements among, and with others, 35–36
discussed, categorized, 26–28
involvement in projects, 28–29, 74–75, 123–124
must respond to ACHP comment, 200
procedures (guidelines, manuals, etc.), internal, 35, 85, 158,
as project overseers, 43–45, 79–81
as project proponent, 39, 74, 81
as project reviewers, 47–49
relationships among, 27–28, 175
responsibility for Section 106 review, 28, 40, 56, 67, 74, 116, 123–127, 162, 172, 180–182,
trust responsibility of toward tribes, 49
Federal Advisory Committees Act (FACA), 92
Federal Aviation Administration (FAA), 44
Federal Communications Commission (FCC), 26, 27, 43, 74, 202–203
Federal connection, importance of finding, 75–76
Federal Deposit Insurance Corporation (FDIC), 44
Federal Energy Regulatory Commission (FERC), 26, 27, 42, 43, 44
Federal Highway Administration (FHWA), 15, 28, 40, 44, 74–75, 93–94, 121, 175, 177, 193–194, 207–208
Federal law, reach of 12, 31–34, 38
   Relationships with state, tribal, local law, 37–38
Federal Preservation Officer (FPO), 93, 219
Finding of no significant impact (FONSI), 60, 120, 192–193
Fish and Wildlife Service, 26, 41, 49
Flag and avoid, 66–67, 96, 140, 184
Footprint fetishism, 65
Forest Glen, Maryland, 14–15
Forest Service, U.S.D.A., 15, 22, 35, 40, 43, 44, 168, 172
Form letters, 112–113
Fort Leavenworth, Kansas, 29

G
Gardner, Anthony, 126
General Services Administration (GSA), 41
Geothermal energy, 15
Gettysburg, 94
Glamis Imperial Mine, 205–207
Government review agencies, 45–49
Grandpa's homestead, 78, 136, 141–142, 144, 146, 150–151, 164–165, 167, 173–174,

H
Hawaii, 16
Hingham, Massachusetts, 16–17
Historic American Buildings Survey/Engineering Record/Landscape Survey (HABS/HAER/HALS), 184–185
Historic property, 13, 19, 29, 57, 58, 65, 66, 82–84, 89, 96, 99, 103, 109, 120–121, 158, 161, 164–165, 171–172, 176–177, 179, 204
Historic resource, 29
Homeland Security, Department of (DHS), 44
Hoopa tribe, 32
Housing and Urban Development, Department of (HUD), 26, 40, 41, 74–75, 165–166, 175, 200

INDEX

I
Idaho, 133
Identification of historic properties, 57, 67, 88, 96–122, 126,
Income tax credits for rehabilitation, 166
Indian tribe(s), tribal 13, 14, 15, 22, 46–47, 49, 55, 58, 84, 85, 79, 89, 92, 102, 105, 108, 109, 113, 115, 118, 123, 137, 145, 147, 152, 163, 165–166, 168, 171, 186, 191, 198, 201, 203, 205–207, 209, 219 *See also* Choctaw tribe; Hoopa tribe; Karuk tribe; Pit River tribe; Quechan tribe; Shasta tribe; Yurok tribe
Intergovernmental relations, 27–28
International agreements, 36–37

J
Japantown, San Jose, California 21
Journey through Hallowed Ground, 94
Judge, Administrative Law (ALJ), 34
Judge Advocate General (JAG), 34

K
Kahoolawe Island 16
Karuk tribe, 32, 166
Katamin, 166
Keatinge, Lea, 159
Klamath River, 32, 166

L
Lawyers, need for, 75–77, 156, 220–221
Leshy, John, 206
Lincoln Historic District 16–17
Local agencies, 39, 40, 41, 42, 44, 45, 53, 57, 74, 77–78, 89, 109, 113, 175,
Local organizations, 53, 78, 89, 105, 111, 219
Local law, 37–38, 56, 77–78, 80, 124, 191, 196, 198, 209, 220
Local significance, 125, 130, 131, 138, 144–145, 153
Los Angeles, 103
Low bid, 69–70

M
Marine Corps, U.S. *See* U.S. Marine Corps
Maryland, 14
Massachusetts Bay Transportation Authority (MBTA), 16–17
Medicine Lake Highlands, 15, 16
Mesa Verde, 160
Mining act, 1872, 205–206
Minnesota, 15–16
Monticello, 94
Mt. Shasta, 58
Mt. Vernon, 160
Murrieta, Joaquin, 131
Mushgigagamongsebe, 21

N
National advocacy groups, 54–55, 89, 219–220
National Conference of State Historic Preservation Officers, 48, 202,
National Environmental Policy Act (NEPA) 13–14, 32–33, 49, 51, 59–61, 69, 76, 80, 84, 85, 101, 106, 107, 109, 112, 120–121, 157–158, 173, 176–178, 192, 196, 204, 205–207, 209–211, 218
National Historic Preservation Act (NHPA)
Section 101(d)(6) of, 49
Section 106 of. *See* Section 106
Section 110 of, 15, 171, 200
Section 304 of, 118
National Oceanic and Atmospheric Administration (NOAA), 45
National Park Service (NPS)   11, 14, 15, 22, 23, 24, 26, 28–29, 33, 41, 46, 47, 92, 119, 121, 125, 126, 157, 170–171, 193, 218
National Register of Historic Places
and the values it recognizes, 30, 126–154
as a list of places, 22, 29, 57, 125,
as a National Park Service division, 22, 125,
criteria, 126–154
criterion (a), 130–131
criterion (b), 131–132, 164
criterion (c), 133–134
criterion (d), 134–135, 139–140, 146–147
criteria considerations, 147–154
50-year rule, 153–154
birthplace or grave, 150–151
cemetery, 151–152
commemorative, 153
moved structure, 150
reconstruction, 152–153
religious place, 149–150
data/documentation requirements for, 142–143, 154–155
eligibility for, 11–12, 23, 24, 25, 49, 57–58, 82–83, 95–98, 115, 118, 126–154, 160, 161–164, 168, 169, 179, 182, 189, 196, 203, 206
exclusion of portable items, 31
explained, 22, 126–154
integrity and, 135, 141–142, 163,
historic contexts and, 145
historical facts and, 145–146
Keeper of, 22, 119, 125, 127–129, 135, 136, 139, 149, 152, 155–157, 161,
landscapes and, 110, 112, 115, 136, 139, 166–168, 205–206, 208
local significance and, 144
nominations to, 23–24, 52, 82, 119, 124, 143–145, 153, 157,
regulations of, 33, 97, 126, 129, 148, 152, 156, 218
uniqueness and, 144–145
National Trust for Historic Preservation, 14–15, 48, 54, 76, 94, 121–122, 178, 190, 193, 197, 219
Native American Graves Protection and Repatriation Act (NAGPRA), 92–93
Native Hawaiian, 9, 13, 16, 48–50, 85, 102, 109–110, 123, 165, 171
Navy, U.S. *See* U.S. Navy
Negotiation Basics, 88
New Jersey, 17
New Mexico, 103, 134

Nongovernmental project proponents, 42–43
North American Free Trade Agreement (NAFTA), 36, 206–207
Norton, Gale, 206
Nuclear Regulatory Commission (NRC), 44
Nunes, Congressman Devin, 126

O
Ojibwe, 21
Oregon, 92–93

P
Panther Meadows, 58
Petaluma, CA, 131
Pit River tribe, 15, 209
Pit River Tribe et al. v. United States Forest Service et al., 209
Plymouth County, Massachusetts, 16
Place(s)
  ancestral, 20, 78, 136, 141–142, 144, 146, 150–151, 184
  architectural, 20, 125, 129, 133, 138, 139–140, 144, 150, 185
  big, 138–139, 205–206
  beautiful, 20, 130,
  as building, structure, site, landscape, 31, 130–152,
  familiar, 20
  historic
    impressing the ACHP about, 198
    and the National Register, 29, 96–98
  natural, 137, 168
  neighborhood, 137–138, 203
  sacred, 19, 131, 133, 149, 206
  scientific, 20, 139–140
  shipwreck as, 35
  spiritual, 30, 36, 58, 130, 137, 143, 149, 205
  traditional, 115, 131, 137–138, 152, 168,
  usual and accustomed, tribal rights to, 35
Police power reserved for local jurisdictions, 37
Potential to cause effects, 82–83
Preferred alternative, 99
Preservation, achieving with Section 106, 14–19, 46, 73–81, 95–117, 123–126, 135–158, 160–162, 172–175, 178–180, 182–190, 200, 218–222
Prince William County, Virginia, 71
Pro bono assistance, 76, 222
Pro-forma review, 61-2
Programmatic agreement, 59, 201–203
Project(s)
  defined, 28–29
  hypothetical example, 56–61
  proponent, 39–43, 50–53, 63,
  supporters, 53
Public comment, involvement, participation, 60, 62, 63, 67–68, 85–86, 89, 101, 112, 142, 154, 158, 173, 198–206, 211
Puget Sound Energy, 42
Purplestone National Park, 170
Pushmataha, Choctaw chief, 132

Q
Quechan tribe, 36, 205–209

R
Recommendations, UNESCO, 36–37
Record of decision (ROD), 60,
Right is not necessarily might, 78
Rosas, Luis, 88
Rural Utility Service, 41

S
Saarinen, Eero, 133
Sacred Lands Film Project, 55
Sanchez, Juan, 89–90
San Jose, California 21
Scoping historic property identification, 98–110
Secretary
  of Agriculture, 48, 197
  of Defense, 175, 199, 200
  of Housing and Urban Development 26, 165, 175, 200
  of the Army, 199
  of the Interior, 26, 48, 83, 87, 117, 118, 126, 165, 200, 206–207
  of Transportation, 208
Section 106 of NHPA
  ACHP comment under, 199–200, 206–208
  applies only to activities of federal agencies, 28, 40, 56, 67, 74, 116, 123–124
  compromise as end product of, 18, 176
  criterion/criteria of adverse effect under, 163–172
    core criterion, 163–165
    alteration, 165–167
    introduction of elements, 169–170
    neglect, 170–171
    physical destruction, 165
    removal, 167
    setting change, 168–169
    transfer, 171–172
    use change, 167–168
  delegation of responsibilities, 40, 74–75, 93, 123,
  determinations under
    "Adverse effect," 162–163, 172–175, 179–180, 189, 193, 196
    "Conditional no adverse effect," 172–173
    "No adverse effect," 162, 163, 172–175, 193
    "No historic properties affected," 161–162
  and direct federal projects, 12, 25, 39, 74, 81
  discoveries under, 204
  emergencies under, 204
  endgame under, 196–201
  examples of adverse effect under. *See* criterion/criteria
  and federal assistance, 12, 38, 43–45, 79–81, 100,
  and federal permits/licenses, 12, 13, 25, 28, 38, 123,
  language of, 24–25
  memorandum of agreement (MOA) under, 59, 67, 167, 180, 183, 190–195
  process, 12, 13, 17, 56–59, 79–92, 96–120, 123–136, 154–157, 160–163, 172–176, 178–180, 189–194, 196–199, 208

INDEX

program alternatives for compliance, 201–204
Purpose of, 18, 72,
Reforming, 210–211
Resolving adverse effects under, 58–59, 179–189, 196–199
Rights of tribes and Native Hawaiians under, 49, 85, 165, 171
Rulemaking under, 33, 47
"Take into account" standard, 11, 25, 123, 160, 179
Shasta tribe, 32
Shortcuts, 62–63
Sierra Club, 54, 190
Snoqualmie Falls, 42
Society for American Archaeology, 54
Sprawl, suburban, 71–72
Standards,
arbitrary, 57, 61, 68
HABS/HAER, 184–185
Secretary of the Interior's (various), 83, 87, 117, 118, 126, 165
SHPO, for identification and documentation, 114–115, 142, 154–155
State, definition of in NHPA, 25
State Historic Preservation Officer (SHPO), 22, 23, 45–46, 57–59, 67–68, 73, 83, 84, 85, 89, 82, 93, 99, 102, 108–109, 112–117, 125, 127–129, 135–139, 142–146, 149, 154–157, 160–163, 168, 172–176, 178, 179, 181–183, 187, 190–194, 196–200, 202–204, 206, 211, 218
State agencies, 41, 44, 74, 75,
State courts, 34,
State laws, 33, 37–38, 56, 206, 209, 220
State Review Board, 125
Stillwater (Bridge), Wisconsin/Minnesota, 15–16
Strategics, 73–79, 95–96, 135–140, 173–174, 179–180
Stuart, J. E. B., 71
Sullivan, Louis, 20
SWCA Environmental Consultants, 222

T

Telecommunications towers, 171, 198, 202–203
The International Group for Historic Aircraft Recovery (TIGHAR), 106
Timing, 73–74,
Traditional cultural property (TCP), 115, 131, 137–138, 152
Trail of Dreams, 36, 205–207
Transportation Coordinating Council (Northern Virginia), 71
Transportation, U.S. Department of. *See* U.S. Department of Transportation

Treaties, Indian, 34–35, 49, 108, 145–146, 151
Tribal Historic Preservation Officer (THPO), 46–47, 84, 99, 101, 127–128, 161–162, 172, 175, 179, 190–191, 197
Tribal law, 37–38, 124,
Trust for Public Land, 55

U

U.S. Air Force, 27, 41
U.S. Army, 14, 27, 28, 40, 41, 43, 203
U.S. Army Corps of Engineers, 28, 40, 41, 43, 64, 92–93, 164, 199, 203–204, 208–209
U.S. Coast Guard, 44
U.S. Code, 24
U.S. Constitution, U.S., 34–35, 108, 149
U.S. Department of Agriculture, 28, 41, 47, 48
See also Forest Service, U.S.D.A.; Secretary of Agriculture
U.S. Department of Defense, 26
See also Secretary of Defense
U.S. Department of Energy, 41
U.S. Department of Homeland Security (DHS), 44
U.S. Department of Housing and Urban Development (HUD), 26, 40, 41, 74–75, 165–166, 175, 200
U.S. Department of Transportation, 28, 40
See also Secretary of Transportation
U.S. Marine Corps, 41
U.S. Navy, 16, 27, 35, 41
U.S. Supreme Court, 34
Undertaking, 24–25, 28, 82–84, 89, 123, 124, 126, 164, 172,
United Nations Educational, Scientific, and Cultural Organization (UNESCO), 36–37
Urban Land Institute, 55

V

Value: historic, architectural, engineering, archaeological, cultural, 29–30, 66, 126–154
Virginia Department of Transportation, 71, 92–93, 121, 128–129, 208

W

Washington, DC, 22, 132, 198
Washington State, 11, 42
Wigwam, great, 131
Windshield survey, 111, 115
Wisconsin, 21
World Trade Center 17, 126, 153
Wright, Frank Lloyd 20, 133

Y

Yurok tribe, 32

About the Author

As a graduate student at the University of California, Riverside, in the early 1970s, Tom King found himself working with the Agua Caliente Cahuilla Tribe in Palm Springs. The tribe wanted to fight off a plan by the Army Corps of Engineers to throw a dam across the tribe's sacred Tahquitz Canyon. A weapon they used in this fight was the then-new federal project review process set up under Section 106 of the National Historic Preservation Act. Seeing Section 106 as a way to save not only the archaeological sites that he was interested in, but all kinds of places that people think are historically or culturally important, King became a specialist in Section 106 review and has done it ever since.

Over the years King has helped Indian tribes, Micronesian and Hawaiian island communities, and local people all over the country use Section 106 to help make federal agencies pay attention to the places they hold dear. Sometimes he and those he's worked with have been successful, other times not. He's also worked in the federal government itself, at the National Park Service, General Services Administration, and Advisory Council on Historic Preservation, and as a contractor for local governments, private companies, Indian tribes, and federal agencies of all kinds. He's the author of six textbooks on aspects of what's come to be called "cultural resource management."

In about 2004, working with ranchers fighting a railroad in New Mexico, horse breeders fighting suburban sprawl in Virginia, Indian tribes dealing with a toxic waste spill on a sacred site, and groups of local residents struggling with federal agencies in Massachusetts, Kentucky, and Ohio, King realized that there was no book—including his—that explained Section 106 for real people, with the perspective of someone trying to save a treasured place from something the feds are planning, assisting, or permitting. This book is the result.

Tom King welcomes contacts from people who need his help and advice, though he is a one-man show and sometimes has trouble responding promptly. He can be contacted at *tfking106@aol.com*. He is affiliated with SWCA Environmental Consultants (*www.swca.com*), but stresses that this book was not approved by SWCA and in no way necessarily reflects SWCA's views. He's also associated with The International Group for Historic Aircraft Recovery (*www.tighar.org*), with whom he spends his spare time doing archaeology in pursuit of Amelia Earhart, but neither TIGHAR nor Earhart has approved this book either.